BIBLE VITAMINS

Brain Research, Neuroplasticity and the Untapped Power of God's Word

Caxton Opere, MD

BIBLE VITAMINS

BIBLE VITAMINS: Brain Research, Neuroplasticity and the Untapped Power of God's Word

ISBN 13: 978-0-9703119-7-9
ISBN 10: 978-0-3119-7-4
Copyright © 2018 Caxton Opere

Published by Divorce Prevention Inc, Frisco TX

All Rights Reserved. Printed in The United States of America. No portion of this book may be reproduced in any form whatsoever without the express written permission of the copyright owner.

All Bible verses are from the Authorized King James Version.

Acknowledgements

Dedicated to the ministers of the Gospel who inspired me during my years of infancy in the word- The late Brother Johnny Ikomi, Bishop Wale Oke, Dr. David Udoh, Dr. Morenike Oloko, Dr. Muyiwa Onabanjo, Professor Chuks Onyeaso, Dr. Winifred Osei, Revd. Joe Olaiya. Thank you for ingraining in me the necessity of imbibing the word of God daily and particularly Bishop Wale Oke, from whom I learnt the motto "No Bible, No Breakfast" approach to starting my day.

To my fathers in the Lord, Bishop C.B. Burroughs Senior still amazingly sharp at 98 years old and Bishop Julius Abiola.

To Pastor Gerald and Mrs. Geni Brooks, Pastor Garrett Hawfitch, Pastor Jonathan Morin, all the pastoral staff and church family at Grace Outreach Center in Plano, Texas. Thank you for your love, prayers and support.

To my greatest support team, my wife and two children. I am thankful for having you in my life and for supporting all of dad's projects.

I owe my feeble knowledge of Hebrew to the teachings of the late Dr. Chuck Missler, John Kostik, as well as the YouTube channel GreekCrusader23.

Cover design: Seyi Opere.

In loving memory of my son,

Oluwaseun Joshua Opere

TABLE OF CONTENTS

Acknowledgements	 3
Preface	 9
Introduction	 11
Chapter 1 The Bible, Cars & Cholesterol	 13
Chapter 2 Old Testament Vitamins	 23
Chapter 3 New Testament Vitamins	 84
Chapter 4 The Bible Changes Your Heart	 120
Chapter 5 Why The Rich Commit Suicide	 125
Chapter 6 How The Bible Got Me My Dream Job	143
Chapter 7 Jesus, Hidden as בְּרֵאשִׁית in Genesis 1:1	148
Chapter 8 Mathematical Symmetry in Genesis 1:1	152
Chapter 9 אֵת: The Untranslatable 4th "Word"	 160
Chapter 10 God's Favorite Numbers	 162
Chapter 11 The Holy Bible or Perfect Bible?	 176
Chapter 12 God's Hemoglobin	 187
Chapter 13 Cooking up Ancient Manuscripts	 190
Chapter 14 Personalizing Bible Vitamins	 194

Preface

Why write a book titled *Bible Vitamins*? To let you know there is raw real power in God's word, accelerate your memorization of multiple Bible verses, and enhance your ability to meditate on God's word. My love for God's word began to develop in the fall of 1985 as a medical student, a few weeks after I surrendered my life to Christ. One morning while in medical school relaxed on the bed and reading my bible, I decided to kick my bible reading up a notch by memorizing a verse. Minutes later, I was meditating on the verse. Today, I still can't recall which verse it was. What I remember was the sudden change in my level of awareness and consciousness and sharpening of my senses that I couldn't otherwise explain. It was as if I suddenly came more alive than ever before. Besides the mental clarity and emotional calmness, I also felt physically stronger. This experience was so powerful, I rushed out of my room to look at myself in the giant bathroom mirrors. I wasn't expecting to see a green monster, but I was experiencing real powerful changes I couldn't explain. As I looked in the mirror, I saw that there was no real change and turned to walk away. But as I turned to walk out of the bathroom, something made me pause, nudging me to turn around again, and look back in that same mirror. I turned around, walked slowly towards the giant mirrors and gazed into my own eyes for some moments. I'm sure I must have said, Oh, my God. A more powerful Caxton was staring back at me through the mirror. There was a force in those eyes, an undeniable power, oozing from the very essence of my being, a power that wasn't there before I gave my life to Jesus Christ. I walked away puzzled but equally excited, fully aware of the reason for this powerful change, accepting Christ. I've never been the same since then. This was my first real encounter with the power in God's word performing divine alchemy between my regenerated spirit, my soul, and the words in the Bible. My conclusion from that experience was that the bible contained far more power than we would ever know and that every born again individual ought to experience divine alchemy with God's word through meditation. A few weeks later, I travelled to see my Muslim grandmother in Lagos. One of her tenants saw me at the bus stop and said, "Wow, you look different?" I smiled, realizing that what I saw in the mirror was now visible to others.

Since then I have been memorizing bible verses, writing them down in small diaries, notebooks and on index cards. Whenever I pulled them out and glanced at the verses, I always feel a sense of calmness as well as a strange sense of aliveness. In 1997, I selected 121 verses for my daily consumption and later that year about 700 verses from Genesis to Revelations that I went through every other day or twice a week. There are over 2,000 bible verses in *Bible Vitamins*, all containing hidden power. Memorize them and meditate on them. They contain important keys and hidden codes for unlocking heaven's treasury vaults and receiving many blessings, power and wise instructions. These words have helped me address countless challenges as I've journeyed through life and my only wish was to have started when I was six years old. Without the words of scripture, there is no way I would have handled the teenage death of my firstborn son. This book is dedicated to him.

If you read *Bible Vitamins* with an open heart, your attitude, behavior, character development, excellence, faith, goodness, hope, integrity and joy will change. That's because as an offspring of the Holy Bible, *Bible Vitamins* operates at the core of your human consciousness and on your mind and spirit to trigger functional and anatomical changes in your brain. These changes are called neuroplasticity and could be detected by special brain scans. Bible verses have an invisible power, hidden from the ordinary eye or unbelieving heart, that once inside the willing heart, can release power of atomic proportions. I know this because I have experienced this power and because I received specific instructions from the Lord to go ahead and publish what I initially felt was an inadequate book.

Bible Vitamins has about 7 percent of the total verses in the Holy Bible. I must confess that in my desperate hunger to have God's word in me after my initial experience, I have read the entire Bible in thirty days. Since then I have also read the entire Bible in sixty days and in ninety days. Bible verses are vitamins. Memorize them, and meditate on them. You'll discover hidden treasures that can change your destiny and your brain may undergo physical and biochemical changes that open up your mind to an entirely new world of creativity, sensitivity, success, purity, joy, peace, love, power and intimacy with God.

Enjoy!

Caxton Opere, MD.

Introduction

Bible Vitamins is an aid to understanding many basic concepts in the Bible and accelerating your ability to memorize multiple bible verses within the shortest possible time. Chapters two and three are the affirmative chapters while the rest are informative chapters. The Bible verses making up the *Vitamins* are taken from all 66 books of the Bible and are located in chapters two and three. So once you finish chapter one, I recommend you skip to chapter four and read to the end. An amazing journey awaits you in these "informative" chapters. Then come back and spend as much time as you desire in chapters two and three. You could also read *Bible Vitamins* like you would any book, that is, chapter by chapter and finish the entire book in a few hours. Figure out what works best for you as you browse through the book. Even if you've read the bible multiple times, you'll still find the insights provided by these informative chapters very refreshing. Then you can dig right into the actual bible verses in chapters two and three for intensified memorization and meditation.

Besides enhancing your spiritual growth, *Bible Vitamins* can instill hope, inspire your faith, build your confidence and empower you. In addition, it answers such questions as *Why do Rich People Commit Suicide, Which Bible Version is Best to Read, Is the Old Testament Still Relevant Today, Does God Have Favorite Numbers, What Day Did Jesus Rise from The Grave*? You'll find the answer to these questions and more as you read the informative chapters.

Many Bible verses in *Bible Vitamins* are abbreviated to accelerate memorization but not to mislead. Such verses may be preceded or followed by a sic sign (...) to indicate that there are words preceding or following the quoted verse in the actual Bible. Check your bible for the complete picture of what the verse is communicating. *Bible Vitamins* is an "aid" and not a "substitute" for the Bible to help you to rapidly memorize bible verses through "template formation" and "hinging".

"Template formation" is a process for learning complex material by breaking the information into smaller bits and pieces with gradually increasing complexity after first laying a foundation so that more complex material can then be added layer by layer using the same topics for a beginner and the expert. This enables the beginner to grasp complex concepts without creating information overload. That's how one person can get a bachelors degree, go on and obtain a masters degree and eventually a PhD in the same field. Template formation is like laying the foundation for a 100-storey skyscraper. As long as you create the right foundation with the right materials, you can keep stacking the floors on each other until you reach the hundredth floor. Just make sure you carefully choose your materials and build wisely. Template formation is how doctors learn to be doctors and engineers are trained to become engineers. All professional training is based on the principles of template formation. Once you have a template, you can teach the same subject to 5th graders and college-bound students alike.

"Hinging" is another learning principle in *Bible Vitamins*. It is a process by which flexible moveable parts are created from a rigid structure in order to increase its versatility. Hinging enables us to think outside the box and create innovative products, services and solutions. Hinging is like taking the 100-storey skyscraper that you built through template formation and turning it into 100 bungalows with a protective dome whenever there's a hurricane alert with the ability to revert back to the original 100-storey skyscraper after the hurricane is over. When hinging is applied to learning the bible, the student becomes more flexible and able to apply the bible verses they've learnt to different life situations with greater speed. Christians who learn the bible without the hinging process are often inflexible and unrealistic. They have a template, but no hinges, a foundation but no flexibility. Individuals in snake-handling churches have a template but no hinges. They are unhinged! *Bible Vitamins* is designed to enable you develop your hinges much faster than the ordinary pace.

To live a truly victorious Christian life, you must have many Bible verses committed to long-term memory and meditate on them regularly. Unfortunately, many Christians only meditate on God's word when they feel they have nothing else to do and are bored when in reality, it should be the first thing besides prayer that they should be taught to do once they receive Christ. You may find many of your favorite bible verses here in *Bible Vitamins*. If not, then here's an opportunity to learn new verses. *Bible Vitamins* is a memory juggler for the layman or seasoned preacher. If you're a preacher, as you imbibe greater volumes of scriptures using *Bible Vitamins*, you will notice a difference in your preaching and its impact on those listening to your message. *Bible Vitamins* can also be an excellent resource for training Christian leaders and disciples of the Gospel of Jesus Christ.

So find a place to relax and enjoy your daily dose of *Bible Vitamins*. Open your heart to God and read, memorize, meditate and recall as many verses as you can. Allow the transforming power of God's word to do its work on your mind and change your brain and perhaps your life for good.

Chapter 1

The Bible, Cars & Cholesterol

From its predicted scientific advances, prophetic revelations, current world events, climate change, and more recently, the neurosciences, there is no document that surpasses the Bible in influence, predictive scientific, historical and mathematical accuracy and transforming power. For example, the book of Nahum, written about 612 BC, described automobiles with headlights. In 1885, about twenty-five hundred years later, Karl Benz finally built the first automobile powered by an internal combustion engine. But even Karl Benz's *Motorwagen* did not have headlights! How could Nahum know fast moving vehicles with headlights would be invented thousands of years ago?

> ... *the chariots shall be with flaming torches in the day of his preparation, and the fir trees shall be terribly shaken. The chariots shall rage in the streets, they shall justle one against another in the broadways: they shall seem like torches, they shall run like the lightnings.* Nahum 2:3-4

Nahum was describing cars in traffic with headlights more than six hundred years before Jesus was born! How can anyone describe cars with headlights on in traffic on dual carriageways at night? What Nahum wrote about in the verses above was absolutely impossible to conceive without God revealing it to him! Yet he did.

Another example of the advanced nature of the Bible can be seen in the book of Isaiah. The Prophet Isaiah predicted the birth of Jesus Christ more than seven hundred years before Jesus was born:

> *Therefore the Lord himself shall give you a sign: Behold, a virgin shall conceive, and bear a son, and shall call his name Immanuel.* Isaiah 7:14

Isaiah predicted not just the birth of Jesus, but also his death:

> *Surely he hath borne our griefs, and carried our sorrows: yet we did esteem him stricken, smitten of God, and afflicted. But he was*

> wounded for our transgressions, he was bruised for our iniquities: the chastisement of our peace was upon him; and with his stripes we are healed. Isaiah 53:4,5

How could Isaiah have known? We couldn't even predict that Google, Apple or Microsoft would be this successful. Otherwise we would all have bought their stock and cashed out millions.

I want you to take a close look at this next verse. See if you can figure out what modern thing was being described here:

> And he had power to give life unto the image of the beast, that the image of the beast should both speak, and cause that as many as would not worship the image of the beast should be killed. Revelation 13:15

Unlike the first two, this one may not be as easy to figure out. The **"image of the beast"** refers to a picture of someone on television or a video streaming device. It seems the Apostle John saw a talking picture on some device. If you were alive two thousand years ago and saw a picture on a gadget that suddenly started talking, you'd probably describe it as an image that was given life. This was what Apostle John saw in Revelation. Almost two thousand years elapsed before television with an "image given life" was finally given to us in the form of television in 1927. The first live video on the Internet was later delivered on June 24, 1993. Today, virtually everyone has a phone that can show live videos. How could the Apostle John have known such gadgets with live images would exist almost two thousand years later? The antichrist can now broadcast live to all these handheld gadgets simultaneously. No one but God could have revealed this to him.

Another example of God's extremely advanced scientific thinking revealed in the Bible is in the prevention of heart disease. Over three thousand years ago, around 1440 BC, God gave Moses specific instructions on lowering the risk of heart attacks and sudden death from cardiovascular disease in the children of Israel:

> It shall be a perpetual statute for your generations throughout all your dwellings, that ye eat neither fat nor blood. Leviticus 3:17

This law was put to the test more than three thousand years later in the early 1990's in a landmark clinical research known as the Scandinavian Simvastatin Survival Study (4S). As a physician regularly taking care of patients with heart attacks and heart disease, this is probably one of the most intriguing scientific discoveries I found in the bible. Exactly 4,444 subjects with high cholesterol (213 to 309mg/dl) and heart disease (angina or heart attacks) from multiple Scandinavian centers were recruited into the trial and divided into two randomly chosen groups. One group would get the 20mg of Simvastatin daily while the other group would get a placebo, or sugar pill. Neither the doctors nor the patients would know who was getting the real pill or the sugar pill therefore the study was called a randomized double blind study. Ever since the results of the 4S were published in the November 1994 issue of the *Lancet* journal, sales of statins have gone through the roof. Sales of statins are now close to $20 billion annually if not higher and sales of atorvastatin (Lipitor®) topped $120 billion between 1996 and 2011. But what did this study show that turned statins into blockbuster drugs? The 4S study showed that reducing blood cholesterol reduced the risk of death and heart attacks. It could be argued that the same or better results could be achieved if the same group avoided eating greasy foods. But that wouldn't make billions for drug companies. Eating greasy foods would raise your cholesterol levels and increase your risk for a heart attack or death. To understand the importance of the Bible's advanced scientific mind, we need to see how effective statins really are and compare this with what the Bible recommends. We can then determine which would be most cost-effective and therefore the best option today.

Greasy foods increase your risk of heart attack and death, cutting down grease with statins decreases that risk by 3.9 percent.

Some details of the 4S study will help you understand the power in the Bible's instructions. In the 4S study, a total of 438 people died, 256 in the placebo group (PG) and 182 in the simvastatin treated group (STG). The 256 people that died in the placebo group represented 11.5% of the people in the PG while the 182 people who died in the STG represented 8.2% of that group. What's the difference in death between the two groups? A mere 3.3%! What if we narrowed the results down and looked only at those that died of coronary heart disease (CHD)? In the PG group, 189 people (8.5%) died of CHD while 111 (5%) died in the STG. The difference between the two groups for coronary death is 3.5%! But how do you think the drug companies will present the 3.5% difference in CHD between both groups to the public and in medical journals? This is how:

"Simvastatin reduced coronary deaths by 41%."

This is perfectly legal, since 5% is 41% lower than 8.5%! When a physician tells a patient that the statin he or she is prescribing will reduce the risk of death by 40%, it is not the absolute truth, but a distorted truth. And the consequences of such misinformation could be an increased risk of dying by patients who place more trust in the statin than in what the Bible recommends, that is, a low fat diet.

> AJ is a mid-level executive in his mid fifties and one of my patients. He was back in the emergency room with chest pain, two days after he had stents placed in his heart to improve blood flow to clogged arteries. He just had a coronary artery bypass three years earlier. So I sat him and his wife down to have a serious talk because his LDL (bad cholesterol) which was through the roof. He admitted that his diet had not changed one bit since his heart surgery but he presumed the prescribed statin would cut down his cholesterol about 50 percent and eliminate his chest pain, no matter what he ate. So did SW, another patient of mine who unfortunately died from "sausages and hot dogs", having placed his trust in statins.

What if these people simply avoided their greasy diets and stuck to healthier diets? Wouldn't that have been more cost-effective than statins? The quality of their lives would actually have been far better. If you want the truth, follow the Bible's instructions. The Bible reveals the truth that sets us free. Man is always seeking an alternative to God's instructions, hoping to beat the odds created by his own disobedience. You've seen the pitiful differences (3.5%) between a placebo and an expensive drug with terrible side effects and therefore very low compliance. Keep in mind that most statin clinical trials usually compare the drug treatments to giving a patient nothing at all and still end up with less than a 4 percent absolute difference.

What if we could find a study that directly or indirectly follows the Bible's instructions? One such study is the *Lifestyle Heart Trial*. The Dean Ornish-style diet used in the *Lifestyle Heart Trial* followed the law in Leviticus 3:17 and not too surprisingly in the study, the average weight loss in patients was 24 pounds with a 37 % drop in bad cholesterol (LDL), a 91% drop in frequency of angina (chest pain), and a visible reversal of the narrowing in the coronary arteries (BUMC Proceedings 2000; 13:351-355). No statin can ever accomplish this feat. Every 1 percent drop in LDL cuts the risk of coronary artery disease by about 2 percent over the lifetime of the individual. Imagine then the impact of a 37% drop in LDL on the patient's quality of life! The Dean Ornish-style diet required avoiding greasy foods, and sticking to, a vegetarian diet. It's impact on heart disease, compared to that of statins is astronomical. So as physicians, if we ignore what the bible says about avoiding greasy foods because we think we have a magic drug to lower cholesterol, we're ignorantly putting our patients at risk.

The average cost per-patient in a clinical trial is $36,500 according to www.quora.com. Based on this estimate, the total cost of the 4S study would be about $162,206,000. Billions of dollars more are spent on statins annually all over the world. One Italian clinical trial showed that only 12.8% of patients continued statin therapy for 4.5 years and the majority stopped by 5.3 months. Praluent, an injectable cholesterol lowering drug approved by the FDA early this year showed similar findings as its predecessors: a death rate of 3.5% in subjects treated with Praluent and 4.1% in those untreated and given a sugar pill instead. The cost? Over $14,000 a year! The financial and health consequences of ignoring the Bible's instructions can be quite drastic!

> *For whosoever eateth the fat of the beast, of which men offer an offering made by fire unto the Lord, even the soul that eateth it shall be cut off from his people.* Leviticus 7:25

Moses' instruction was simple: cut out the grease or face dire consequences. Today, there are so many people eating themselves to death while on statins and arriving in the hospital with heart attacks or strokes and a look of disbelief. Most were hoping that a small statin pill without the necessary changes in their diets or behaviors should have protected them. And some of these are men and women that have worked hard all their lives only to drop dead when they should be enjoying their families while in retirement. They had been assured that the statin was the key to a 35% or greater improvement in their health.

There are at least fifteen other bible verses written thousands of years ago telling us not to eat fat but to burn it? Exodus 29:13; Leviticus 3:16, 4:19, 4:26, 4:31, 4:35, 6:12, 7:31, 8:16, 8:20, 9:10, 9:20, 16:25, 17:6 and 18:17. Moses was not a cardiologist and the ample evidence against greasy diets came more than three thousand years ago. To have such knowledge written down clearly in more than one bible verse by non-scientists in an "archaic" book written over three thousand years ago is, truly amazing. How could this be, except an advanced scientific mind was providing the information?

What other issues did the bible address thousands of years ago that scientists are still spending millions confirming today? Exercise is another example. According to a Stanford study published in the July 2, 1998 issue of the *New England Journal of Medicine*, exercise doubled the fall in bad cholesterol (LDL) by 14-20% when combined with diet. The bible recommends exercise:

> *Bodily exercise profiteth little: but godliness is profitable unto all things...* I Timothy 4:8

How about anger? According to a *Harvard School of Public Health* study published by Dr. Kawachi and colleagues in 1996, anger, a trait the bible recommended that we tone down or avoid completely thousands of years ago, tripled the risk of heart attacks. What exactly does the Bible have to say about anger? A lot, but one verse makes it clear that we'd be foolish to let anger rule our spirits:

> *Be not hasty in thy spirit to be angry: for anger resteth in the bosom of fools.* Ecclesiastes 7:9

Another verse warns us to avoid anger penetrating into our subconscious minds:

> *Be ye angry, and sin not: let not the sun go down upon your wrath.* Ephesians 4:26

While patience is a desired virtue, anger is a detriment to almost anyone. Anger poisons your body systems. Dr. Mittelman, a cardiologist, showed in a study of over 1600 patients that a patient's risk for a heart attack doubled within two hours of an anger episode.

My final example is about a relatively new scientific concept called neuroplasticity. For hundreds of years, scientists had thought that once we reach a certain age, no new cell growth, development or positive changes could occur in the brain. Over the last four decades alone, enough scientific evidence has accumulated confirming that the brain is not a fixed structure as we previously thought. Neuroplasticity is the brain's ability to reorganize itself structurally and functionally due to learning, challenges, insults, habits, attitudes and behaviors. These structural and functional changes start at the molecular level and involve the nerve cells in the brain, creating new connections with each other regardless of a person's age, even after damage to the brain such as follows a stroke. Science has basically shown us that we can change not only our minds but also our physical brains. Today, neuroscientists now agree that the brain is a constantly changing organ capable of healing and regeneration even in advanced age. Today, neuroplasticity is to scientists, what Einstein's theory of relativity was to physicists in the early 1900's when Einstein first published his paper on relativity.

> If you want to get a cab driver's license in London, you need to spend about 4 years memorizing a maze of about 25,000 streets, as well as several other tourist attractions, within a 10-kilometer radius around Charring Cross. This is a really tough mental ordeal causing specific brain changes studied

by scientists such as Dr. Ellen Maguire and Dr. Vanessa Sluming. Dr. Maguire and colleagues observed increases in grey matter in the posterior hippocampus of the brains of the taxi drivers when compared with non-taxi drivers matched for age, intelligence and education. This change was dramatic.

In another study, Dr. Vanessa Sluming and colleagues compared the brain scans of professional male symphony orchestra musicians with those of non-musicians. Both groups were matched according to age, sex, right- or left-handedness and IQ. The musicians showed a statistically significant increase in their grey matter in the left inferior frontal gyrus of Broca's area. In addition, the musicians did not have the normal shrinking of brain cells that occurred with age in non-musicians. In another similar study published in the October 8 2003 issue of the *Journal of Neuroscience*, the brains of non-musicians were again compared with those of amateur and professional musicians. Professional musicians practicing an hour or more a day had the greatest increases in specific areas of their brain; the left cerebellum responsible for balance and movement: the left Heschl's gyrus, that processes sound and language and the left inferior frontal gyrus associated with inhibiting action in response to a signal to stop. There was no increase in the grey matter in non-musicians in these areas. Amateur musicians had an increase in grey matter somewhere in between the two groups. Could the brains of the professional musicians have always been larger and is that why they chose to become musicians? Quite possible but there is evidence that training your brain musically can enlarge these parts too. In a study published in the September 2008 issue of the *Journal of Neuroscience*, musical training in non-musically trained adults was shown to cause the same changes in brain structure.

The following bible verses, some written over three thousand years ago, suggest the writers knew of the brain's capacity for change:

And these words, which I command thee this day, shall be in thine heart. Deuteronomy 6:6

Bind them upon thy fingers, write them upon the table of thine heart. Proverbs 7:3

This book of the law shall not depart out of thine mouth; but thou shalt meditate therein day and night, that thou mayest observe to do according to all that is written therein: for then thou shalt make thy way prosperous, and then thou shalt have good success.
Joshua 1:8

A new heart also will I give you, and a new spirit will I put within you: and I will take away the stony heart out of your flesh, and I will give you an heart of flesh. Ezekiel 36:26

Finally, brethren, whatsoever things are true, whatsoever are honest, whatsoever things are just, whatsoever things are pure, whatsoever things are lovely, whatsoever things are of good report; if there be any virtue, and if there be any praise, think on these things. Philippians 4:8

And be not conformed to this world: but be ye transformed by the renewing of your mind... Romans 12:2

For as he thinketh in his heart, so is he... Proverbs 23:7

And be renewed in the spirit of your mind Ephesians 4:23

The authors of these verses seem quite convinced that we can change our lives by thinking, meditating and by changing the information we feed our brain. This change may take seconds or decades. But whenever these changes take place in our lives, there will be corresponding changes in our brain structure and function. But how could these prophets have known this? They didn't have CAT scans, PET scans, functional MRI's, EEG's or even simple x-rays. From reading the entire Bible over thirty times, I am convinced that there is no other tool on this planet that can reprogram the brain for optimal functioning like the Bible could. I'd like to leave you one final example of the Bible's power with four bible verses and the story of a young lady from the late Reverend Kenneth Hagin Senior.

For the word of God is quick, and powerful, and sharper than any two edged sword, piercing even to the dividing asunder of soul and spirit, and of the joints and marrow, and is a discerner of the thoughts and intents of the heart. (Hebrews 4:12)
    (Words that rapidly penetrate the deepest parts of our being)

...and the sword of the Spirit, which is the word of God. (Ephesians 6:17)
    (Words that can cut through the realm of the invisible world)

So shall my word be that goeth forth out of my mouth: it shall not return unto me void, but it shall accomplish that which I please, and it shall prosper in the thing whereto I sent it. (Isaiah 55:11)
(Words too powerful to be stopped once sent on a mission!)

It is the spirit that quickeneth; the flesh profiteth nothing: the words that I speak unto you, they are spirit and they are life. John 6:63

Years ago, KB, a young girl with a developmental abnormality that made her relatively mute but scream intermittently without provocation, was taken to a weeklong Kenneth Hagin Sr. revival tent meeting. She was always an embarrassment to her family in social gatherings and intermittently screamed at the tent meeting that first day. Her sister could barely hold her down or keep her quiet while they both sat in the front row. The next day, she was back in the same front row with her sister. She did not make as much noise the second day. By the third or fourth day she was quiet. By the time the meeting ended she came to the tent, bible in hand, and quietly read along with the preacher. Years later, while in a city, Reverend Hagin recalled in *The Healing Anointing*, a beautiful young lady with her family running up to him and introducing herself. When he couldn't remember who she was, she reminded him she was the screaming young girl at the tent meeting.

All KB had to do was hear the words of scripture. Whatever tormented her poor little soul had created changes in her brain that made it impossible for her to function as a normal human being. These brain changes may have been detectable by Positron Emission Tomography (PET) scans of the brain. I know from experience that Reverend Kenneth preaches the undiluted word of God and I can imagine KB hearing many verses of the bible during that tent meeting. Those words must have created neuroplastic changes in her brain. What KB experienced was a miracle. All she did was hear the words of scripture and a divine alchemy took place between her mind and these words as she heard them. There was a power in the words she heard that day as no one prayed for her or laid hands on her. Neither did she have any faith to draw any conclusions from the preacher's words. The word just worked. May the word also work for you the day you need a miracle, in Jesus' name. Amen.

If these words get deep into your soul through memorization and meditation, they will initiate a transformation in you at the molecular level, one so powerful, you could become an entirely new human being, assisted of course by the power of the Holy Spirit:

> *Therefore if any man be in Christ, he is a new creature: old things are passed away; behold all things are become new.*
> II Corinthians 5:17

The words in the bible are written to change your life from the inside out, if you will put them in your heart and obey them. In the next two chapters, you will experience some of the most powerful words in the entire universe. These words have the uncanny ability to penetrate the deepest levels of human consciousness, far beyond the structural and functional changes currently measurable by science, to effect those changes, at the spiritual level. At such a higher level of conscious awareness, it will be impossible for you to bow before any man or any problem. It was this powerful transforming effect of the word of God that three young boys encountered and therefore refused to bow before any man or any idol, even in the face of death:

> *Shadrach, Meshach, and Abednego, answered and said to the king, O Nebuchadnezzar, we are not careful to answer thee in this matter. If it be so, our God whom we serve is able to deliver us from the burning fiery furnace, and he will deliver us out of thine hand, O king. But if not, be it known unto thee, O king, that we will not serve thy gods, nor worship the golden image which thou hast set up. Then was Nebuchadnezzar full of fury, and the form of his visage was changed against Shadrach, Meshach and Abednego...*
> Daniel 3:16-19

God instilled neuroplasticity into the very nature of humans and inspired the 40 authors of the Bible to write 31,101 verses over a span of 1500 years. God has hidden the most powerful code for changing lives in the words of the Bible. This change is called neuroplasticity. He gave us a very powerful piece of eternity, wrapped it with human words, and allowed it to be placed in printed form, in the bible. That's why some of us know there is something powerful and sacred hidden in the nature of the words in the bible. The Bible contains the antidotes for sin, failure, depression, divorce, pornography, fear, destructive behaviors, addiction, self-sabotage and all manner of evil plaguing the human mind and the human race. God's word was designed to help us in time of need, understand our purpose on earth, as well as his ultimate plan for mankind.

Chapter 2

Old Testament Vitamins

Genesis
1:1 In the beginning God created the heaven and the earth
1:2 And the earth was without form and void; and darkness was upon the face of the deep. And the Spirit of God moved upon the face of the waters
1:3 And God said, Let there be light: and there was light
1:4 And God saw the light, that it was good: and God divided the light from the darkness
1:26 And God said, Let us make man in our image, after our likeness, and let them have dominion over...
1:27 So God created man in his own image, in the image of God created he him; male and female created he them
1:28 And God blessed them, and God said unto them, Be fruitful and multiply, and replenish the earth, and subdue it; and have dominion...
1:29 And God said, Behold I have given you...
1:31 And God saw everything that he had made, and behold, it was very good...
2:17 But of the tree of knowledge of good and evil, thou shalt not eat of it: for in the day that thou eatest thereof thou shalt surely die
2:18...It is not good that the man should be alone, I will make him an help meet for him
2:22 And the rib, which the Lord God had taken from man, made he a woman, and brought her unto the man
2:23 And Adam said, This is now bone of my bones, flesh of my flesh
2:24 Therefore shall a man leave his father and his mother, and shall cleave unto his wife: and they shall be one flesh
3:3 But of the fruit of the tree which is in the midst of the garden, God hath said, Ye shall not eat of it, neither shall ye touch it, lest ye die
3:6 And when the woman saw that the tree was good for food, and that it was pleasant to the eyes...
3:11 And he said, Who told thee that thou wast naked?...
3:12 And the man said, The woman whom thou gavest...
3:13...And the woman said, The serpent beguiled me...
3:15 And I will put enmity between thee and the woman, and between thy seed and her seed; it shall bruise thy head, and thou shalt bruise his heel

3:16 Unto the woman he said, I will greatly multiply thy sorrow and thy conception...
3:17 And unto Adam he said...cursed is the ground for thy sake
3:19 In the sweat of thy face shalt thou eat bread...
3:24 ...cursed is the ground for thy sake; in sorrow shalt thou eat of it all the days of thy life
4:8 ...Cain rose up against Abel his brother and slew him
6:2...sons of God saw the daughters of men that they were fair...
6:3 And the Lord said, My spirit shall not always strive with man
6:5 And God saw that the wickedness of man was great in the earth, and that every thought of the imagination of his heart was only evil continually
6:6 And it repented the Lord that he had made man on the earth, and it grieved him at his heart
6:7 And the Lord said, I will destroy man whom I have created...
11:6 And the Lord said, Behold, the people is one, and they have all one language... now nothing will be restrained from them, which they have imagined to do
11:7 ...let us go down, and there confound their language, that they may not understand one another's speech
11:8 So the Lord scattered them abroad from thence...
12:1 Now the Lord had said unto Abram, Get thee out of thy country, and from thy kindred, and from thy father's house, unto a land that I will shew thee
12:2 And I will make of thee a great nation...
12:3 And I will bless them that bless thee, and curse him that curseth thee: and in thee shall all the families of the earth be blessed
12:4 So Abram departed, as the Lord had spoken unto him...
13:2 And Abram was very rich in cattle and in silver and in gold
17:13 ...and my covenant shall be in your flesh for an everlasting covenant
18:14 ...Is anything too hard for the Lord? ...thou shalt have a son
18:19 For I know him, that he will command his children and his household after him, and he shall keep the way of the Lord...
22:12 ...for now I know that thou fearest God, seeing thou hast not withheld thy son, thine only son from me
22:17 ...I will multiply thy seed as the stars of the heaven... and thy seed shall possess the gate of his enemies
22:18 And in thy seed shall all the nations of the earth be blessed; because thou hast obeyed my voice
26:12 Then Isaac sowed in that land, and received in the same year an hundred-fold: and the Lord blessed him
26:32 ...We have found water
28:17 ... and this is the gate of heaven

28:22 ...and of all that thou shalt give me I will surely give the tenth unto thee
32:26 ...I will not let thee go, except thou bless me
32:28 ...for as a prince as thou power with God and with man and hath prevailed
37:8 ...And they hated him yet the more for his dreams...
39:2 And the Lord was with Joseph, and he was a prosperous man...
41:51 ...Manasseh, For God, said he, hath made me forget my toil, and all my father's house
41:52 ...Ephraim, For God hath caused me to be fruitful in the land of my affliction
49:24 But his bow abode in strength, and the arms of his hands were made strong by the hands of the mighty God of Jacob...
50:1 And Joseph said unto them, Fear not: for am I in the place of God?
50:20 ...ye thought evil against me; but God meant it unto good...

Exodus

1:21 And it came to pass, because the midwives feared God, that he made them houses
2:24 And God heard their groaning, and God remembered his covenant with...
3:14 And God said unto Moses, I AM THAT I AM...
4:1 And Moses answered and said, But, behold, they will not believe me...
14:13 ...Fear ye not, stand still and see the salvation of the Lord, which he will show to you today: for the Egyptians whom ye have seen today, ye shall see them again no more forever
14:14 The Lord shall fight for you, and ye shall hold your peace
14:18 And the Egyptians shall know that I am the Lord, when I have gotten me honour upon Pharaoh...
14:22 And the children of Israel went into the midst of the sea upon the dry ground...
15:3 The Lord is a man of war: the Lord is his name
15:10 ...they sank as lead in the mighty waters
16:30 So the people rested on the seventh day
25:8 And let them make me a sanctuary; that I may dwell among them
25:40 And look that thou make them after their pattern, which was shewed thee in the mount
32:22 ...thou knowest the people, that they are set on mischief
33:20 ...for there shall no man see me, and live
34:14 For thou shalt worship no other god: for the Lord, whose name is Jealous, is a jealous God

35:2 ...a sabbath of rest to the Lord: whosoever doeth work therein shall be put to death
40:16 Thus did Moses: according to all that the Lord commanded him, so did he

Leviticus

2:13 ...with all thine offerings thou shalt offer salt
3:17 It shall be a perpetual statute for your generations throughout all your dwellings, that ye eat neither fat nor blood
6:13 The fire shall ever be burning upon the altar; it shall never go out
11:45 ...ye shall therefore be holy, for I am holy
18:22 Thou shalt not lie with mankind, as with womankind: it is abomination
18:23 Neither shalt thou lie with any beast to defile thyself therewith...
18:24 Defile not ye yourselves in any of these things...
19:28 Ye shall not make any cuttings in your flesh for the dead, nor print any marks upon you...
19:31 Regard not them that have familiar spirits, neither ask after wizards to be defiled by them...
19:32 Thou shalt rise up before the hoary head, and honour the face of the old man...
19:33 And if a stranger sojourn with thee in your land, ye shall not vex him
19:35 Ye shall do no unrighteousness in judgment...
20:7 Sanctify yourselves therefore, and be ye holy: for I am the Lord your God
20:9 For everyone that curseth his father or his mother shall be surely put to death...
20:10 And the man that commiteth adultery with another man's wife ...shall surely be put to death
20:13 If a man also lie with mankind, as he lieth with a woman, both of them have committed an abomination: they shall surely be put to death...
26:4 Then I will give you rain in due season, and the land shall yield her increase, and the trees of the field shall yield their fruit
26:8 And five of you shall chase an hundred, and hundred of you shall put ten thousand to flight: and your enemies shall fall before you by the sword
26:9 For I will have respect unto you, and make you fruitful, and multiply you...

Numbers

6:24 The Lord bless thee and keep thee

6:25 The Lord make his face shine upon thee, and be gracious unto thee
6:26 The Lord lift up his countenance upon thee, and give thee peace
23:8 How shall I curse whom God hath not cursed...
23:19 God is not a man that he should lie...
32:23 ...and be sure your sin will find you out
35:33 ...the land cannot be cleansed of the blood that is shed therein, but by the blood of him that shed it

Deuteronomy

1:8 Behold, I have set the land before you: go in and possess...
2:3 Ye have compassed this mountain long enough: turn you...
2:24 ...begin to possess it, and contend with him in battle
2:31 ...begin to possess, that thou mayest inherit his land
4:15 Take ye therefore good heed unto yourselves...
4:16 Lest ye corrupt yourselves...
4:24 For the Lord thy God is a consuming fire, even a jealous God
4:29 But if from thence thou shalt seek the Lord thy God, thou shalt find him, if thou seek him with all thy heart and with all thy soul
4:39 Know therefore this day, and consider it in thine heart, that the Lord he is God in heaven above, and upon the earth beneath: there is none else
5:7 Thou shalt have none other gods before me
5:16 Honour thy father and thy mother ... that it may go well...
5:17 Thou shalt not kill
5:18 Neither shalt thou commit adultery
5:19 Neither shalt thou steal
5:20 Neither shalt thou bear false witness against thy neighbor
5:21 Neither shalt thou desire thy neighbour's wife, neither shalt thou covet thy neighbour's house, his field or...
5:29 O that there were such an heart in them, that they would fear me, and keep all my commandments always, that it may be well with them, and with their children forever
6:6 And these words, which I command thee this day, shall be in thine heart
6:7 And thou shalt teach them diligently unto thy children...
6:8 And thou shalt bind them for a sign upon thine hand, and they shall be as frontlets between thine eyes
6:11 ...when thou shalt have eaten and be full
6:12 Then beware...
6:15 For the Lord thy God is a jealous God among you lest the anger of the Lord thy God be kindled against thee, and destroy thee from off the face of the earth

6:16 Ye shall not tempt the Lord your God...
7:3 Neither shalt thou make marriages with them...
7:9 Know therefore that the Lord thy God, he is God, the faithful God, which keepeth covenant and mercy with them that love him and keep his commandments to a thousand generations
7:10 And repayeth them that hate him to their face, to destroy them...
7:14 Thou shalt be blessed above all people: there shall not be male or female barren among you or among your cattle
7:15 And the Lord will take away from thee all sickness, and will put none of the evil diseases of Egypt, which thou knowest, upon thee
7:18 Thou shalt not be afraid of them...
7:26 Neither shall thou bring an abomination into thine house, lest thou be a cursed thing like it...
8:2 ...to humble thee, and to prove thee, to know what was in thine heart...
8:18 But thou shalt remember the Lord thy God: for it is he that giveth thee power to get wealth
8:19 ...if thou do at all forget the Lord thy God, and walk after other gods, and serve them, I testify against you this day that ye shall surely perish
9:5 Not for thy righteousness or for the uprightness of thine heart ...but for the wickedness of these nations the Lord thy God doth drive them out from before thee...
9:6 ...for thou art a stiffnecked people
10:16 Circumcise therefore the foreskin of your heart, and be no more stiffnecked
11:8 Therefore ye shall keep all the commandments which I command you this day, that ye may be strong, and go in and possess the land...
11:26 Behold, I set before you this day a blessing and a curse
11:27 A blessing if ye obey the commandments of the Lord...
11:28 And a curse, if ye will not obey the commandments of the Lord your God, but turn aside out of the way...
12:23 Only be sure that thou eat not the blood: for the blood is the life...
13:4 Ye shall walk after the Lord your God, and fear him, and keep his commandments, and obey his voice, and ye shall serve him, and cleave unto him
15:1 At the end of every seven years thou shalt make a release
16:19 ...neither take a gift: for a gift doth blind the eyes of the wise...
17:17 Neither shall he multiply wives to himself...
18:22 When a prophet speaketh in the name of the Lord, if the thing follow not, nor come to pass...

19:10 That innocent blood be not shed in the land...
19:16 If a false witness rise up against any man to testify against him that which is wrong
19:19 Then shall ye do unto him, as he had thought to do unto his brother...
20:3 ...let not your hearts faint, fear not and do not tremble...
20:4 For the Lord your God is he that goeth with you, to fight for you against your enemies: let not your hearts faint, fear not, and do not tremble, neither be ye terrified because of them
21:9 So shalt thou put away the guilt of innocent blood from among you, when thou shalt do that which is right in the sight of the Lord
22:1 Thou shalt not see thy brother's ox or his sheep go astray and hide thyself from them...
22:5 The woman shall not wear that which pertaineth to a man, neither shall a man put on a woman's garment...
22:28 If a man find a damsel that is a virgin, which is not betrothed, and lay hold on her, and lie with her...
23:2 A bastard shall not enter the congregation of the Lord; even to his tenth generation...
23:13 And thou shalt have a paddle upon thy weapon; and it shall be when thou ease thyself abroad, thou shalt dig therewith, and shalt cover that which cometh from thee
23:18 Thou shalt not bring the hire of a whore or the price of a dog into the house of the Lord...
24:1 ...let him write her a bill of divorcement, and give it in her hand, and send her out of his house
24:4 Her former husband, which sent her away, may not take her again to be his wife...
24:5 When a man hath taken a new wife, he shall not go out to war, neither shall he be charged with any business...
24:14 Thou shalt not oppress an hired servant...
24:16 The fathers shall not be put to death for the children, neither shall children be put to death for the fathers...
28:2 And all these blessings shall come on thee and overtake thee, if thou shalt hearken diligently unto the voice of the Lord thy God
28:3 Blessed shall thou be in the city, and blessed shall thou be in the field
28:4 Blessed shall be the fruit of thy body and the fruit of thy ground, and the fruit of thy cattle, the increase of thy kine, and the flocks of thy sheep,
28:5 Blessed shall be thy basket and thy store
28:6 Blessed shall thou be when thou comest in, and blessed shall thou be when thou goest out

28:7 The Lord shall cause thine enemies that rise up against thee to be smitten before thy face: they shall come out against thee one way and they shall flee before thee seven ways

28:8 The Lord shall command the blessings upon thee in thy storehouses, and in all that thou settest thine hand unto: and he shall bless thee in the land which the Lord thy God giveth thee

29:9 Keep therefore the words of this covenant, and do them, that ye may prosper in all that ye do

29:29 The secret things belong unto the Lord our God: but those things which are revealed belong unto us and to our ...

30:11 For this commandment... is not hidden from thee, neither is it far off

30:14 But the word is very nigh unto thee, in thy mouth, and in thy heart, that thou mayest do it

30:15 See, I have set before thee this day life and good, death and evil

30:17 But if thine heart turn away, so that thou wilt not hear...

30:19 I call heaven and earth to record this day against you, that I have set before you life and death, blessing and cursing, therefore choose life, that both thou and thy seed may live

32:10 ...he instructed him, he kept him as the apple of his eye

32:12 So the Lord alone did lead him, and there was no strange god with him

32:13 He made him ride on the high places of the earth, that he might eat the increase of the fields; and he made him to suck honey out of the rock, and oil out of the flinty rock

32:39 See now that I, even I, am he, and there is no god with me: I kill, and I make alive, I wound and I heal: neither is there any that can deliver out of my hand

32:52 Yet thou shalt see the land before thee; but thou shalt not go thither unto the land...

33:19 ...for they shall suck of the abundance of the seas, and of treasures hidden in the sand

34:7 And Moses was an hundred and twenty years old...his eye was not dim, nor his natural force abated

34:9 And Joshua the son of Nun was full of the spirit of wisdom; for Moses had laid his hands upon him...

Joshua

1:3 Every place that the sole of your feet shall tread upon, that have I given unto you...

1:5 There shall not any man be able to stand before thee all the days of thy life: as I was with Moses, so I will be with thee: I will not fail thee nor forsake thee

1:6 Be strong and of a good courage...

1:7 Only be thou strong and very courageous...
1:8 This book of the law shall not depart out of thy mouth: but thou shall meditate therein day and night, that thou mayest observe to do according to all that is written therein: for then thou shalt make thy way prosperous, and then thou shalt have good success
1:9 Have not I commanded thee? Be strong, and of a good courage; be not afraid, neither be thou dismayed: for the Lord thy God is with thee withersoever thou goest
2:12 ...shew kindness unto my father's house, and give me a true token
2:18 ...thou shalt bind this line of scarlet thread in the window...
3:5 ...Sanctify yourselves: for tomorrow the Lord will do wonders among you
3:17 And the priests... stood firm on dry ground in the midst of Jordan...
5:9 ...This day have I rolled away the reproach of Egypt from off you...
5:12 And the manna ceased...
11:15 As the Lord commanded Moses his servant, so did Moses command Joshua, and so did Joshua; he left nothing undone that the Lord commanded Moses
11:19 There was not a city that made peace with the children of Israel, save the Hivites...
14:12 Now therefore give me this mountain...
18:12 ...Go and walk through the land, and describe it, and come again to me...
21:43 And the Lord gave unto Israel all the land which he sware to give unto their fathers...
21:45 ...all came to pass
23:10 One man of you shall chase a thousand: for the Lord your God, he it is that fighteth for you...
23:14 ... not one thing hath failed of all the good things which the Lord your God spake concerning you...
24:15 ... choose you this day whom ye will serve ...but as for me and my house, we will serve the Lord

Judges

3:2 ...that the generations of the children of Israel might know, to teach them war...
4:8 ...If thou wilt go with me, then I will go...
11:34 And Jephthah came to Mizpeh unto his house, and behold his daughter came out...
16:1 Then Samson went to Gaza, and saw there an harlot...
16:22 Howbeit the hair of his head began to grow again...

18:9 ...and are ye still? Be not slothful to go, and to enter to possess the land
21:25 In those days there was no king in Israel: every man did that which was right in his own eyes

Ruth

2:2 ...I shall find grace
2:12 The Lord recompense thy work, and a full reward be given thee of the Lord God of Israel under whose wings thou art come to trust
2:13 ...Let me find favour in thy sight, my lord...
3:6 ...and did according to all that her mother in-law bade her
3:10 ...Blessed be thou of the Lord...thou hast shewed more kindness in the latter than at the beginning...
3:16 ...Who art thou, my daughter?
3:18... Sit still... for the man will not be in rest till he have finished the thing this day
4:13 The Lord gave her conception, and she bare a son

I Samuel

1:10 And she was in bitterness of soul, and prayed unto the Lord, and wept sore
1:17... Go in peace: And the God of Israel grant thee thy petition that thou hast asked of him
2:4 The bows of the mighty men are broken, and they that stumbled are girded with strength
2:9 He will keep the feet of his saints, and the wicked shall be silent in darkness; for by strength shall no man prevail
2:21 And the Lord visited Hannah, so that she conceived, and bare three sons and two daughters
2:30 ...for them that honour me, I will honour
3:10 ...Then Samuel answered, Speak; for thy servant heareth
3:19 And Samuel grew, and the Lord was with him, and did let none of his words fall to the ground
3:21 ...for the Lord revealed himself to Samuel in Shi-loh by the word of the Lord
7:10 ...and Samuel cried unto the Lord for Israel; and the Lord heard him
7:13 So the Philistines were subdued...
10:6 And the Spirit of the Lord will come upon thee... and thou shalt be turned into another man
14:6 ...for there is no restraint to the Lord to save by many or by few
15:22 ...to obey is better than sacrifice, and to hearken than the fat of rams

15:23 For rebellion is as the sin of witchcraft, and stubbornness is as iniquity and idolatory. Because thou hast rejected the word of the Lord, he hath also rejected thee from being king
15:28 ...The Lord hath rent the kingdom of Israel from thee this day, and hath given it to a neighbour of thine...
16:7 ...for the Lord seeth not as man seeth; for man looketh on the outward appearance, but the Lord looketh on the heart
16:13 Then Samuel took the horn of oil and anointed him...and the Spirit of the Lord came upon David...
16:23 ...when the evil spirit from God was upon Saul...David took an harp, and played
17:36 Thy servant slew both the lion and the bear: and this uncircumcised Philistine shall be as one of them...
17:45 ...Thou comest to me with a sword and with a spear, and with a shield: but I come to thee in the name of the Lord of hosts, the God of the armies of Israel, whom thou hast defiled
17:46 This day will the Lord deliver thee into mine hand; and I will smite thee, and take thine head from thee...
17:47 ...for the battle is the Lord's, and he will give you *(Goliath)* into our hands *(emphasis mine)*
17:50 So David prevailed over the Philistine with a sling and with a stone...
18:14 And David behaved himself wisely in all his ways; and the Lord was with him
21:8...the king's business required haste
23:16 ... and strengthened his hand in God
24:15 The Lord therefore be judge, and judge between me and thee...and deliver me out of thine hand
25:36 ...his wife had told him these things, that his heart died within him, and he became as a stone
26:9 ...for who can stretch forth his hand against the Lord's anointed, and be guiltless?
26:12 ...because a deep sleep from the Lord was fallen upon them
28:15...God is departed from me, and answereth me no more...
30:8 Pursue: for thou shalt surely overtake them, and without fail recover all
30:18 And David recovered all that the Amalekites had carried away...

II Samuel

8:14 ...And the Lord preserved David whithersoever he went
8:15 And David reigned over all Israel; and David executed judgment and justice unto all his people
11:2 ...David arose from his bed... and saw a woman washing herself... very beautiful...

12:7 And Nathan said to David, thou art the man...
12:12 For thou didst it secretly, but I will do this thing before all Israel, and before the sun
13:15 ...the hatred wherein he hated her was greater than the love wherewith he had loved her
15:31 ...O Lord, I pray thee, turn the counsel of Ahithophel into foolishness
18:33 ...O my son Absalom, my son, my son Absalom...
22:33 God is my strength and power and he maketh my way perfect
22:35 He teacheth my hands to war so that a bow of steel is broken by mine arms
24:24 ...neither will I offer burnt offerings unto the Lord my God of that which doth cost me nothing...
24:25 ...So the Lord was intreated for the land, and the plague was stayed from Israel

I Kings
2: 2 ...be thou strong therefore, and shew thyself a man
3:9 Give therefore thy servant an understanding heart to judge thy people, that I may discern between good and bad
3:26...Let it be neither mine nor thine, but divide it
4:1 And God gave Solomon wisdom and understanding exceeding much, and largeness of heart, even as the sand that is on the seashore
8:1...the cloud filled the house of the Lord
8:11 So that the priests could not stand to minister because of the cloud: for the glory of the Lord had filled the house of the Lord
10:7 ...thy wisdom and prosperity exceedeth the fame which I heard
13:4 ...And his hand, which he put forth against him, dried up...
20:28 ...Thus saith the Lord, Because the Syrians have said, The Lord is God of the hills, but he is not God of the valleys, therefore will I deliver all this great multitude into thine hand, and ye shall know that I am the Lord
21:19 ...Hast thou killed, and also taken possession...

II Kings
1:10 ...if I be a man of God, then let fire come down from heaven, and consume thee and thy fifty...
2:21 ...Thus saith the Lord, I have healed these waters; there shall not be from thence any more death or barren land
3:27 Then he took his eldest son ...and offered him for a burnt offering upon the wall...

4:2 ...Thine handmaid hath not any thing in the house, save a pot of oil
6:6 ...and the iron did swim
6:16 And he answered, Fear not: for they that be with us are more than they that be with them
6:18 ...Elisha prayed unto the Lord... Smite this people with blindness. And he smote them with blindness
8:6 ...Restore all that was hers
11:1 ...Athaliah ...arose and destroyed all the seed royal
17:17 ...used divination and enchantments, and sold themselves to do evil in the sight of the Lord...
19:3 ...This day is a day of trouble, and of rebuke, and blasphemy: for the children are come to the birth, and there is not strength to bring forth
19:14 And Hezekiah received the letter... and spread it before the Lord
19:19 ...save thou us out of his hand, that all the kingdoms of the earth may know that thou art the Lord God...

I Chronicles

4:10 And Jabez called on the God of Israel, saying, Oh that thou wouldest bless me indeed, and enlarge my coast, and that thine hand might be with me, and that thou wouldest keep me from evil, that it may not grieve me...
12:32 And of the children of Issachar, which were men that had understanding of the times, to know what Israel ought to do...
16:11 Seek the Lord and his strength, seek his face continually
16:21 He suffered no man to do them wrong: yea, he reproved kings for their sakes
16:22 Saying, touch not mine anointed, and do my prophets no harm
16:27 Glory and honour are in his presence; strength and gladness are in his place
17:27 ...for thou blessest, O Lord, and it shall be blessed for ever
26:8 ...able men for strength for the service...
28:20 And David said to Solomon his son, Be strong and of a good courage, and do it: fear not...
29:11 Thine, O Lord, is the greatness, and the power, and the glory, and the victory, and the majesty...
29:12 Both riches and honour come of thee, and thou reignest over all; and in thine hand is power and might; and in thine hand it is to make great, and to give strength unto all
29:13 Now therefore, our God, we thank thee, and praise thy glorious name

II Chronicles

5:14 ...for the glory of the Lord had filled the house of God
7:14 If my people, which are called by my name, shall humble themselves, and pray, and seek my face and turn from their wicked ways; then will I hear from heaven, and will forgive their sins, and will heal their land
13:12 And, behold, God himself is with us for our captain
14:11...Lord, it is nothing with thee to help, whether with many, or with them that have no power: help us, O Lord our God; for we rest on thee, and in thy name we go against this multitude`...
15:7 Be ye strong therefore, and let not your hands be weak: for your work shall be rewarded
16:9 For the eyes of the Lord run to and fro throughout the whole earth, to show himself strong on the behalf of those whose heart is perfect towards him
17:6 And his heart was lifted up in the ways of the Lord
18:21 ...I will go out and be a lying spirit in the mouth of all his prophets...
18:23 Then Zedekiah...smote Micaiah upon the cheek, and said Which way went the Spirit of the Lord from me to speak unto thee
18:26 ...feed him with bread of affliction...
18:30 ...Fight ye not with small or great, save only with the king...
19:6...Take heed what ye do: for ye judge not for man, but for the Lord...
19:11...Deal courageously, and the Lord shall be with the good
20:2...There cometh a great multitude against thee...
20:3 And Jehoshaphat feared, and set himself to seek the Lord...
20:12 O our God, wilt thou not judge them? for we have no might against this great company that cometh against us; neither know we what to do: but our eyes are upon thee
20:15 ...Be not afraid nor dismayed by reason of this great multitude; for the battle is not yours, but God's
20:17 Ye shall not need to fight in this battle: set yourselves, stand ye still, and see the salvation of the Lord with you...
20:20 ...Believe in the Lord your God so shall ye be established; believe his prophets, so shall ye prosper
20:22 And when they began to sing and to praise, the Lord set ambushments against the children of Ammon, Moab and...
20:27...the Lord had made them to rejoice over their enemies
29:5 ...carry forth the filthiness out of the holy place
30:7 And be not ye like your fathers, and like your brethren...
30:8 Now be ye not stiffnecked, as your fathers were, but yield yourselves unto the Lord...

30:9 For if ye turn again unto the Lord, your brethren and your children shall find compassion before them that led them captive...
32:7 Be strong and courageous, be not afraid or dismayed... for there be more with us than with them
32:8 With him is an arm of flesh; but with us is the Lord our God to help us, and to fight our battles...
32:30 ...And Hezekiah prospered in all his works
32:31 ...in the business of the ambassadors...God left him
36:16 But they mocked the messengers of God, and despised his words, and misused his prophets... till there was no remedy

Ezra

6:7 Let the work of this house of God alone
6:22 ...for the Lord had made them joyful and turned the heart of the king of Assyria unto them to strengthen their hands in the work of the house of God, the God of Israel
7:10 For Ezra had prepared his heart to seek the law of the Lord, and to do it, and to teach...
8:21 Then I proclaimed a fast there, at the river of Ahava, that we might afflict ourselves before our God, to seek of him a right way for us, and for our little ones, and for all our substance
8:23 So we fasted and besought our God for this: and he was intreated of us
10:10 ...Ye have transgressed, and have taken strange wives, to increase the trespass of Israel
10:11 ...separate yourselves from the people of the land and from strange wives

Nehemiah

2:12 ...neither told I any man what my God had put in my heart to do at Jerusalem
2:18 ...let us build the wall of Jerusalem, that we be no more a reproach
2:20 The God of heaven, he will prosper us; therefore we his servants will arise and build
4:4 Hear O our God; for we are despised: and turn their reproach upon their own head...
4:6 ...for the people had a mind to work
4:14 ...fight for your brethren, your sons, and your daughters, your wives, and your houses
4:20...our God shall fight for us
6:9 For they all made us afraid... now therefore, O God, strengthen my hands
8:10 ...for the joy of the Lord is your strength

Esther

2:15 ...And Esther obtained favor in the sight of all them that looked upon her

4:14 ...who knoweth whether thou art come into the kingdom for such a time as this?

4:16 ...I also and my maidens will fast likewise; and so will I go in unto the king, which is not according to the law: and if I perish, I perish

6:13 ...If Mordecai be of the seed of the Jews, before whom thou hast begun to fall, thou shalt not prevail against him, but shalt surely fall before him

Job

1:6 Now there was a day when the sons of God came to present themselves before the Lord, and Satan came also among them

1:21 ...Naked came I out of my mother's womb, and naked shall I return thither: the Lord gave, and the Lord hath taken away; blessed be the name of the Lord

1:22 In all this Job sinned not, nor charged God foolishly

2:9 ...curse God, and die

2:10 ...In all this did not job sin with his lips

3:25 For the thing which I greatly feared is come upon me...

4:17 Shall mortal man be more just than God? shall a man be more pure than his maker?

5:2 For wrath killeth the foolish man, and envy slayeth the silly one

5:8 I would seek unto God, and unto God would I commit my cause

5:9 Which doeth great things and unsearchable, marvelous things without number

5:12 He disappointed the devices of the crafty, so that their hands cannot perform their enterprise

5:17 Behold, happy is the man whom God correcteth: therefore despise not thou the chastening of the Lord

5:18 For he maketh sore, and bindeth up: he woundeth and his hands make whole

5:19 He shall deliver thee in six troubles: yea in seven there shall no evil befall thee

5:20 In famine he shall redeem thee from death, and in war from the power of the sword

5:21 Thou shalt be hid from the scourge of the tongue: neither shalt thou be afraid of destruction when it cometh

5:22 At destruction and famine thou shalt laugh: neither shalt thou be afraid of the beasts of the earth

5:23 For thou shalt be in league with the stones of the field: and the beasts of the field shall be at peace with thee
6:6 Can that which is unsavoury be eaten without salt
6:24 Teach me and I will hold my tongue: and cause me to understand wherein I have erred
6:25 How forcible are right words...
8:2 ...how long shall the words of thy mouth be like a strong wind
8:3 Doth God pervert judgement? or doth the almighty pervert justice?
8:7 Though thy beginning was small, yet thy latter end should greatly increase
8:22 They that hate thee will be clothed with shame
9:4 He is wise in heart, and mighty in strength: who hath hardened himself against him and prospered
9:20 If I justify myself, mine own mouth shall condemn me...
10:12 Thou hast granted me life and favour, and thy visitation hath preserved my spirit
10:15 If I be wicked, woe unto me; and if I be righteous, yet will I not lift up my head...
11:7 Canst thou by searching find out God...
12:5 He that is ready to slip with his feet is as a lamp despised in the thought of him that is at ease
12:12 With the ancient is wisdom; and in length of days understanding
13:4 But ye are forgers of lies, ye are all physicians of no value
13:15 Though he slay me, yet will I trust in him: but I will maintain mine own ways before him
14:1 Man that is born of a woman is of few days, and full of trouble
14:7 For there is hope of a tree, if it be cut down, that it will sprout again, and that the tender branch thereof will not cease
14:8 Though the root thereof wax old in the earth, and the stock thereof die in the ground
14:9 Yet through the scent of water it will bud, and bring forth boughs like a plant
14:14 ...all the days of my appointed time will I wait until my change come
15:14 What is man that he should be clean? and he which is born of a woman, that he should be righteous?
15:15 Behold, he putteth no trust in his saints; yea, the heavens are not clean in his sight
15:16 How much more abominable and filthy is man, which drinketh iniquity like water?
15:31 Let not him that is deceived trust in vanity; for vanity shall be his recompence
16:2 I have many such things: miserable comforters are ye all

16:16 My face is foul with weeping, and on my eyelids is the shadow of death
17:9 ...he that hath clean hands shall be stronger and stronger
18:5 Yea, the light of the wicked shall be put out, and the spark of his fire shall not shine
18:14 His confidence shall be rooted out of his tabernacle, and it shall bring him to the king of terrors
18:16 His roots shall be dried up beneath, and above shall his branch be cut off
19:25 For I know that my redeemer liveth and that he shall stand at the latter day upon the earth
20:5 That the triumphing of the wicked is short, and the joy of the hypocrite but for a moment

Job 22:21-29
22:21 Acquaint now thyself with him and be at peace: thereby good shall come unto thee
22:22 Receive I pray thee, the law from his heart, and lay up his words in thine heart
22:23 If thou return to the almighty, thou shalt be built up, thou shalt put away iniquity far from thy tabernacles
22:24 Then shalt thou lay up gold as dust, and the gold of O'phir as the stones of the brooks
22:25 Yea, the almighty shall be thy defense and thou shalt have plenty of silver
22:26 For then shalt thou have thy delight in the Almighty and shalt lift thy face unto God
22:27 Thou shalt make thy prayer unto him, and he shalt hear thee, and thou shalt pay thy vows
22:28 Thou shalt also decree a thing and it shall be established unto thee: and the light shall shine upon thy ways
22:29 When men are cast down, then thou shalt, say There is lifting up: and he shall save the humble person
23:6 Will he plead against me with his great power? No; but he would put strength in me
23:10 But he knoweth the way that I take: when he hath tried me I shall come forth like gold
23:12 Neither have I gone back from the commandment of his lips; I have esteemed the words of his mouth more than my necessary food
26:14 Lo, these are parts of his ways: but how little is heard of him? But the thunder of his power who can understand?
28:12 But where shall wisdom be found? and where is the place of understanding?
28:15 It cannot be gotten for gold, neither shall silver be weighed for the price thereof

28:18 ...for the price of wisdom is above rubies
29:6 When I washed my steps with butter...
29:15 I was eyes to the blind, and feet was I to the lame
29:16 I was a father to the poor...
31:9 If mine heart hath been deceived by a woman...
31:29 If I rejoiced at the destruction of him that hated me, or lifted up myself when evil found him
31:30 Neither have I suffered my mouth to sin by wishing a curse to his soul
31:33 If I covered my transgressions as Adam, by hiding mine iniquity in my bosom
33:3 My words shall be of the uprightness of my heart: and my lips shall utter knowledge clearly
33:26 He shall pray unto God, and he will be favorable unto him: and he shall see his face with joy: for he will render unto man his righteousness
33:27 He looketh upon men, and if any say, I have sinned, and perverted that which was right, and it profited me not
33:28 He will deliver his soul from going into the pit, and his life shall see the light
34:10 ...far be it from God, that he should do wickedness; and from the Almighty that he should commit iniquity
34:12 Yea, surely God will not do wickedly, neither will the Almighty pervert judgment
34:18 Is it fit to say to a king, Thou art wicked? and to princes, Ye are ungodly?
34:22 There is no darkness, nor shadow of death, where the workers of iniquity may hide themselves
34:23 For he will not lay upon man more than right; that he should enter into judgment with God
34:29 When he giveth quietness, who then can make trouble...
34:32 That which I see not teach thou me; if I have done iniquity, I will do no more
35:9 By reason of the multitude of oppressions they make the oppressed to cry: they cry out by reason of the arm of the mighty
35:10 But none saith, Where is God my maker, who giveth songs in the night
35:13 Surely God will not hear vanity, neither will the Almighty regard it
36:5 Behold, God is mighty, and despiseth not any...
36:6 He preserveth not the life of the wicked: but giveth right to the poor
36:11 If they obey and serve him, they shall spend their days in prosperity, and their years in pleasures
37:19 Teach us what we shall say unto him; for we cannot order our speech by reason of darkness

37:23 Touching the Almighty, we cannot find him out: he is excellent in power, and in judgment, and in plenty of justice: he will not afflict
38:12 Hast thou commanded the morning since thy days; and caused the dayspring to know his place
40:7 Gird up thy loins now like a man...
41:27 He esteemeth iron as straw, and brass as rotten wood
42:10 And the Lord turned the captivity of Job, when he prayed for his friends...
42:12 So the Lord blessed the latter end of Job more than his beginning...

Psalms

1:1 Blessed is the man that walketh not in the counsel of the ungodly, nor standeth in the way of sinners, nor sitteth in the seat of the scornful
1:2 But his delight is in the law of the Lord, and in his law doth he meditate day and night
1:3 And he shall be like a tree planted by the rivers of water, that bringeth forth his fruit in his season; his leaf also shall not wither; and whatsoever he doeth shall prosper
2:8 Ask of me and I will give thee the heathen for thine inheritance, and the uttermost parts of the earth for thy possession
2:11 Serve the Lord with fear, and rejoice with trembling
2:12 Kiss the Son, lest he be angry, and ye perish from the way... Blessed are all they that put their trust in him
3:2 Many there be which say of my soul, There is no help for him in God
3:3 But thou, O Lord, art a shield for me; my glory, and the lifter up of mine head
3:4 I cried unto the Lord with my voice, and he heard me out of his holy hill. Selah
3:5 I laid me down and slept; I awaked for the Lord sustained me
3:6 I will not be afraid of ten thousands of people, that have set themselves against me round about
4:4 ...commune with your own heart upon your bed, and be still. Selah
4:7 Thou hast put gladness in my heart, more than in the time that their corn and their wine increased
4:8 I will both lay me down in peace, and sleep: for thou Lord only makest me dwell in safety
5:1 Give ear to my words, O Lord, consider my meditation
5:2 Hearken unto the voice of my cry, my King, and my God: for unto thee will I pray

5:11 But let all those that put their trust in thee rejoice: let them ever shout for joy, because thou defendest them: let them also that love thy name be joyful in thee
5:12 For thou Lord, wilt bless the righteous; with favor wilt thou compass him as with a shield
6:1 O Lord, rebuke me not in thy anger, neither chasten me...
6:2 Have mercy upon me, O Lord; for I am weak: O Lord, heal me; for my bones are vexed
6:6 I am weary with my groaning... I water my couch with my tears
6:7 Mine eye is consumed because of grief; it waxed old...
7:9 Oh let the wickedness of the wicked come to an end...
7:10 My defense is of God which saveth the upright in heart
7:11 God judgeth the righteous, and God is angry with the wicked everyday
7:14 Behold he travaileth with iniquity, and hath conceived mischief, and brought forth falsehood
7:15 He made a pit, and digged it, and is fallen into the ditch which he made
7:16 His mischief shall fall upon his own head, and his violent dealing shall come down upon his own pate
9:6 O thou enemy, destructions are come to a perpetual end...
9:9 The Lord also will be a refuge for the oppressed...
9:17 The wicked shall be turned into hell, and all the nations that forget God
9:18 For the needy shall not alway be forgotten...
10:15 Break thou the arm of the wicked and the evil man...
11:3 If the foundations be destroyed, what can the righteous do
12:6 The words of the Lord are pure words: as silver tried in a furnace of earth, purified seven times
13:1 How long will thou forget me, O Lord? for ever?
13:5 But I have trusted in thy mercy; my heart shall rejoice in thy salvation
14:1 The fool hath said in his heart, there is no God...
15:1 Lord, who shall abide in thy tabernacle? who shall dwell in thy holy hill?
16:1 Preserve me O God, for in thee do I put my trust
16:3 But to the saints that are in the earth, and to the excellent, in whom is all my delight
16:5 The Lord is the portion of mine inheritance and of my cup: thou maintainest my lot
16:6 The lines are fallen unto me in pleasant places; yea, I have a goodly heritage
16:7 I will bless the Lord who hath given me counsel: my reins also instruct me in the night seasons

16:8 I have set the Lord always before me: because he is at my right hand, I shall not be moved
16:10 For thou wilt not leave my soul in hell; neither wilt thou suffer thine Holy One to see corruption
16:11 Thou wilt show me the path of life: in thy presence is fullness of joy; at thy right hand there are pleasures for evermore
17:3 ...I am purposed that my mouth shall not transgress
17:5 Hold up my goings in thy paths, that my footsteps slip not
17:8 Keep me as the apple of the eye, hide me under the shadow of thy wings
17:15 As for me, I will behold thy face in righteousness: I shall be satisfied when I awake, with thy likeness
18:1 I will love thee O Lord, my strength
18:2 The Lord is my rock, and my fortress, and my deliverer; my God, my strength, in whom I will trust; my buckler, and the horn of my salvation, and my high tower
18:3 I will call upon the Lord, who is worthy to be praised: so shall I be saved from mine enemies
18:19 He brought me forth also into a large place; he delivered me, because he delighted in me
18:32 It is God that girdeth me with strength and maketh my way perfect
18:39 For thou hast girdeth me with strength unto the battle: thou hast subdued under me those that rose up against me
19:7 The law of the Lord is perfect, converting the soul: the testimony of the Lord is sure, making wise the simple
19:8 The statutes of the Lord are right, rejoicing the heart: the commandment of the Lord is pure, enlightening the eyes
19:9 The fear of the Lord is clean, enduring forever: the judgments of the Lord are true and righteous altogether
19:10 More to be desired are they than gold, yea, than much fine gold: sweeter also than honey and the honeycomb
19:11 Moreover by them is thy servant warned: and in keeping of them there is great reward
19:12 Who can understand his errors? Cleanse thou me from hidden faults
19:13 Keep back thy servant also from presumptuous sins; let them not have dominion over me...
19:14 Let the words of my mouth, and the meditation of my heart be acceptable in thy sight, O Lord my strength, and my redeemer
20:1 The Lord hear thee in the day of trouble; the name of the God of Jacob defend thee
20:2 Send thee help from thee sanctuary, and strengthen thee out of Zion
20:7 Some trust in chariots, and some in horses: but we will remember the name of the Lord

21:7 For the king trusteth in the Lord, and through the mercy of the most High he shall not be moved
22:1 My God, my God, why hast thou forsaken me...
23:1 The Lord is my shepherd, I shall not want
23:2 He maketh me to lie down in green pastures: he leadeth me beside the still waters
23:3 He restoreth my soul...
24:1 The earth is the Lord's, and the fullness thereof; the world, and they that dwell therein
25:1 Unto thee, O Lord, do I lift up my soul
25:2 O my God I trust in thee, let me not be ashamed, let not my enemies triumph over me
25:4 Shew me thy ways, O Lord teach me thy paths
25:9 The meek will he guide in judgment: and the meek will he teach his way
25:14 The secret of the Lord is with them that fear him; and he will show them his covenant
27:1 The Lord is my light and my salvation, whom shall I fear? The Lord is the strength of my life, of whom shall I be afraid?
27:2 When the wicked, even mine enemies and my foes, came upon me to eat up my flesh, they stumbled and fell
27:4 One thing have I desired of the Lord, that will I seek after; that I may dwell in the house of the Lord all the days of my life...
27:5 For in the time of trouble he shall hide me in his pavilion...
27:6 And now shall mine head be lifted up above mine enemies...
27:7 Hear, O Lord, when I cry...
27:10 When my father and my mother forsake me, then the Lord will take me up
27:13 I had fainted, unless I had believed to see the goodness of the Lord in the land of the living
27:14 Wait on the Lord: be of good courage, and he shall strengthen thine heart: wait, I say, on the Lord
28:7 The Lord is my strength and shield; my heart trusted in him, and I am helped: therefore my heart greatly rejoiceth; and with my song will I praise him
29:2 Give unto the Lord the glory due unto his name...
29:4 The voice of the Lord is powerful... full of majesty
29:7 The voice of the Lord divideth the flames of fire
30:1 O Lord my God, I cried unto thee, and thou hast healed me
30:5 For his anger endureth but a moment; in his favor is life: weeping may endure for a night, but joy cometh in the morning
31:1 In thee O Lord, do I put my trust; let me never be ashamed; deliver me in thy righteousness
31:3 For thou art my rock and my fortress; therefore for thy name's sake lead me, and guide me

31:4 Pull me out of the net that they have laid privily for me: for thou art my strength
31:18 Let the lying lips be put to silence...
31:23 O love the Lord, all ye his saints: for the Lord preserveth the faithful, and plentifully rewardeth the proud doer
32:1 Blessed is he whose transgression is forgiven, whose sin is covered
32:6 For this shall everyone that is godly pray unto thee in a time when thou mayest be found...
32:8 I will instruct thee and teach thee in the way which thou shalt go: I will guide thee with mine eye
32:10 Many sorrows shall be to the wicked, but he that trusteth in the Lord, mercy shall compass him about
33:6 By the word of the Lord were the heavens made...
33:8 Let all the earth fear the Lord: let all the inhabitants of the world stand in awe of him
33:9 For he spake, and it was done; he commanded, and it stood fast
33:16 There is no king saved by the multitude of an host: a mighty man is not delivered by much strength
34:1 I will bless the Lord at all times: his praise shall continually be in my mouth
34:7 The angel of the Lord encampeth round about them that fear him, and delivereth them
34:9 O fear the Lord ye his saints...
34:19 Many are the afflictions of the righteous: but the Lord delivereth him out of them all
34:21 Evil shall slay the wicked...
34:22 The Lord redeemeth the soul of his servants: and none of them that trust in him shall be desolate
35:26 Let them be ashamed and brought to confusion that rejoice at mine hurt...
35:27 Let them shout for joy, and be glad, that favour my righteous cause...
36:7 How excellent is thy loving kindness O God! Therefore the children of men put their trust under the shadow of thy wings
37:1 Fret not thyself because of evil doers, neither be thou envious against the workers of iniquity
37:2 For they shall soon be cut down like grass and wither as the green herb
37:3 Trust in the Lord, and do good, so shalt thou dwell in the land, and verily thou shalt be fed
37:4 Delight thyself in the Lord; and he shall give thee the desires of thine heart
37:5 Commit thy way unto the Lord; trust also in him; and he shall bring it to pass

37:6 And he shall bring forth thy righteousness as the light, and thy judgment as the noonday

37:7 Rest in the Lord and wait patiently for him: fret not thyself because of him who prospereth in his way, because of the man who bringeth wicked devices to pass

37:8 Cease from anger, and forsake wrath: fret not thyself in anywise to do evil

37:9 For evildoers shall be cut off: but those that wait upon the Lord, they shall inherit the earth

37:10 For yet a little while, and the wicked shall not be: yea, thou shalt diligently consider his place, and it shall not be

37:11 But the meek shall inherit the earth; and shall delight themselves in the abundance of peace

37:23 The steps of a good man are ordered by the Lord: and he delighteth in his way

37:24 Though he fall, he shall not be utterly cast down: for the Lord upholdeth him with his hand

37:25 I have been young, and now am old; yet have I not seen the righteous forsaken, nor his seed begging bread

37:31 The law of his God is in his heart, none of his steps shall slide

39:1 I said, I will take heed to my ways, that I sin not with my tongue: I will keep my mouth with a bridle, while the wicked is before me

39:5 ...verily every man at his best state is altogether vanity

39:8 Deliver me from all my transgressions: make me not the reproach of the foolish

40:1 I waited patiently for the Lord: and he inclined unto me, and heard my cry

40:2 He brought me up also out of an horrible pit, out of the miry clay, and set my feet upon a rock, and established my goings

40:3 And he hath put a new song in my mouth, even praise unto our God: many shall see it and fear...

40:8 I delight to do thy will O my God: yea thy law is within my heart

41:1 Blessed is he that considereth the poor, the Lord will deliver him in time of trouble

41:4 I said Lord, be merciful unto me: heal my soul: for I have sinned against thee

41:11 By this I know that thou favorest me, because mine enemy doth not triumph over me

42:1 As the hart panteth after the water brooks, so panteth my soul after thee, O God

42:7 Deep calleth unto deep at the noise of thy waterspouts: all thy waves and thy billows are gone over me

42:8 Yet the Lord will command his loving kindness in the daytime, and in the night his song shall be with me, and my prayer unto the God of my life
42:11 Why art thou cast down, O my soul? And why art thou disquieted within me? hope thou in God...
44:4 Thou art my King, O God: command deliverances for Jacob
44:26 Arise for our help, and redeem us for thy mercies' sake
45:6 Thy throne, O God is for ever and ever: the sceptre of thy kingdom is a right scepter
45:7 Thou lovest righteousness, and hatest wickedness...
46:1 God is our refuge and strength, a very present help in trouble
46:4 There is a river, the streams whereof shall make glad the city of God, the holy place of the tabernacles of the most high
46:5 God is in the midst of her; she shall not be moved...
46:10 Be still, and know that I am God...
47:9 ...for the shields of the earth belong unto God...
48:1 Great is the Lord, and greatly to be praised in the city of our God, in the mountain of his holiness
48:14 For this God is our God for ever and ever: he will be our guide even unto death
49:3 My mouth shall speak of wisdom; and the meditation of my heart shall be of understanding
49:15 But God will redeem me from the power of the grave: for he shall receive me
50:2 Out of Zion, the perfection of beauty, God hath shined
50:5 Gather my saints together unto me; those that have made a covenant with me by sacrifice
50:10 For every beast of the field is mine, and the cattle upon a thousand hills
50:23 Whoso offereth praise glorifieth me: and to him that ordereth his conversation aright will I show the salvation of God
51:1 Have mercy upon me, O God, according to thy lovingkindness: according to the multitude of thy tender mercies blot out my transgressions
51:2 Wash me thoroughly from mine iniquity, and cleanse me from my sin
51:3 For I acknowledge my transgressions: and my sin is ever before me
51:4 Against thee, thee only, have I sinned, and...
51:5 Behold I was shapen in iniquity; and in sin did my mother conceive me
51:6 Behold, thou desirest truth in the inward parts: and in the hidden part thou shalt make me to know wisdom
51:7 Purge me with hyssop and I shall be clean: wash me, and I shall be whiter than snow

51:8 Make me to hear joy and gladness, that the bones which thou hast broken may rejoice
51:9 Hide thy face from my sins, and blot out all mine iniquities
51:10 Create in me a clean heart, O God; and renew a right spirit within me
51:11 Cast me not away from thy presence; and take not thy holy spirit from me
51:12 Restore unto me the joy of thy salvation; and uphold me with thy free spirit
51:13 Then will I teach transgressors thy ways; and sinners shall be converted unto thee
51:15 O Lord, open thou my lips, and my mouth will show forth thy praise
53:1 The fool hath said in his heart, there is no God...
53:2 God looked down from heaven upon the children of men, to see if there were any that did understand, that did seek God
54:1 Save me, O God, by thy name, and judge me by thy strength
54:2 Hear my prayer, O God; give ear to the words of my mouth
55:22 Cast thy burden upon the Lord and he shall sustain thee: he shall never suffer the righteous to be moved
56:9 When I cry unto thee, then shall mine enemies turn back: this I know; for God is for me
56:11 In God I have put my trust: I will not be afraid what man can do to me
57:1 Be merciful unto me, O God, be merciful unto me: for my soul trusteth in thee: yea in the shadow of thy wings will I make my refuge until these calamities be over past
57:5 Be thou exalted, O God, above the heavens, let thy glory be...
59:1 Deliver me from mine enemies, O my God: defend me...
59:2 Deliver me from the workers of iniquity, and save me from...
59:9 Because of his strength will I wait upon thee: for God is my defence
60:11 Give us help from trouble, for vain is the help of man
60:12 Through God we shall do valiantly: for he it is that shall tread down our enemies
61:1 Hear my cry O God; attend unto my prayer
61:2 From the end of the earth will I cry unto thee, when my heart is overwhelmed: lead me to the rock that is higher than I
62:1 Truly my soul waiteth upon God: from him cometh my salvation
62:2 He only is my rock and my salvation; he is my defence; I shall not be greatly moved
62:5 My soul, wait thou only upon God; for my expectation is from him
62:7 In God is my salvation and my glory: the rock of my strength, and my refuge, is in God

62:10 Trust not in oppression, and become not vain in robbery: if riches increase, set not your heart upon them
62:11 God hath spoken once; twice have I heard this that power belongeth unto God
63:1 O God, thou art my God; early will I seek thee: my soul thirsteth for thee, my flesh longeth for thee in a dry and thirsty land, where no water is
63:2 To see thy power and thy glory, so as I have seen thee in the sanctuary
63:3 Because thy loving kindness is better than life, my lips shall praise thee
63:5 My soul shall be satisfied as with marrow and fatness; and my mouth shall praise thee with joyful lips
64:1 Hear my voice, O God in my prayer: preserve my life from fear of the enemy
64:2 Hide me from the secret counsel of the wicked; from the insurrection of the workers of iniquity
64:7 But God shall shoot at them with an arrow; suddenly shall they be wounded
65:2 O thou that hearest prayer, unto thee shall all flesh come
65:11 Thou crownest the year with thy goodness; and thy paths drop fatness
66:3 Say unto God, how terrible art thou in thy works! through the greatness of thy power shall thine enemies submit themselves unto thee
66:12 Thou hast caused men to ride over our heads; we went through fire and through water but thou broughtest us out into a wealthy place
66:18 If I regard iniquity in my heart, the Lord will not hear me
66:20 Blessed be God, which hath not turned away my prayer, nor his mercy from me
67:5 Let the people praise thee, O God; let all the people praise...
67:6 Then shall the earth yield her increase; and God, even our own God, shall bless us
67:7 God shall bless us; and all the ends of the earth shall fear him
68:1 Let God arise, let his enemies be scattered...
68:6 God setteth the solitary in families: he bringeth out those which are bound with chains
68:11 The Lord gave the word: great was the company of those that published it
68:18 Thou hast ascended on high, thou hast led captivity captive: thou hast received gifts for men
68:19 Blessed be the Lord, who daily loadeth us with benefits...
68:20 He that is our God is the God of salvation...
68:28 Thy God hath commanded thy strength: strengthen, O God, that which thou hast wrought for us

68:35 ...the God of Israel is he that giveth strength and power unto his people. Blessed be God
69:5 O God thou knowest my foolishness; and my sins are not hid from thee
69:9 For the zeal of thine house hath eaten me up...
70:1 Make haste, O God, to deliver me; make haste to help me, O Lord
70:2 Let them be ashamed and confounded that seek after my soul
71:1 In thee, O Lord, do I put my trust: let me never be put to confusion
73:25 Whom have I in heaven but thee? and there is none upon earth that I desire beside thee
73:26 My flesh and my heart faileth: but God is the strength of my heart, and my portion forever
74:20 ...the dark places of the earth are full of the habituations of cruelty
74:21 O let not the oppressed return ashamed...
75:6 For promotion cometh neither from the east, nor from the west, nor from the south
77:13 ...who is so great a God as our God?
78:41 ...tempted God, and limited the Holy One of Israel
81:9 There shall no strange God be in thee, neither shall thou worship any strange god
83:15 So persecute them with thy tempest, and make them afraid with thy storm
83:18 That men may know that thou whose name alone is JEHOVAH, art the most high over all the earth
84:7 They go from strength to strength, every one of them in Zion appeareth before God
84:10 For a day in thy courts is better than a thousand, I had rather be a doorkeeper in the house of my God...
84:11 For the Lord God is a sun and shield: the Lord will give grace and glory: no good thing will he withhold from them that walk uprightly
84:12 O Lord of hosts, blessed is the man that trusteth in thee
86:17 Show me a token for good; that they which hate me may see it, and be ashamed...
89:9 Thou rulest the raging of the sea: when the waves thereof arise, thou stillest them
89:16 In thy name shall they rejoice all the day: and in thy righteousness shall they be exalted
89:17 For thou art the glory of their strength: and in thy favor our horn shall be exalted
89:21 With whom my hand shall be established: mine arm also shall strengthen him

89:34 My covenant will I not break, nor alter the thing that is gone out of my lips
90:4 For a thousand years in thy sight are but as yesterday...
90:10 The days of our years are threescore years and ten...
90:12 So teach us to number our days, that we may apply our hearts unto wisdom
90:15 Make us glad according to the days wherein thou hast afflicted us, and the years wherein we have seen evil
90:17 And let the beauty of our God be upon us: and establish thou the work of our hands upon us...
91:1 He that dwelleth in the secret place of the most High shall abide under the shadow of the Almighty
91:5 Thou shalt not be afraid for the terror by night...
91:6 ...nor for the destruction that wasteth at noonday
91:7 A thousand shall fall at thy side, and ten thousand at thy right hand: but it shall not come nigh thee
91:8 Only with thine eyes shalt thou behold and see the reward of the wicked
91:9 Because thou hast made the LORD, which is my refuge, even the most High, thy habitation
91:10 There shall no evil befall thee, neither shall any plague come nigh thy dwelling
91:11 For he shall give his angels charge over thee, to keep thee...
91:14 Because he hath set his love upon me, therefore will I deliver him: I will set him on high, because he hath known my name
91:15 He shall call upon me, and I will answer him: I will be with him in trouble; I will deliver him and honour him
91:16 With long life will I satisfy him, and show him my salvation
92:1 It is a good thing to give thanks unto the Lord, and to sing praises unto thy name, O most High
92:4 For thou, Lord, hast made me glad through thy work: I will triumph in the works of thy hands
92:9 ...all the workers of iniquity shall be scattered
92:10 But my horn shalt thou exalt like the horn of an unicorn: I shall be anointed with fresh oil
94:19 In the multitude of thy thoughts within me thy comforts delight my soul
100:4 Enter into his gates with thanksgiving, and into his courts with praise: be thankful unto him and bless his name
102:13 Thou shalt arise, and have mercy upon Zion: for the time to favour her, yea, the set time, is come
103:1 Bless the Lord, O my soul: and all that is within me, bless his holy name
103:3 Who forgiveth all thine iniquities; who healeth all thy diseases

103:4 Who redeemeth thy life from destruction; who crowneth thee with loving kindness and tender mercies
103:5 Who satisfieth thy mouth with good things; so that thy youth is renewed like the eagle's
103:7 He made known his ways unto Moses, his acts unto the children of Israel
103:10 He hath not dealt with us after our sins; nor rewarded us according to our iniquities
103:14 For he knoweth our frame; he remembereth that we are dust
104:4 Who maketh his angels spirits; his ministers a flaming fire
104:27 These all wait upon thee; that thou mayest give them their meat in due season
104:34 My meditation of him shall be sweet: I will be glad in the Lord
105:3 Glory ye in his holy name: let the heart of them rejoice that seek the Lord
105:4 Seek the Lord and his strength: seek his face evermore
105:14 He suffered no man to do them wrong: yea, he reproved kings for their sakes
105:15 Saying, Touch not mine anointed, and do my prophets no harm
107:16 For he hath broken the gates of brass, and cut the bars of iron in sunder
107:20 He sent his word, and healed them, and delivered...
108:12 Give us help from trouble: for vain is the help of man
108:13 Through God we shall do valiantly: for it is he that shall tread down our enemies
109:1 Hold not thy peace, O God of my praise
109:4 For my love they are my adversaries: but I give myself unto prayer
109:26 Help me, O Lord my God: O save me according to...
109:29 Let my adversaries be clothed with shame...
110:2 The Lord shall send the rod of thy strength out of Zion: rule thou in the midst of thine enemies
110:3 Thy people shall be willing in the day of thy power...
111:10 The fear of the Lord is the beginning of wisdom ...
112:1 ...Blessed is the man that feareth the Lord, that delighteth greatly in his commandments
112:2 His seed shall be mighty upon earth
112:3 Wealth and riches shall be in his house: and his righteousness endureth forever
112:5 A good man showeth favour and lendeth: he will guide his affairs with discretion
112:10 ...the desire of the wicked shall perish
113:3 From the rising of the sun unto the going down of the same...

113:7 He raiseth up the poor out of the dust, and lifteth the needy out of the dunghill
113:8 That he may set him with princes, even with the princes of his people
113:9 He maketh the barren woman to keep house, and to be a joyful mother of children
115:14 The Lord shall increase you more and more, you and your children
116:15 Precious in the sight of the Lord is the death of his saints
118:9 It is better to trust in the Lord than to put confidence in princes
118:17 I shall not die, but live, and declare the works of the Lord
118:22 The stone which the builders refused is become the head stone of the corner
118:29 O, give thanks unto the Lord; for he is good: for his mercy endureth forever

Psalm 119
119:9 Wherewithal shall a young man cleanse his way? By taking heed thereto according unto thy word
119:11 Thy word have I hid in mine heart that I might not sin against you
119:18 Open thou mine eyes that I may behold wondrous things out of thy law
119:28 My soul melteth for heaviness: strengthen thou me according unto thy word
119:29 Remove from me the way of lying: and grant me thy law graciously
119:32 I will run the way of thy commandments, when thou shalt enlarge my heart
119:34 Give me understanding, and I shall keep thy law...
119:35 Make me to go in the path of thy commandments; for therein do I delight
119:37 Turn away mine eyes from beholding vanity and quicken thou me in the way
119:46 And I will speak of thy testimonies also before kings, and will not be ashamed
119:47 And I will delight myself in thy commandments which I have loved
119:48 My hands also will I lift up unto thy commandments, which I have loved; and I will meditate in thy statutes
119:49 Remember the word unto thy servant, upon which thou hast caused me to hope
119:62 At midnight I will rise to give thanks unto thee because...
119:63 I am a companion of all them that fear thee, and of them that keep thy precepts

119:68 Thou art good, and doest good; teach me thy statutes
119:71 It is good for me that I have been afflicted; that I might learn thy statutes
119:74 They that fear thee will be glad when they see me; because I have hoped in thy word
119:80 Let my heart be sound in thy statutes; that I be not ashamed
119:89 For ever, O Lord, thy word is settled in heaven
119:93 I will never forget thy precepts for with them thou hast quickened me
119:97 O how love I thy law! It is my meditation all the day
119:99 I have more understanding than all my teachers: for thy testimonies are my meditation
119:103 How sweet are thy words unto my taste! Yea sweeter than honey to my mouth
119:105 Thy word is a lamp unto my feet and a light unto my path
119:130 The entrance of thy words giveth light; it giveth understanding to the simple
119:133 Order my steps in thy word: and let not any iniquity have dominion over me
119:162 I rejoice at thy word, as one that findeth great spoil
119:165 Great peace have they which love thy law and nothing shall offend them
119:173 Let thine hand help me; for I have chosen thy precepts
120:1 In my distress I cried unto the Lord and he heard me
120:2 Deliver my soul, O Lord, from lying lips, and from a deceitful tongue
120:7 I am for peace: but when I speak, they are for war
121:1 I will lift up mine eyes unto the hills, from whence cometh...
121:2 My help cometh from the Lord, which made heaven and...
121:3 He will not suffer thy foot to be moved: he that keepeth thee will not slumber
121:6 The sun shall not smite thee by day, nor the moon by night
122:6 Pray for the peace of Jerusalem: they shall prosper that...
122:7 Peace be within thy walls and prosperity within thy palaces
123:1 Unto thee lift I up mine eyes, O thou that dwelleth in the heavens
123:2 Behold, as the eyes of servants look unto the hand of their masters, and as the eyes of a maiden unto the hand of her mistress; so our eyes wait upon the Lord our God, until that he have mercy upon us
123:3 Have mercy upon us, O Lord, have mercy upon us: for we are exceedingly filled with contempt
124:6 Blessed be the Lord, who hath not given us as a prey to their teeth
124:7 Our soul is escaped as a bird out of the snare of the fowlers: the snare is broken and we are escaped

124:8 Our help is in the name of the Lord, who made heaven and earth
125:1 They that trust in the Lord shall be as mount Zion which cannot be removed, but abideth for ever
125:3 For the rod of the wicked shall not rest upon the lot of the righteous...
126:1 When the Lord turned again the captivity of Zion, we were like them that dream
126:5 They that sow in tears shall reap in joy
127:1 Except the Lord build the house, they labour in vain ...
127:2 ...for so he giveth his beloved sleep
127:3 Lo, children are an heritage of the Lord: and the fruit of the womb is his reward
128:3 Thy wife shall be as a fruitful vine by the sides of thine house: thy children like olive plants round about thy table
128:6 Yea thou shalt see thy children's children, and peace upon Israel
131:2 Surely I have behaved and quieted myself, as a child that is weaned of his mother
132:8 Arise, O Lord, into thy rest; thou, and the ark of thy strength
133:1 Behold, how good and how pleasant it is for brethren to dwell together in unity
135:5 For I know that the Lord is great, and that our Lord is above all gods
135:6 Whatsoever the Lord pleased, that did he in heaven, and in earth, in the seas, and all deep places
138:2 ...for thou hast magnified thy word above all thy name
138:3 In the day when I cried, thou answeredst me and strengthenedst me with strength in my soul
138:7 Though I walk in the midst of trouble, thou wilt revive me...
138:8 The Lord will perfect that which concerneth me...
139:14 I will praise thee for I am fearfully and wonderfully made...
139:16 ...in thy book all my members were written, which in continuance were fashioned, when as yet there was none of them
139:17 How precious also are thy thoughts unto me, O God! How great is the sum of them!
139:23 Search me, O God, and know my heart: try me, and know...
140:4 Keep me, O Lord, from the hands of the wicked...
144:1 Blessed be the Lord my strength, which teacheth my hands to war and my fingers to fight
144:2 My goodness, and my fortress; my high tower, and my deliverer; my shield, and he in whom I trust; who subdueth my...
145:9 The Lord is good to all: and his tender mercies are over all his works
145:15 The eyes of all wait upon thee; and thou givest them their meat in due season

145:16 Thou openest thine hand, and satisfieth the desire of every living thing
145:17 The Lord is righteous in all his ways, and holy in all his...
147:3 He healeth the broken in heart, and bindeth up their wounds
147:5 Great is our Lord, and of great power: his understanding is infinite
147:13 For he hath strengthened the bars of thy gates; he hath blessed thy children within thee
149:4 For the Lord taketh pleasure in his people: he will beautify the meek with salvation
149:6 Let the high praises of God be in their mouth, and a two-edged sword in their hand
149:8 To bind their kings with chains, and their nobles with fetters of iron
150:6 Let everything that hath breath praise the Lord. Praise ye the Lord

Proverbs

1:5 A wise man will hear, and will increase learning; and a man of understanding shall attain unto wise counsels
1:7 The fear of the Lord is the beginning of knowledge but fools despise wisdom and instruction
1:8 My son, hear the instruction of thy father, and forsake not the law of thy mother
1:9 For they shall be an ornament of grace unto thy head, and chains about thy neck
1:20 Wisdom crieth without; she uttereth her voice in the streets
1:32 ...the prosperity of fools shall destroy them
1:33 But whoso hearkeneth unto me shall dwell safely, and shall be quiet from fear of evil
2:3 Yea, if thou criest after knowledge, and liftest up thy voice for understanding
2:4 If thou seekest her as silver, and searchest for her as for hid treasures
2:5 Then shalt thou understand the fear of the Lord, and find the knowledge of God
2:6 For the Lord giveth wisdom: out of his mouth cometh knowledge and understanding
2:7 He layeth up sound wisdom for the righteous: he is a buckler to them that walk uprightly
2:10 When wisdom entereth into thine heart and knowledge is pleasant unto thy soul
2:11 Discretion shall preserve thee, understanding shall keep thee
2:18 For her house inclineth unto death, and her paths unto the dead

2:19 None that go unto her returneth again, neither take they hold of the paths of life

3:1 My son forget not my law; but let thine heart keep my commandments

3:2 For length of days, and long life, and peace, shall they add to thee

3:3 Let not mercy and truth forsake thee: bind them about thy neck; write them upon the table of thine heart

3:4 So shall thou find favour and good understanding in the sight of God and man

3:5 Trust in the lord with all thine heart; and lean not unto thine own understanding

3:6 In all thy ways acknowledge him, and he shall direct thy paths

3:7 Be not wise in thine own eyes: fear the Lord and depart from evil

3:8 It shall be health to thy navel and marrow to thy bones

3:9 Honour the Lord with thy substance, and with the firstfruits of all thine increase

3:10 So shall thy barns be filled with plenty, and thy presses shall burst out with new wine

3:13 Happy is the man that findeth wisdom, and the man that getteth understanding

3:14 For the merchandise of it is better than the merchandise of silver and the gain thereof than fine gold

3:15 She is more precious than rubies: and all the things thou canst desire are not to be compared unto her

3:16 Length of days is in her right hand; and in her left hand riches and honour

3:17 Her ways are ways of pleasantness, and all are paths are peace

3:18 She is a tree of life to them that lay hold upon her and happy is everyone that retaineth her

3:19 The Lord by wisdom hath founded the earth; by understanding hath he established the heavens

3:21 My son, let not them depart from thine eyes: keep sound wisdom and discretion:

3:22 So shall they be life unto thy soul and grace unto thy neck

3:23 Then shalt thou walk in thy way safely, and thy foot shall not stumble

3:26 For the Lord shall be thy confidence, and shall keep thy foot from being taken

3:35 The wise shall inherit glory: but shame shall be the promotion of fools

4:5 Get wisdom, get understanding: forget it not; neither decline from the words of my mouth

4:6 Forsake her not, and she shall preserve thee: love her, and she shall keep thee
4:7 Wisdom is the principal thing; therefore get wisdom: and with all thy getting get understanding
4:8 Exalt her, and she shall promote thee: she shall bring thee to honour, when thou dost embrace her
4:9 She shall give to thine head an ornament of grace: a crown of glory shall she deliver to thee
4:13 Take fast hold of instruction; let her not go: keep her for she is thy life
4:14 Enter not into the path of the wicked, and go not in the way of evil men
4:15 Avoid it, pass not by it, turn from it, and pass away
4:18 But the path of the just is as the shining light, that shineth more and more unto the perfect day
4:20 My son, attend unto my words; incline thine ear unto my sayings
4:21 Let them not depart from thine eyes; keep them in the midst of thine heart
4:22 For they are life unto those that find them, and health unto all their flesh
4:23 Keep thy heart will all diligence; for out of it are the issues of life
4:24 Put away from thee a forward mouth, and perverse lips put far from thee
4:25 Let thine eyes look right on, and let thine eyelids look straight before thee
4:26 Ponder the path of thy feet, and let all thy ways be established
5:18 Let thy fountain be blessed: and rejoice with the wife of thy youth
5:19 Let her be as the loving hind and pleasant roe; let her breasts satisfy thee at all times; and be thou ravished always with her love
6:6 Go to the ant thou sluggard; consider her ways and be wise:
6:7 Which, having no guide, overseer, or ruler
6:8 Provideth her meat in the summer, and gathereth her food in the harvest
6:9 How long wilt thou sleep, O sluggard? When wilt thou arise out of thy sleep?
6:10 Yet a little sleep, a little slumber, a little folding of the hands to sleep
6:11 So shall thy poverty come as one that travelleth, and thy want as an armed man
6:26 For by means of a whorish woman a man is brought to a piece of bread: and the adulteress will hunt for the precious life
6:27 Can a man take fire in his bosom, and his clothes not be burnt

6:32 But whoso committeth adultery with a woman lacketh understanding: he that doeth it destroyeth his own soul

7:2 Keep my commandments and live; and my law as the apple of thine eye

7:3 Bind them upon thy fingers, write them upon the table of...

7:4 Say unto wisdom, thou art my sister; and call understanding thy kinswoman

8:11 For wisdom is better than rubies; and all the things that may be desired are not to be compared to it

8:15 By me kings reign, and princes decree justice

8:17 I love them that love me; and those that seek me early...

8:18 Riches and honour are with me, yea, durable riches and righteousness

8:19 My fruit is better than gold; and my revenue than choice silver

8:21 That I may cause those that love me to inherit substance; and I will fill their treasures

9:8 Reprove not a scorner, lest he hate thee: rebuke a wise man and he will love thee

9:10 The fear of the Lord is the beginning of wisdom: and the knowledge of the holy is understanding

9:11 For by me thy days shall be multiplied, and the years of thy life shall be increased

10:4 He becometh poor that dealeth with a slack hand: but the hand of the diligent maketh rich

10:7 The memory of the just is blessed: but the name of the wicked shall rot

10:14 Wise men lay up knowledge: but the mouth of the foolish is near destruction

10:19 In the multitude of words there wanteth not sin

10:22 The blessing of the Lord, it maketh rich, and he added no sorrow with it

10:26 As vinegar to the teeth, and as smoke to the eyes, so is the sluggard to them that sent him

11:4 Riches profit not in the day of wrath: but righteousness...

11:13 A talebearer revealeth secrets...

11:14 Where no counsel is, the people fall: but in the multitude of counselors there is safety

11:16 A gracious woman retaineth honour: and strong men retain riches

11:19 As righteousness tendeth to life: so he that pursueth evil pursueth it to his own death

11:22 As a jewel of gold in a swine's snout, so is a fair woman which is without discretion

11:25 The liberal soul shall be made fat: and he that watereth...

11:29 He that troubleth his own house shall inherit the wind: and the fool shall be servant to the wise of heart

11:30 ...he that winneth souls is wise
12:1 Whoso loveth instruction loveth knowledge
12:4 A virtuous woman is a crown to her husband: but she that maketh ashamed is rottenness in his bones
12:11 He that tilleth his land shall be satisfied with bread...
12:14 A man shall be satisfied with good by the fruit of his mouth...
12:15 The way of a fool is right in his own eyes, but he that hearkeneth unto counsel is wise
12:16 A fool's wrath is presently known: but a prudent man covereth shame
12:23 A prudent man concealeth knowledge: but the heart of fools proclaimeth foolishness
12:24 The hand of the diligent shall bear rule: but the slothful shall be under tribute
12:27 The slothful man roasteth not that which he took in hunting: but the substance of a diligent man is precious
13:1 A wise son heareth his father's instructions...
13:3 He that keepeth his mouth keepeth his life: but he that openeth wide his lips shall have destruction
13:7 There is that maketh himself rich yet hath nothing...
13:13 Whoso despiseth the word shall be destroyed
13:16 Every prudent man dealeth with knowledge: but a fool layeth open his folly
13:18 Poverty and shame shall be to him that refuseth instruction...
13:20 He that walketh with wise men shall be wise: but a companion of fools shall be destroyed
13:22 A good man leaveth an inheritance to his children's children...
14:1 Every wise woman buildeth her house: but the foolish plucketh it down with her hands
14:9 Fools make a mock at sin: but among the righteous there is favour
14:10 The heart knoweth its own bitterness...
14:12 There is a way which seemeth right unto a man, but the end thereof are the ways of death
14:17 He that is soon angry dealeth foolishly: and a man of wicked devices is hated
14:23 In all labour there is profit: but the talk of the lips tendeth only to penury
14:24 The crown of the wise is their riches, but the foolishness of fools is folly
14:26 In the fear of the Lord is strong confidence: and his children shall have a place of refuge
14:27 The fear of the Lord is a fountain of life, to depart from the snares of death

14:29 He that is slow to wrath is of great understanding: but he that is hasty of spirit exalteth folly
14:30 A sound heart is the life of the flesh: but envy the rottenness of the bones
14:33 Wisdom resteth in the heart of him that hath understanding...
14:34 Righteousness exalteth a nation: but sin is a reproach to any people
15:1 A soft answer turneth away wrath: but grievous words stir up anger
15:2 The tongue of the wise useth knowledge aright: but the mouth of fools poureth out foolishness
15:4 A wholesome tongue is a tree of life: but perverseness therein is a breach in the spirit
15:5 A fool despiseth his father's instruction: but he that regardeth reproof is prudent
15:10 Correction is grievous unto him that forsaketh the way: and he that hateth reproof shall die
15:19 The way of a slothful man is as an hedge of thorns...
15:20 A wise son maketh a glad father...
15:21 Folly is joy to him that is destitute of wisdom...
15:22 Without counsel purposes are disappointed: but in the multitude of counselors they are established
15:23 A man hath joy by the answer of his mouth...
15:30 The light of the eyes rejoiceth the heart...
16:3 Commit thy works unto the Lord, and thy thoughts shall be established
16:5 Every one that is proud in heart is an abomination to the Lord: though hand join in hand, he shall not be unpunished
16:6 By mercy and truth iniquity is purged: and by the fear of the Lord men depart from evil
16:7 When a man's ways please the Lord, he maketh even his enemies to be at peace with him
16:8 Better is a little with righteousness than great revenues without right
16:9 A man's heart deviseth his way: but the Lord directeth his steps
16:20 He that handleth a matter wisely shall find good: and whoso trusteth in the Lord, happy is he
16:22 Understanding is a wellspring of life unto him that hath it: but the instruction of fools is folly
16:24 Pleasant words are as an honeycomb, sweet to the soul, and health to the bones
16:25 There is a way that seemeth right unto a man, but the end thereof are the ways of death

16:32 He that is slow to anger is better than the mighty; and he that ruleth his spirit than he that taketh a city
17:1 Better is a dry morsel, and quietness therewith, than an house full of sacrifices with strife
17:2 A wise servant shall have rule over a son that causeth shame...
17:10 A gift is as a precious stone in the eyes of him that hath it: whithersoever it turneth, it prospereth
17:13 Whoso rewardeth evil for good, evil shall not depart from...
17:20... he that hath a perverse tongue falleth into mischief
17:24 Wisdom is before him that hath understanding; but the eyes of a fool are in the ends of the earth
17:27 He that hath knowledge spareth his words; and a man of understanding is of an excellent spirit
17:28 Even a fool, when he holdeth his peace, is counted wise: and he that shutteth his lips is esteemed a man of understanding
18:4 The words of a man's mouth are as deep waters, and a wellspring of wisdom as a flowing brook
18:7 A fool's mouth is his destruction, and his lips are the snare of his soul
18:9 He also that is slothful in his work is brother to him that is a great waster
18:10 The name of the Lord is a strong tower: the righteous runneth into it, and is safe
18:13 He that answereth a matter before he heareth it, it is folly and shame unto him
18:14 The spirit of a man will sustain his infirmity; but a wounded spirit who can bear
18:16 A man's gift maketh room for him, and bringeth him before great men
18:20 A man's belly shall be satisfied with the fruit of his mouth; and with the increase of his lips shall he be filled
18:21 Death and life are in the power of the tongue: and they that love it shall eat the fruit thereof
18:22 Whoso findeth a wife findeth a good thing, and obtaineth favour of the Lord
19:2 Also, that the soul be without knowledge, it is not good...
19:11 The discretion of a man deferreth his anger; and it is his glory to pass over a transgression
19:15 Slothfulness casteth into a deep sleep; and an idle soul...
20:1 Wine is a mocker, strong drink is raging: and whosoever is deceived thereby is not wise
20:3 It is an honour for a man to cease from strife...
20:11 Even a child is known by his doings...
20:13 Love not sleep, lest thou cometh to poverty; open...
20:17 Bread of deceit is sweet to a man, but afterwards...

20:18 Every purpose is established by counsel: and with good advice make war
20:20 Whoso curseth his father or his mother, his lamp...
20:27 The spirit of man is the candle of the Lord, searching all the inward parts of the belly
20:30 The blueness of a wound cleanseth away evil: so do stripes the inward parts of the belly
21:1 The king's heart is in the hand of the Lord...
21:5 The thoughts of the diligent tend only to plenteousness...
21:9 It is better to dwell in the corner of the housetop, than with a brawling woman in a wide house
21:13 Whoso stoppeth his ears at the poor, he also shall cry himself, but shall not be heard
21:17 He that loveth pleasure shall be a poor man: he that loveth wine and oil shall not be rich
21:21 He that followeth after righteousness and mercy findeth life, righteousness, and honour
21:22 A wise man scaleth the city of the mighty, and casteth down the strength of the confidence thereof
21:23 Whoso keepeth his mouth and his tongue keepeth his soul from troubles
21:25 The desire of the slothful killeth him; for his hands refuse to labour
21:27 The sacrifice of the wicked is abomination: how much...
21:30 There is no wisdom nor understanding nor counsel against the Lord
21:31 The horse is prepared against the day of battle: but safety is of the Lord
22:1 A good name is rather to be chosen than great riches...
22:4 By humility and the fear of the Lord are riches, and honour, and life
22:6 Train up a child in the way he should go: and when he is old, he will not depart from it
22:13 The slothful man saith, There is a lion without...
22:15 Foolishness is bound in the heart of a child; but the rod of correction will drive it far from him
22:24 Make no friendship with an angry man...
22:28 Remove not the ancient landmarks which thy fathers have set
22:29 Seest thou a man diligent in his business? he shall stand before kings; he shall not stand before mean men
23:4 Labour not to be rich: cease from thine own wisdom
23:13 Withhold not correction from the child: for if thou beatest him with the rod, he shall not die
23:27 For a whore is a deep ditch; and a strange woman is a narrow pit

24:3 Through wisdom is an house builded; and by understanding it is established
24:4 And by knowledge shall the chambers be filled with all precious and pleasant riches
24:5 A wise man is strong; yea a man of knowledge increaseth strength
24:6 For by wise counsel thou shalt make thy war: and in the multitude of counselors there is safety
24:10 If thou faint in the day of adversity, thy strength is small
24:14 So shall the knowledge of wisdom be unto thy soul: when thou hast found it, then there shall be a reward, and thy expectation shall not be cut off
24:17 Rejoice not when thine enemy falleth...
24:27 Prepare thy work without, and make it fit for thyself in the field; and afterwards build thine house
25:2 It is the glory of God to conceal a thing: but the honour of kings to search out a matter
25:5 Take away the wicked from before the king, and his throne shall be established in righteousness
25:6 Put not forth thyself in the presence of the king, and stand not in the place of great men
25:7 For better it is that he be said unto thee, Come up hither; than that thou shouldest be put lower...
25:11 A word fitly spoken is like apples of gold in pictures of silver
25:14 Whoso boasteth himself of a false gift is like clouds and wind without rain
25:15 ...a soft tongue breaketh the bone
25:17 Withdraw thy foot from thy neighbour's house; lest he be weary of thee and hate thee
25:21 If thine enemy be hungry, give him bread to eat; and if he be thirsty, give him water to drink
25:22 For thou shalt heap coals of fire upon his head
25:24 It is better to dwell in the corner of the housetop, than with a brawling woman and in a widehouse
25:27 It is not good to eat much honey: so for men to search their own glory is not glory
25:28 He that hath no rule over his own spirit is like a city that is broken down and without walls
26:2 As the bird by wandering, as the swallow by flying so the curse causeless shall not come
26:4 Answer not a fool according to his folly, lest thou be like unto him
26:5 Answer a fool according to his folly, lest he be wise in his own conceit
26:11 As a dog returneth to his vomit, so a fool returneth to his...
26:14 As the door turneth upon his hinges, so doth the slothful...

26:16 The sluggard is wiser in his own conceit than seven men that can render a reason

26:22 The words of a talebearer are as wounds and they go down...

27:1 Boast not thyself of to morrow; for thou knowest not what a day may bring forth

27:2 Let another man praise thee and not thine own mouth, a stranger and not thine own lips

27:4 Wrath is cruel, and anger is outrageous; but who is able to stand before envy

27:5 Open rebuke is better than secret love

27:6 Faithful are the wounds of a friend; but the kisses of an enemy are deceitful

27:17 Iron sharpeneth iron; so a man sharpeneth the countenance of his friend

27:18 ...he that waiteth on his master shall be honoured

27:22 Though thou shouldest bray a fool in a mortar among wheat with a pestle, yet will not his foolishness depart from him

27:23 Be thou diligent to know the state of thy flocks...

27:24 For riches are not forever: and doth the crown endure to every generation

28:1 The wicked flee when no man pursueth: but the righteous are bold as a lion

28:8 He that by usury and unjust gain increaseth his substance, he shall gather it for him that will pity the poor

28:13 He that covereth his sins shall not prosper: but whoso confesseth and forsaketh them shall have mercy

28:19 He that tilleth his land shall have plenty of bread...

28:26 He that trusteth in his own heart is a fool...

29:10 The bloodthirsty hate the upright: but the just seek his soul

29:11 A fool uttereth all his mind: but a wise man keepeth it in till afterwards

29:15 The rod and reproof give wisdom: but a child left to himself bringeth his mother to shame

29:17 Correct thy son and he shall give the rest; yea, he shall give delight unto thy soul

29:18 Where there is no vision, the people perish: but he that keepeth the law happy is he

29:23 A man's pride shall bring him low: but honour shall uphold the humble in spirit

29:27 An unjust man is an abomination to the just: and he that is upright in the way is abomination to the wicked

30:2 Surely I am more brutish than any man

30:5 Every word of God is pure: he is a shield unto them that put their trust in him

30:11 There is a generation that curseth their father, and doth not bless their mother
30:12 There is a generation that are pure in their own eyes, but are not washed from their filthiness
31:3 Give not thy strength unto women, nor thy way to that which destroyeth kings
31:10 Who can find a virtuous woman? For her price is above rubies
31:11 The heart of her husband doth safely trust in her, so that he shall have no need of spoil
31:12 She will do him good and not evil all the days of her life
31:16 She considereth a field, and buyeth it: with the fruit of her hands she planted a vineyard
31:26 She openeth her mouth with wisdom; and in her tongue is the law of kindness
31:27 She looketh well to the ways of her household, and eateth not the bread of idleness
31:30 Favour is deceitful, and beauty is vain: but a woman that feareth the Lord, she shall be praised

Ecclesiastes

1:18 For in much wisdom is much grief: and he that increaseth knowledge increaseth sorrow
3:1 To every thing there is a season, and a time to every purpose under the heaven
3:11 He hath made everything beautiful in his time
4:9 Two is better than one; because they have a reward for their labour
4:10 For if they fall, the one will lift up his fellow: but woe to him that is alone when he falleth...
4:12 ... a threefold cord is not quickly broken
5:2 Be not rash with thy mouth, and let not thine heart be hasty to utter anything before God...
5:3 For a dream cometh through the multitude of business; and a fool's voice is known by multitude of words
5:9 As he came forth of his mother's womb, naked shall he return to go as he came
5:11 When goods increase, they are increased that eat them...
7:8 Better is the end of a thing than the beginning thereof: and the patient in spirit is better than the proud in spirit
7:9 Be not hasty in thy spirit to be angry for anger resteth in the bosom of fools
7:19 Wisdom strengtheneth the wise more than ten mighty men which are in the city
8:4 Where the word of a king is, there is power...

8:8 ...neither shall wickedness deliver those that are given to it
8:11 Because sentence against an evil work is not executed speedily, therefore the heart of the sons of men is fully set in them to do evil
9:4 ...for a living dog is better than a dead lion
9:10 Whatsoever thy hand findeth to do, do it with thy might; for there is no work, nor device, nor knowledge, nor wisdom, in the grave, whither thou goest
9:11 ...the race is not to the swift, nor the battle to the strong...
9:17 The words of wise men are heard in quiet more than the cry of him that ruleth among fools
9:18 Wisdom is better than weapons of war...
10:1 Dead flies cause the ointment of the apothecary to send forth a stinking savour: so doth a little folly him that is in reputation for wisdom and honour
10:8 He that diggeth a pit shall fall into it; and whoso breaketh an hedge, the serpent shall bite him
10:10 If the iron be blunt, and he do not whet the edge, then must he put to more strength: but wisdom is profitable to direct
10:14 A fool is also full of words...
10:15 The labour of the foolish wearieth everyone of them, because he knoweth not how to go to the city
10:18 By much slothfulness the building decayeth...
10:19 ...money answereth all things
11:1 Cast thy bread upon the waters: for thou shalt find it after many days
12:1 Remember now thy creator in the days of thy youth...

Song of Solomon
2:4 He brought me to the banqueting house, and his banner over me was love
6:3 I am my beloved's, and my beloved is mine...
6:5 Turn away thine eyes from me, for they have overcome me...
8:6 Set me as a seal upon thine heart, as a seal upon thine arm: for love is strong as death...
8:7 Many waters cannot quench love, neither can the floods drown it:

Isaiah
1:5 ...the whole head is sick and the whole heart faint
1:16 Wash you, make you clean, put away the evil of your doings from before mine eyes, cease to do evil
1:17 Learn to do well, seek judgment, relieve the oppressed, judge the fatherless, plead for the widow

1:18 Come now, and let us reason together, saith the Lord: though your sins be as scarlet, they shall be as white as snow, though they be red like crimson, they shall be as wool

1:19 If ye be willing and obedient, ye shall eat the good of the land

1:25 And I will turn my hand upon thee, and purely purge away thy dross, and take away all thy tin

2:2 And it shall come to pass in the last days, that the mountain of the Lord's house shall established in the top of the mountains, and shall be exalted above the hills, and all nations shall flow unto it

3:12 As for my people, children are their oppressors, and women rule over them...

4:1 And in that day seven women shall take hold of one man...

4:5 ...for upon all the glory shall be a defence

5:13 Therefore my people are gone into captivity, because they have no knowledge...

5:20 Woe unto them that call evil good, and good evil...

6:5 Then said I, Woe is me! for I am undone; because I am a man of unclean lips, and I dwell in the midst of a people of unclean lips...

7:14 ...Behold, a virgin shall conceive, and bear a son, and shall call his name Immanuel

8:9 Associate yourselves, O ye people, and ye shall be broken in pieces...

8:10 Take counsel together, and it shall come to nought; speak the word, and it shall not stand: for God is with us.

8:13 Sanctify the Lord of hosts himself; and let him be your fear, and let him be your dread

8:20 To the law and to the testimony: if they speak not according to this word, it is because there is no light in them

9:4 For thou hast broken the yoke of his burden, and the staff of his shoulder, the rod of his oppressor, as in the day of Midian

9:6 For unto us a child is born, unto us a son is given: and the government shall be upon his shoulder: and his name shall be called Wonderful, Counsellor, The mighty God, The everlasting Father, The Prince of Peace

9:7 Of the increase of his government and peace there shall be no end...

9:16 For the leaders of this people cause them to err; and they that are led of them are destroyed

9:19 Through the wrath of the Lord of hosts is the land darkened, and the people shall be as the fuel of the fire...

10:1 Woe unto them that decree unrighteous decrees...

10:27 And it shall come to pass in that day, that his burden shall be taken away from off thy shoulder, and his yoke from off thy neck, and the yoke shall be destroyed because of the anointing

11:1 And there shall come forth a rod out of the stem of Jesse, and a Branch shall grow out of his roots

11:2 And the spirit of the Lord shall rest upon him, the spirit of wisdom and understanding, the spirit of counsel and might, the spirit of knowledge and of the fear of the Lord
11:3 And shall make him of quick understanding in the fear of the Lord; and he shall not judge after the sight of his eyes, neither reprove after the hearing of his ears
12:3 Therefore with joy shall ye draw water out of the wells of salvation
13:11 And I will punish the world for their evil, and the wicked for their iniquity; and I will cause the arrogancy of the proud to cease...
14:5 The Lord hath broken the staff of the wicked, and the sceptre of the rulers
14:12 How art thou fallen from heaven, O Lucifer, son of the morning! how art thou cut down to the ground, which didst weaken the nations
14:13 For thou hast said in thine heart, I will ascend into heaven, I will exalt my throne above the stars of God
14:15 Yet thou shalt be brought down to hell, to the sides of the pit
19:2 And I will set the Egyptians against the Egyptians: and they shall fight every one against his brother, and every one against his neighbor, city against city, and kingdom against kingdom
19:14 The Lord hath mingled a perverse spirit in the midst thereof: and they have caused Egypt to err in every work thereof as a drunken man staggereth in his vomit
25:1 O Lord, thou art my God; I will exalt thee, I will praise thy name; for thou hast done wonderful things; thy counsels of old are faithfulness and truth
25:7 And he will destroy in this mountain the face of the covering cast over all people, and the vail that is spread over all nations
25:8 He will swallow up death in victory; and the Lord God will wipe away tears from off all faces...
26:3 Thou wilt keep him in perfect peace, whose mind is stayed on thee: because he trusteth in thee
26:4 Trust ye in the Lord forever: for in the Lord JE-HO-VAH is everlasting strength
26:9 With my soul have I desired thee in the night; yea, with my spirit within me will I seek thee early...
28:6 ...and for strength to them that turn the battle to the gate
28:16 ...I lay in Zion for a foundation a stone, a tried stone...
28:18 And your covenant with death shall be disannulled...
32:17 And the work of righteousness shall be peace; and the effect of righteousness quietness and assurance for ever
33:6 And wisdom and knowledge shall be the stability of thy times, and strength of salvation...

33:22 For the Lord is our judge, the Lord is our lawgiver, the Lord is our king; he will save us
35:3 Strengthen ye the weak hands, and confirm the feeble knees
38:5 ...I have heard thy prayer, I have seen thy tears: behold I...
40:8 The grass withereth, the flower fadeth: but the word of our God shall stand for ever
40:28 Hast thou not known? Hast thou not heard, that the everlasting God, the Lord, the Creator of the ends of the earth, fainteth not, neither is weary? There is no searching of his understanding
40:29 He giveth power to the faint; and to them that have no might he increaseth strength
40:30 Even the youths shall faint and be weary, and the young men shall utterly fall:
40:31 But they that wait upon the Lord shall renew their strength; they shall mount up with wings as eagles; they shall run and not be weary; and they shall walk, and not faint
41:10 Fear thou not; for I am with thee: be not dismayed; for I am thy God: I will strengthen thee; yea, I will help thee; yea, I will uphold thee with the right hand of my righteousness
41:11 Behold all they that were incensed against thee shall be ashamed and confounded: they shall be as nothing; and they that strive with thee shall perish
41:12 Thou shalt seek them, and shall not find them, even them that contended with thee...
41:13 For I the Lord will hold thy right hand, saying unto thee, Fear not; I will help thee
41:15 Behold, I will make thee a new sharp threshing instrument having teeth; thou shalt thresh the mountains, and beat them small, and shalt make the hills as chaff
41:17 When the poor and needy seek water, and there is none, and their tongue faileth for thirst, I the Lord will hear them, I the God of Israel will not forsake them
41:18 I will open rivers in high places, and fountains in the midst of the valleys: I will make the wilderness a pool of water, and the dry land springs of water
41:21 Produce your cause saith the Lord; bring forth your strong reasons, saith the King of Jacob
42:4 He shall not fail nor be discouraged, till he have set judgement in the earth...
42:8 I am the Lord: that is my name: and my glory will I not give to another...
43:1 ...Fear not: for I have redeemed thee, I have called thee by thy name; thou art mine
43:2 When thou passest through the waters, I will be with thee; and through the rivers, they shall not overflow thee: when thou

walkest through the fire thou shalt not be burned; neither shall the flame kindle upon thee

43:11 I, even I, am the Lord; and beside me there is no saviour

43:18 Remember ye not the former things, neither consider the things of old

43:19 Behold, I will do a new thing; now it shall spring forth; shall ye not know it? I will even make a way in the wilderness, and rivers in the desert

43:25 I even I, am he that blotteth out thy transgressions for mine own sake...

44:3 For I will pour water on him that is thirsty, and floods upon the dry ground: I will pour my spirit upon thy seed, and my blessing upon thine offspring

44:22 I have blotted out, as a thick cloud, thy transgressions, and as a cloud, thy sins: return unto me; for I have redeemed thee

44:26 That confirmeth the word of his servant, and performeth the counsel of his messengers...

45:2 I will go before thee, and make the crooked places straight: I will break in pieces the gates of brass, and cut in sunder the bars of iron:

45:3 I will give thee the treasures of darkness, and hidden riches of secret places...

45:11 Thus saith the Lord, the Holy One of Israel, and his Maker, Ask me of things to come concerning my sons, and concerning the work of my hands command ye me

45:13 I have raised him up in righteousness, and I will direct all his ways: he shall build my city, and he shall let go my captives, not for price nor reward, saith the Lord of hosts

45:22 Look unto me, and be ye saved, all the ends of the earth: for I am God, and there is none else

46:9 Remember the former things of old: for I am God, and there is none else; I am God and there is none like me

46:10 Declaring the end from the beginning and from ancient times the things that are not yet done, saying, My counsel shall stand, and I will do all my pleasure

48:17 ...I am the Lord thy God which teacheth thee to profit, which leadeth the by the way that thou shalt go

48:18 O that thou hadst hearkened to my commandments! then had thy peace been as a river, and thy righteousness as the waves of the sea

48:22 There is no peace saith the Lord, unto the wicked

49:15 Can a woman forget her suckling child that she should not have compassion on the son of her womb? Yea they may forget, yet will I not forget thee

49:23 And kings shall be thy nursing fathers, and their queens thy nursing mothers...

49:25 But thus saith the Lord, Even the captives of the mighty shall be taken away, and the prey of the terrible shall be delivered: for I will contend with him that contendeth with thee, and I will save thy children

50:4 The Lord God hath given me the tongue of the learned, that I should know how to speak a word in season to him that is weary...

50:7 For the Lord God will help me; therefore shall I not be confounded: therefore have I set my face like a flint, and I know that I shall not be ashamed

51:12 I, even I, am he that comforteth you: who art thou, that thou shouldest be afraid of a man that shall die, and of the son of man which shall be made as grass

52:1 Awake, awake; put on thy strength, O Zion; put on thy beautiful garments, O Jerusalem, the holy city: for henceforth there shall no more come unto thee the uncircumcised and the unclean

52:2 Shake thyself from the dust; arise, and sit down, O Jerusalem: loose thyself from the bands of thy neck, O captive daughter of Zion

53:5 But he was wounded for our transgressions, he was bruised for our iniquities: the chastisement of our piece was upon him; and with his stripes, we are healed

53:6 All we like sheep have gone astray; we have turned every one to his own way; and the Lord hath laid on him the iniquity of us all

54:1 Sing, O barren, thou that didst not bear; break forth into singing, and cry aloud, thou that didst not travail with child: for more are the children of the desolate than the children of the married wife

54:2 Enlarge the place of thy tent, and let them stretch forth the curtains of thine habitations: spare not, lengthen thy cords, and strengthen thy stakes

54:3 For thou shalt break forth on the right hand and on the left; and thy seed shall inherit the gentiles and cause the desolate cities to be inhabited

54:4 Fear not; for thou shalt not be ashamed: neither be thou confounded; for thou shalt not be put to shame: for thou shalt forget the shame of thy youth, and shalt not remember the reproach of thy widowhood anymore

54:12 And I will make thy windows of agates, and thy gates of carbuncles, and all thy borders of pleasant stones

54:13 And all thy children shall be taught of the Lord; and great shall be the peace of thy children

54:14 In righteousness shalt thou be established: thou shalt be far from oppression ...

54:15 ...whosoever shall gather together against thee shall fall for thy sake

54:17 No weapon that is formed against thee shall prosper; and every tongue that shall rise against thee in judgment thou shalt condemn. This is the heritage of the servants of the Lord, and their righteousness is of me, saith the Lord

55:8 For my thoughts are not your thoughts, neither are your ways my ways, saith the Lord

55:9 For as the heavens are higher than the earth, so are my ways higher than your ways, and my thoughts than your thoughts

55:10 For as the rain cometh down, and the snow from heaven, and returneth not thither, but watereth the earth, and maketh it bring forth and bud, that it may give seed to the sower, and bread to the eater

55:11 So shall my word be that goeth forth out of my mouth: it shall not return unto me void, but it shall accomplish that which I please, and it shall prosper in the thing whereto I sent it

56:7 Even them will I bring to my holy mountain, and make them joyful in my house of prayer

56:10 His watchmen are blind: they are all ignorant, they are all dumb dogs, they cannot bark; sleeping, lying down, loving to slumber

57:13 ...but he that putteth his trust in me shall possess the land, and shall inherit my holy mountain

57:18 I have seen his ways, and will heal him: I will lead him also, and restore comforts unto him and to his mourners

57:19 I create the fruit of the lips...

58:6 Is not this the fast that I have chosen? to loose the bands of wickedness, to undo the heavy burdens, and to let the oppressed go free, and that ye break every yoke?

58:7 Is it not to deal thy bread to the hungry, and that thou bring the poor that are cast out to thy house? when thou seest the naked, that thou cover him; and that thou hide not thyself from thine own flesh?

58:8 Then shall thy light break forth as the morning, and thy health shall spring forth speedily: and thy righteousness shall go before thee; the glory of the Lord shall be thy rereward

58:9 Then shalt thou call, and the Lord shall answer; thou shalt cry, and he shall say, Here I am...

59:1 Behold the Lord's hand is not shortened, that it cannot save; neither his ear heavy, that it cannot hear

59:2 But your iniquities have separated between you and your God, and your sins have hid his face from you that he will not hear

59:15 Yea, truth faileth; and he that departeth from evil maketh himself a prey...

59:19 …When the enemy shall come in like a flood, the Spirit of the Lord shall lift up a standard against him
60:1 Arise, shine; for the light is come, and the glory of the Lord is risen upon thee
60:17 For brass I will bring gold, and for iron I will bring silver, and for wood brass, and for stones iron…
60:18 Violence shall no more be heard in thy land, wasting nor destruction within thy borders
60:20 Thy sun shall no more go down; neither shall thy moon withdraw itself: for the Lord shall be thine everlasting light, and the days of thy mourning shall be ended
61:1 The Spirit of the Lord God is upon me; because the Lord hath anointed me to preach good tidings unto the meek
61:6 But ye shall be named the Priests of the Lord: men shall call you the Ministers of our God: ye shall eat the riches of the gentiles, and in their glory shall ye boast yourselves
61:7 For your shame ye shall have double…
62:6 I have set watchmen upon thy walls, O Jerusalem…
63:9 In all their affliction he was afflicted…
64:6 We are all as an unclean thing, and all our righteousness are as filthy rags…
66:2 …but to this man will I look, even to him that is poor and of a contrite spirit, and trembleth at my word
66:9 Shall I bring to the birth, and not cause to bring forth? saith the Lord

Jeremiah

1:5 Before I formed thee in the belly I knew thee; and before thou camest forth out of the womb I sanctified thee, and I ordained thee a prophet unto the nations
1:12 …for I will hasten my word to perform it
1:17 Thou therefore gird up thy loins, and arise, and speak unto them, all that I command thee: be not dismayed at their faces, lest I confound thee before them
1:18 For, behold, I have made thee this day a defenced city, and an iron pillar, and brasen walls against the whole land…
1:19 And they shall fight against thee; but they shall not prevail against thee; for I am with thee saith the Lord, to deliver thee
2:5 Thus saith the Lord, What iniquity have your fathers found in me, that they are gone far from me, and have walked after vanity, and are become vain
2:19 Thine own wickedness shall correct thee…
3:15 And I will give you pastors according to mine heart, which shall feed you with knowledge and understanding

4:3 For thus saith the Lord to the men of Judah and Jerusalem, Break up your fallow ground, and sow not among thorns
5:25 ...your sins have witholden good things from you
5:31 The prophets prophesy falsely, and the priests bear rule by their means; and my people love to have it so...
7:3 ...Amend your ways and your doings, and I will cause you to dwell in this place
7:16 Therefore pray not thou for this people, neither lift up cry nor prayer for them...for I will not hear thee
7:23 ...walk ye in all the ways that I have commanded you, that it may be well unto you
8:7 ...my people know not the judgment of the Lord
8:10 ...everyone from the least even unto the greatest is given to covetousness, from the prophet even unto the priest...
8:15 We looked for peace, but no good came; and for a time of health, and behold trouble
8:22 Is there no balm in Gilead...
9:5 And they will deceive everyone his neighbour, and will not speak the truth
9:6 Thine habitation is in the midst of deceit; through deceit they refuse to know me, saith the Lord
10:12 He hath made the earth by his power, he hath established the world by his wisdom, and hath stretched out the heaven by his discretion
10:21 For the pastors are become brutish, and have not sought the Lord: therefore they shall not prosper, and all their flocks shall be scattered
10:23 O Lord, I know that the way of man is not in himself: it is not in man that walketh to direct his steps
10:24 O Lord, correct me, but with judgment; not in thine anger, lest thou bring me to nothing
12:8 Mine heritage is unto me as a lion in the forest; it crieth out against me: therefore have I hated it
12:10 Many pastors have destroyed my vineyard, they have trodden my portion under foot...
13:23 Can the Ethiopian change his skin, or the leopard his spots? then may ye also do good that are accustomed to do evil
15:16 Thy words were found and I did eat them; and thy word was unto me the rejoicing of mine heart...
15:21 And I will deliver thee out of the hand of the wicked, and I will deliver the from the hand of the terrible
17:5 Thus saith the Lord; cursed be the man that trusteth in man...
17:7 Blessed is the man that trusteth in the Lord, and whose hope the Lord is
17:9 The heart is deceitful above all things, and desperately wicked: who can know it?

17:14 Heal me, O Lord, and I shall be healed; save me and I shall be saved: for thou art my praise

17:17 Be not a terror unto me: thou art my hope in the day of evil

18:8 If that nation, against whom I have pronounced, turn from their evil, I will repent of the evil that I thought to do unto them

20:9 ...But his word was in mine heart as a burning fire shut up in my bones...

20:11 But the Lord is with me as a mighty terrible one: therefore my persecutors shall stumble, and they shall not prevail: they shall be greatly ashamed; for they shall not prosper: their everlasting confusion shall never be forgotten

22:13 Woe unto him that buildeth his house by unrighteousness, and his chambers by wrong; that useth his neighbour's service without wages, and giveth him not for his work

22:22 The wind shall eat up all thy pastors, and thy lovers shall go into captivity...

23:36 ...ye have perverted the words of the living God...

29:7 And seek the peace of the city whither I have caused you to be carried away captives, and pray unto the Lord for it: for in the peace thereof shall ye have peace

29:9 For they prophesy falsely in my name: I have not sent them, saith the Lord

29:11 For I know the thoughts that I think toward you, saith the Lord, thoughts of peace, and not of evil, to give you an expected end

29:13 And ye shall seek me, and find me, when ye shall search for me with all your heart

30:17 For I will restore health unto thee, and I will heal thee of thy wounds, saith the Lord

31:25 For I have satiated the weary soul, and I have replenished every sorrowful soul

32:17 Ah Lord God! Behold thou hast made the heaven and the earth by thy great power and stretched out arm, and there is nothing too hard for thee

32:27 Behold, I am the Lord, the God of all flesh: is there anything too hard for me?

32:39 And I will give them one heart, and one way, that they may fear me for ever, for the good of them, and of their children after...

32:40 And I will make an everlasting covenant with them, that I will not turn away from them, to do them good; but I will put my fear in their hearts, that they shall not depart from me

32:41 Yea, I will rejoice over them to do them good, and I will plant them in this land assuredly with my whole heart and with my whole soul

33:3 Call unto me, and I will answer thee, and shew thee great and mighty things, which thou knowest not

35:6 ...We will drink no wine...
42:3 That the Lord thy God may show us the way wherein we may walk, and the thing that we may do
48:10 Cursed be he that doeth the work of the Lord deceitfully, and cursed be he that keepeth his sword back from blood
51:20 Thou art my battle axe and weapons of war...

Lamentations
3:22 It is of the Lord's mercies that we are not consumed, because his compassions fail not
3:23 They are new every morning: great is thy faithfulness
3:26 It is good that a man should both hope and quietly wait for the salvation of the Lord
3:31 For the Lord will not cast off for ever
3:32 But though he cause grief, yet will he have compassion according to the multitude of his mercies
3:36 To subvert a man in his cause, the Lord approveth not
3:40 Let us search and try our ways, and turn again to the Lord
3:41 Let us lift up our heart with our hands unto God in the heavens
5:2 Our inheritance is turned to strangers, our houses to aliens
5:16 The crown is fallen from our head: woe unto us that we have sinned

Ezekiel
3:19 Yet if thou warn the wicked, and he turn not from his wickedness, nor from his wicked way, he shall die in his iniquity; but thou hast delivered thy soul
9:4 ...set a mark upon the foreheads of the men that sigh and that cry for all the abominations that be done in the midst thereof
9:9 ...the land is full of blood, and the city full of perverseness...
18:20 The soul that sinneth, it shall die. The son shall not bear the iniquity of the father...
18:26 When a righteous man turneth away from his righteousness, and comitteth iniquity, and dieth in them; for his iniquity that he hath done shall he die
18:27 Again, when the wicked man turneth away from his wickedness that he hath committed, and doeth that which is lawful and right, he shall save his soul
18:30 ...Repent, and turn yourselves from all your transgressions; so iniquity shall not be your ruin
22:26 Her priests have violated my law, and have profaned mine holy things...
23:45 ...because they are adulteresses, and blood is in their hands
24:13 In thy filthiness is lewdness...
24:23 ...but ye shall pine away for your iniquities

25:17 And I will execute great vengeance upon them with furious rebukes
28:12* ...Thou sealest up the sum, full of wisdom, and perfect in beauty
28:13* Thou hast been in the Eden of God...
28:14* Thou art the anointed cherub that covereth; and I have set thee so: thou wast upon the holy mountain of God...
28:15* Thou wast perfect in thy ways from the day that thou wast created, till iniquity was found in thee
28:17 *Thine heart was lifted up because of thy beauty, thou hast corrupted thy wisdom by reason of thy brightness...
28:18* ...therefore will I bring forth a fire from the midst of thee, it shall devour thee...
33:6 But if the watchman see the sword come, and blow not...
33:11 ...I have no pleasure in the death of the wicked: but that the wicked turn from his way and live
33:13 ...if he trust to his own righteousness, and commit iniquity, all his righteousness shall not be remembered...
33:15 If the wicked restore...he shall surely live, he shall not die
33:31 ...for with their mouth they show much love, but their heart goeth after their covetousness
34:2 Woe be to the shepherds of Israel that do feed themselves...
34:26 And I will make them and the places round about my hill a blessing; and I will cause the shower to come down in his season; there shall be showers of blessing
36:26 A new heart also will I give you, and a new spirit will I put within you: and I will take away the stony heart out of your flesh, and I will give you an heart of flesh
36:27 And I will put my spirit within you, and cause you to walk in my statutes, and ye shall keep judgments, and do them
36:29 I will also save you from all your uncleannesses...
37:4 Again he said unto me, Prophesy upon these bones, and say unto them, O ye dry bones, hear the word of the Lord
44:9 No stranger, uncircumcised in heart, nor uncicrcumcised in flesh, shall enter into my sanctuary...
44:21 Neither shall any priest drink wine, when they enter into the inner court
44:23 And they shall teach my people the difference between the holy and profane, and cause them to discern between the unclean and the clean
* Satan, Lucifer. See Isaiah 14:12

Daniel
1:20 And in all matters of wisdom and understanding that the king inquired of them, he found them ten times better than all the magicians and astrologers that were in all his realm

3:17 If it be so, our God whom we serve is able to deliver us from the burning fiery furnace...
5:14 I have even heard of thee, that the spirit of the gods is in thee, and that light and understanding and excellent wisdom is found in thee
6:23 ...and no manner of hurt was found upon him, because he believed in his God
10:12 ...from the first day... thy words were heard, and I am come for thy words
11:32 ...but the people that do know their God shall be strong and do exploits

Hosea

2:19 And I will betroth thee unto me forever...
4:6 My people are destroyed for lack of knowledge: because thou hast rejected knowledge, I will also reject thee...
7:9 Strangers have devoured his strength, and he knoweth it not...
10:12 Sow to yourselves in righteousness, reap in mercy; break up your fallow ground: for it is time to seek the Lord, till he come and rain righteousness upon you
13:14 I will ransom them from the power of the grave; I will redeem them from death...

Joel

2:15 Blow the trumpet in Zion, sanctify a fast, call a solemn assembly
2:25 And I will restore to you, the years that the locust hath eaten, the cankerworm, and the caterpiller, and the palmer worm, my great army which I sent among you
2:26 And ye shall eat in plenty, and be satisfied, and praise the name of the Lord your God, that hath dealt wondrously with you: and my people shall never be ashamed
2:28 And it shall come to pass afterward, that I will pour out my spirit upon all flesh; and your sons and your daughters shall prophesy, your old men shall dream dreams, your young men shall see visions
3:10 ... let the weak say, I am strong

Amos

3:3 Can two walk together except they be agreed?
3:7 Surely the Lord God will do nothing, but he revealeth his secret unto his servants the prophets
4:12 ...Prepare to meet thy God, O Israel
5:6 Seek the Lord, and ye shall live...
6:1 Woe to them that are at ease in Zion...

8:11 ...I will send a famine in the land, not a famine of bread, nor a thirst for water, but of hearing the words of the Lord
8:12 ...they shall run to and fro to seek the word of the Lord, and shall not find it

Obadiah
4 Though thou exalt thyself as the eagle, and though thou set thy nest among the stars, thence will I bring thee down, saith the Lord
17 But upon mount Zion shall be deliverance, and there shall be holiness; and the house of Jacob shall possess their possession

Jonah
1:2 Arise, go to Nineveh, that great city, and cry against it...
2:8 They that observe lying vanities forsake their own mercy
2:10 And the Lord spake unto the fish, and it vomited out Jonah upon the dry ground

Micah
3:8 But truly I am full of power by the spirit of the Lord ...
5:4 And he shall stand and feed in the strength of the Lord, in the majesty of the name of the Lord his God...
5:9 Thine hand shall be lifted up upon thine enemies, and all thine enemies shall be cut off
6:8 ...what doth the Lord require of thee, but to do justly, and to love mercy, and to walk humbly with thy God
7:8 ...when I sit in darkness, the Lord shall be a light unto me
7:18 ...he retaineth not his anger for ever, because he delighteth in mercy

Nahum
1:3 The Lord is slow to anger, and great in power, and will not at all acquit the wicked
1:7 The Lord is good, a strong hold in the day of trouble; and he knoweth them that trust in him
1:9 ...affliction shall not rise the second time
1:12 ...Though I have afflicted thee, I will afflict thee no more
1:13 For now will I break his yoke from off of thee, and will burst thy bonds in sunder
3:4 Because of the multitude of the whoredoms of the wellfavoured harlot...

Habakkuk
1:13 Thou art of purer eyes than to behold evil, and canst not look on iniquity

2:2 ...Write the vision, and make it plain upon tables, that he may run that readeth it
2:4 ...but the just shall live by his faith
2:14 For the earth shall be filled with the knowledge of the glory of the Lord, as the waters cover the sea
3:2 ...O Lord, revive thy work in the midst of the years...
3:17 Although the fig tree shall not blossom, neither shall fruit be in the vines; the labour of the olive shall fail, and the fields shall yield no meat; the flock shall be cut off from the fold, and there shall be no herd in the stalls:
3:18 Yet I will rejoice in the Lord, I will joy in the God of my salvation
3:19 The Lord God is my strength, and he will make my feet like hinds' feet, and he will make me to walk upon mine high places...

Zephaniah

2:3 Seek ye the Lord, all ye meek of the earth, which have wrought his judgment...
3:17 The Lord thy God in the midst of thee is mighty; he will save, he will rejoice over thee with joy, he will rest in his love, he will joy over thee with singing

Haggai

1:6 Ye have sown much and bring in little; ye eat, but ye have not enough; ye drink, but ye are not filled with drink; ye clothe you, but there is none warm; and he that earneth wages earneth wages to put it into a bag with holes
1:9 Ye looked for much, and, lo, it came to little; and when ye brought it home, I did blow upon it...
2:4 Yet now be strong, O Zerubabel, saith the Lord; and be strong, O Joshua, son of Josedech, the high priest; and be strong, all ye people of the land, saith the Lord, and work: for I am with you, saith the Lord
2:8 The silver is mine, and the gold is mine, saith the Lord of hosts
2:9 The glory of this latter house shall be greater than of the former, saith the Lord of hosts...

Zechariah

2:8 ...for he that toucheth you toucheth the apple of his eye
4:6 ...Not by might, nor by power, but by my Spirit, saith the Lord of hosts
4:9 ...The hands of Zerubabel have laid the foundation of this house; his hands shall also finish it...
4:10 For who hath despised the day of small things...
6:8 ...quieted my spirit in the north country

8:13 And it shall come to pass that as ye were a curse among the heathen, O house of Judah, and house of Israel; so will I save you, and ye shall be a blessing: fear not, but let your hands be strong
10:1 Ask ye of the Lord rain in the time of the latter rain; so the Lord shall make bright clouds, and give them showers of rain, to every one grass in the field
13:1 In that day there shall be a fountain opened to the house of David and to the inhabitants of Jerusalem for sin and for uncleanness

Malachi

1:11 For from the rising of the sun even unto the going down of the same my name shall be great among the Gentiles
2:1 And now, O ye priests, this commandment is for you
2:2 If ye will not hear, and if ye will not lay it to heart, to give glory to my name…I will even send a curse upon you…
2:3 Behold, I will corrupt your seed, and spread dung upon your faces…
2:5 My covenant was with him of life and peace; and I gave them to him for the fear wherewith he feared me…
2:6 The law of truth was in his mouth, and iniquity was not found in his lips: he walked with me in peace and equity, and did turn many away from iniquity
2:7 For the priest's lip should keep knowledge, and they should seek the law at his mouth: for he is the messenger of the Lord of hosts
3:10 Bring ye all the tithes into the storehouse, that there may be meat in mine house, and prove me now herewith, saith the Lord of hosts, if I will not open you the windows of heaven, and pour you out a blessing, that there shall not be room enough to receive it
3:11 And I will rebuke the devourer for your sakes, and he shall not destroy the fruits of your ground; neither shall your vine cast her fruit before the time in the field saith the Lord of hosts
3:12 And all nations shall call you blessed: for ye shall be a delightsome land, saith the Lord of hosts
4:2 But unto you that fear my name shall the Sun of righteousness arise with healing in his wings…

Chapter 3

New Testament Vitamins

Matthew
1:23 Behold, a virgin shall be with child, and shall bring forth a son, and they shall call his name Emmanuel, which being interpreted is, God with us
2:12 And being warned of God in a dream that they should not return to Herod, they departed into their own country another way
3:2 ...Repent ye: for the kingdom of heaven is at hand
3:10 And now also the axe is laid unto the root of the trees: therefore every tree which bringeth not forth good fruit is hewn down, and cast into the fire
3:11 I indeed baptize you with water unto repentance: but he that cometh after me is mightier than I, whose shoes I am not worthy to bear: he shall baptize you with the Holy Ghost, and with fire
4:4 It is written, man shall not live by bread alone, but by every word that proceedeth out of the mouth of God
4:17 From that time Jesus began to preach, and to say, Repent: for the kingdom of heaven is at hand
4:19 And he saith unto them, Follow me, and I will make you fishers of men
5:3 Blessed are the poor in spirit; for theirs is the kingdom of heaven
5:4 Blessed are they that mourn: for they shall be comforted
5:5 Blessed are the meek: for they shall inherit the earth
5:11 Blessed are they which are persecuted for righteousness' sake: for theirs is the kingdom of heaven
5:13 Ye are the salt of the earth...
5:14 Ye are the light of the world...
5:16 Let your light so shine before men, that they may see your good works and glorify your Father which is in heaven
5:19 Whosoever shall break one of these least commandments, and shall teach men so, he shall be called the least in the kingdom of heaven...
5:20 For I say unto you, That except your righteousness shall exceed the righteousness of the scribes and Pharisees, ye shall in no case enter into the kingdom of heaven
6:6 But thou, when thou prayest, enter into thy closet, and when thou hast shut thy door, pray to thy Father which is in secret; and thy Father which seeth in secret shall reward the openly
6:10 Thy kingdom come, thy will be done in earth, as it is in heaven
6:14 For if ye forgive men their trespasses, your heavenly Father will also forgive you

6:21 For where your treasure is, there will your heart be also
6:22 The light of the body is the eye: if therefore thine eye be single, thy whole body shall be full of light
6:23 But if thine eye be evil, thy whole body shall be full of darkness. If therefore the light that is in thee be darkness, how great is that darkness
6:24 No man can serve two masters: for either he will hate the one, and love the other...
6:33 But seek ye first the kingdom of God, and his righteousness; and all these things shall be added unto you
6:34 Take therefore no thought for the morrow: for the morrow shall take thought for the things of itself. Sufficient unto the day is the evil thereof
7:3 And why beholdest thou the mote that is in thy brother's eye, but considerest not the beam that is in thine own eye
7:6 Give not that which is holy unto the dogs, neither cast ye your pearls before swine...
7:7 Ask, and it shall be given you; seek and ye shall find; knock and it shall be opened unto you
7:8 For everyone that asketh receiveth; and he that seeketh findeth; and to him that knocketh it shall be opened
7:13 Enter ye in at the strait gate: for wide is the gate, and broad is the way, that leadeth to destruction, and many there be which go in...
7:14 Because strait is the gate, and narrow is the way, which leadeth unto life, and few there be that find it
7:15 Beware of false prophets, which come to you in sheep's clothing, but inwardly they are ravening wolves
7:16 Ye shall know them by their fruit...
7:21 Not every one that saith unto me, Lord, Lord, shall enter into the kingdom of God
8:8...but speak the word only, and my servant shall be healed
8:10...I have not found so great faith, no, not in Israel
8:22 But Jesus said unto him, Follow me: and let the dead bury their dead
8:26 And he saith unto them, Why are ye fearful, O ye of little faith?
*8:29...What have we to do with thee, Jesus, thou Son of God...
9:29 Then touched he their eyes saying, According to your faith...
9:37 ...The harvest truly is plenteous, but the laborers are few
10:1 And when he had called unto him his twelve disciples, he gave them power against unclean spirits, to cast them out, and to heal all manner of sickness and all manner of disease
10:16 ...be ye therefore wise as serpents and harmless as doves
10:22 And ye shall be hated of all men for my name's sake...
10:30 But the very hairs of your head are numbered
10:31 Fear ye not therefore, ye are of more value than many sparrows

10:32 Whosoever therefore shall confess me before men, him will I confess also before my Father which is in heaven
10:33 But whosoever shall deny me before men, him will I also deny before my Father which is in heaven
10:34 Think not that I am come to send peace on earth: I came not to send peace, but a sword
10:36 And a man's foes shall be they of his own household
10:38 And he that taketh not his cross, and followeth after me, is not worthy of me
10:39 He that findeth his life shall lose it: and he that loseth his life for my sake shall find it
10:40 He that receiveth you receiveth me...
11:12 And from the days of John the Baptist until now, the kingdom of heaven suffereth violence and the violent take it by force
11:28 Come unto me, all ye that labor and are heavy laden, and I will give you rest
12:25 ...every city or house divided against itself shall not stand
12:30 He that is not with me is against me and he that gathereth not with me scattereth abroad
12:31 ...but the blasphemy against the Holy Ghost shall not be forgiven unto men
12:36 But I say unto you, That every idle word that men shall speak they shall give account thereof in the day of judgment
12:37 For by thy words thou shalt be justified, and by thy words thou shalt be condemned
13:8 But other fell unto good ground, and brought forth fruit, some an hundredfold, some sixtyfold, some thirtyfold
13:9 Who hath ears to hear, let him hear
13:11 ...Because it is given unto you to know the mysteries of the kingdom of heaven...
13:15 For this people's heart is waxed gross, and their ears dull of hearing, and their eyes they have closed...
14:36 And besought him that they might only touch the hem of his garment: and as many as touched were made perfectly whole
16:19 And I will give unto thee the keys of the kingdom of heaven: and whatsoever thou shalt bound on earth shall be bound in heaven: and whatsoever thou shalt lose on earth shall be loosed in heaven
16:24 ...If any man will come after me, let him deny himself, and take up his cross, and follow me
16:26 For what is a man profited if he shall gain the whole world, and lose his own soul...
*17:21 Howbeit this kind goeth not out but by prayer and fasting
18:3 ...Except ye be converted, and become as little children, ye shall not enter into the kingdom of heaven
*18:11 For the Son of man is come to save that which was lost

18:18 Verily I say unto you, Whatsoever ye shall bind on earth shall be bound in heaven: and whatsoever ye shall lose on earth shall be loosed in heaven
19:9 Whosoever shall put way his wife except it be for fornication, and shall marry another, commiteth adultery
19:24 It is easier for the camel to go through the eye of a needle than for a rich man to enter into the kingdom of heaven
20:32 What will ye that I shall do unto you?
21:22 And all things, whatsoever ye shall ask in prayer believing, ye shall receive
22:37 Thou shalt love the Lord thy God with all thy heart, and with all thy soul, and with all thy mind
22:39 ...Thou shalt love thy neighbor as thyself
24:24 For there shall arise false Christs, and false prophets...
24:42 Watch therefore: for ye know not what hour your Lord doth come
25:30 And cast ye the unprofitable servant into outer darkness...
26:40 ...What, could ye not watch with me one hour
26:41 Watch and pray, that ye enter not into temptation: the spirit indeed is willing, but the flesh is weak
26:52 ...For all they that take the sword shall perish by the sword
28:6 He is not here: for he is risen. Come see the place where the Lord lay
28:18 ...All power is given unto me in heaven and in earth
28:19 Go ye therefore, and teach all nations, baptizing them in the name of the Father, and of the Son, and of the Holy Ghost
28:20 Teaching them to observe all things whatsoever I have commanded you: and, lo, I am with you alway, even unto the end of the world...

Mark

1:17 And Jesus said unto them, Come ye after me, and I will make you to become fishers of men
3:5 ...Stretch forth thine hand...
3:11 And unclean spirits, when they saw him, fell down before him, and cried saying, Thou art the Son of God
4:39 And he arose, and rebuked the wind, and said unto the sea, Peace be still, And the wind ceased, and there was a great calm
5:39 The damsel is not dead, but sleepeth
5:41 Tali-tha cumi, which is, being interpreted, Damsel, I say unto thee, arise
6:31 ...Come ye yourselves apart into a desert place, and rest...
6:42 And they did all eat and were filled
6:56 ...and as many as touched him were made whole

7:15 There is nothing from without a man, that entering into him can defile him: but the things which come out of him, those are they that defile the man
*7:16 If any man have ears to hear, let him hear
7:21 For from within, out of the heart of men proceed evil thoughts, adulteries, fornications...
7:23 All these evil things come from within, and defile the man
9:24 ...Lord, I believe, help thou my unbelief
*9:44 Where their worm dieth not, and the fire is not quenched
9:47 And if thine eye offend thee, pluck it out: it is better for thee to enter into the kingdom of God with one eye, than having two eyes to be cast into hell fire
10:23 ...How hardly shall they that have riches enter into the kingdom of God
10:44 And whosoever of you will be the chiefest, shall be servant of all
10:45 For even the Son of man came not to be ministered unto, but to minister, and to give his life a ransom for many
11:23 ...whosoever shall say unto this mountain, Be thou removed and be thou cast into the sea; and shall not doubt in his heart, but shall believe that those things which he saith shall come to pass; he shall have whatsoever he saith
11:24 Therefore I say unto you, what things soever ye desire, when ye pray, believe that ye receive them, and ye shall have them
11:25 And when ye stand praying, forgive, if ye have ought against any: that your Father also which is in heaven may forgive you your trespasses
*11:26 But if ye do not forgive, neither will your Father which is in heaven forgive your trespasses
13:22 For false Christs and false prophets shall rise, and shall shew signs and wonders, to seduce, if it were possible, even the elect
13:31 Heaven and earth shall pass away: but my words shall not pass away
16:4 And when they looked, they saw that the stone was rolled away: for it was very great
16:9 Now when Jesus was risen early the first day of the week...
16:15 Go ye into the world and preach the gospel to every creature
16:16 He that believed and is baptized shall be saved; but he that believeth not shall be damned
16:17 And these signs shall follow them that believe; in my name they shall cast out devils; they shall speak with new tongues
16:18 They shall take up serpents; and if they drink any deadly thing, it shall not hurt them; they shall lay hands on the sick and they shall recover

Luke

1:13 ...thy prayer is heard...
1:30 And the angel said unto her, Fear not, Mary: for thou hast found favour with God
1:31 And, behold, thou shalt conceive in thy womb, and bring forth a son, and shalt call his name JESUS
1:36 ...and this is the sixth month with her, who was called barren
1:37 For with God nothing shall be impossible
2:40 And the child grew, and waxed strong in spirit, filled with wisdom: and the grace of God was upon him
2:52 And Jesus increased in wisdom and stature and in favour with God and man
4:24 And he said, Verily I say unto you, No prophet is accepted in his own country
4:32 And they were astonished at his doctrine: for his word was with power
4:35 And Jesus rebuked him, saying, Hold thy peace and come out of him. And when the devil had thrown him in the midst, he came out of him, and hurt him not
5:16 And he withdrew himself into the wilderness and prayed
5:17 ...and the power of the Lord was present to heal them
6:12 ...he went out into a mountain to pray, and continued all night in prayer to God
6:19 And the whole multitude sought to touch him: for there went virtue out of him, and healed them all
6:24 Woe unto you that are rich...
6:26 Woe unto you, when all men shall speak well of you...
6:27 ...Love your enemies, do good to them that hate you
6:28 Bless them that curse you, and pray for them which despitefully use you
6:29 And unto him that smiteth thee on the one cheek offer...
6:30 Give to every man that asketh of thee; and of him that taketh away thy goods ask them not again
6:31 And as you would that men should do to you, do ye also to...
6:38 Give and it shall be given unto you, good measure pressed down, shaken together, and running over shall men give into your bosom. For with the same measure that ye mete withal it shall be measured to you again
6:41 And why beholdest thou the mote that is in thy brother's eye...
6:43 For a good tree bringeth not forth corrupt fruit...
6:48 He is like a man which built an house, and digged deep...
7:21 And in that same hour he cured many of their infirmities...
7:35 But wisdom is justified of all her children
8:18 Take heed therefore how you hear...

8:21 ...My mother and my brethren are those which hear the word of God, and do it.
8:25 And he said unto them, Where is your faith?...
8:45 And Jesus said, who touched me...
9:23 ...If any man will come after me, let him deny himself, and take up his cross daily, and follow me
9:24 For whosoever will save his life shall lose it: but whosoever will lose his life for my sake, the same shall save it
9:26 For whosoever shall be ashamed of me and of my words, of him shall the Son of man be ashamed, when he shall come in his own glory, and in his Father's, and of the holy angels
9:29 And as he prayed, the fashion of his countenance was altered...
9:62 ...No man, having put his hand to the plough, and looking back, is fit for the kingdom of God
10:18 And he said unto them, I beheld Satan as lightning fall from heaven
10:19 Behold I give unto you power to tread on serpents and scorpions and over all the power of the enemy: and nothing shall by any means hurt you
14:11 For whosoever exalteth himself shall be abased, and he that humbleth himself shall be exalted
14:26 If any man come to me, and hate not his father, and mother, and wife, and children, and brethren, and sisters, yea, and his own life also, he cannot be my disciple
14:33 So likewise, whosoever he be of you that forsaketh not all that he hath, he cannot be my disciple
15:7 ...joy shall be in heaven over one sinner that repenteth, more than over ninety and nine just persons which need no repentance
16:10 He that is faithful in that which is least is faithful also in much...
16:13 ...Ye cannot serve God and mammon
17:32 Remember Lot's wife
*17:36 Two men shall be in the field; the one shall be taken, and the other left
18:24...How hardly shall they that have riches enter the kingdom of heaven
21:19 In your patience, possess ye your souls
22:32 But I have prayed for thee, that thy faith fail not: and when thou art converted, strengthen thy brethren
24:49 But tarry ye in the city of Jerusalem, until ye be endued with power from on high

John
1:1 In the beginning was the Word, and the Word was with God, and the Word was God
1:2 The same was in the beginning with God

1:3 All things were made by him; and without him was not anything made that was made
1:4 In him was life; and the life was the light of men
1:12 But as many as received him, to them gave he power to become the sons of God...
1:13 Which were born, not of blood, nor of the will of the flesh, nor of the will of man, but of God
1:14 And the Word was made flesh, and dwelt among us...
1:16 And of his fullness have all we received, and grace for grace
1:17 For the law was given by Moses, but grace and truth came by Jesus Christ
1:18 No man hath seen God at any time...
2:7 Jesus saith unto them, fill the waterpots with water...
2:15 And when he had made a scourge of small cords, he drove them all out of the temple...
2:24 But Jesus did not commit himself unto them, because he knew all men
3:3 Except a man be born again, he cannot see the kingdom of God
3:5 ...Verily, verily, I say unto thee, Except a man be born of water and of the Spirit, he cannot see the kingdom of God
3:6 That which is born of the flesh is flesh; and that which is born of the Spirit is spirit
3:7 Marvel not that I say unto thee, Ye must be born again
3:16 For God so loved the world, that he gave his only begotten Son, that whosoever believeth in him should not perish, but have everlasting life
3:17 For God sent not his Son into the world to condemn the world; but that the world through him might be saved
3:19 And this is the condemnation, that light is come into the world, and men loved darkness rather than light, because their deeds were evil
3:20 For everyone that doeth evil hateth the light, neither cometh to the light, because their deeds were evil
3:21 But he that doeth truth cometh to the light, that his deeds may be made manifest, that they are wrought in God
3:30 He must increase, but I must decrease
3:34 For he whom God hath sent speaketh the words of God: for God giveth not the Spirit by measure unto him
3:35 The Father loveth the Son, and hath given all things into his hand
4:23 But the hour cometh and now is when the true worshippers shall worship the Father in spirit and in truth; for the Father seeketh such to worship him
4:24 God is a Spirit, and they that worship him must worship him in spirit and in truth
4:34 ...My meat is to do the will of him that sent me, and to finish his work

4:44 For Jesus testified… a prophet hath no honour in his own country
*5:4 For an angel went down at a certain season into the pool…
5:8 Jesus saith unto him, Rise up, take thy bed, and walk
5:24 He that heareth my word, and believeth on him that sent me, hath everlasting life, and shall not come into condemnation; but is passed from death unto life
5:26 For as the Father hath life in himself; so hath he given to the Son to have life in himself
6:27 Labour not for the meat which perisheth…
6:37 All that the Father giveth me shall come to me; and he that cometh to me I will in no wise cast out
6:63 It is the spirit that quickeneth; the flesh profiteth nothing: the words that I speak unto you, they are spirit, and they are life
7:38 He that believeth on me, as the scripture hath said, out of his belly shall flow rivers of living water
8:7 …He that is without sin among you, let him first cast a stone at her
8:11 …Neither do I condemn thee: go, and sin no more
8:12 …he that followeth me shall not walk in darkness but shall have the light of life
8:32 And ye shall know the truth, and the truth shall make you free
8:36 If the Son therefore shall make you free, ye shall be free indeed
8:56 Your father Abraham rejoiced to see my day: and he saw it, and was glad
8:58 Jesus said unto them, Verily, verily, I say unto you, Before Abraham was, I am
9:4 I must work the works of him that sent me, while it is day: the night cometh when no man can work
9:25 …one thing I know, that, whereas I was blind, now I see
9:40 …Are we blind also?
10:9 I am the door: by me if any man enter in, he shall be saved…
10:10 The thief cometh not, but for to steal, and to kill, and to destroy: I am come that they might have life, and that they might have it more abundantly
10:17 Therefore doth my Father love me, because I lay down my life, that I might take it again
10:27 My sheep hear my voice, and I know them, and they follow me
10:30 I and my Father are one
11:4 This sickness is not unto death, but for the glory of God, that the son of God might be glorified thereby
11:25 I am the resurrection, and the life; he that believeth in me, though he were dead, yet shall he live
11:43 And when he thus had spoken, he cried with a loud voice, Lazarus, come forth
11:44 …Loose him, and let him go
12:10 But the chief priests consulted that they might put Lazarus also to death

12:24 Verily, verily, I say unto you, except a corn of wheat fall into the ground and die, it abideth alone: but if it die, it bringeth forth much fruit

12:25 He that loveth his life shall lose it; and he that hateth his life in this world shall keep it unto life eternal

12:43 For they loved the praise of men more than the praise of God

13:16 ...the servant is not greater than his lord...

13:35 By this shall men know ye are my disciples if ye have love one for another

14:1 Let not your heart be troubled: ye believe in God, believe also in me

14:2 In my Father's house are many mansions: if it were not so, I would have told you so. I go to prepare a place for you

14:6 Jesus saith unto him, I am the way, the truth, and the life: no man cometh unto the Father, but by me

14:9 ...he that hath seen me hath seen the Father...

14:13 And whatsoever ye shall ask in my name, that will I do, that the Father may be glorified in the Son

14:14 If ye shall ask any thing in my name, I will do it

14:15 If ye love me, keep my commandments

14:16 And I will pray the Father, and he shall give you another Comforter, that he may abide with you forever

14:17 Even the Spirit of truth; whom the world cannot receive, because it seeth him not, neither knoweth him...

14:20 At that day ye shall know that I am in my Father, and ye in me, and I in you

14:21 He that hath my commandments, and keepeth them, he it is that loveth me: and he that loveth me shall be loved of my Father, and I will love him, and will manifest myself to him

14:26 But the Comforter, which is the Holy Ghost, whom the Father will send in my name, he shall teach you all things...

14:27 Peace I leave with you, my peace I give unto you: not as the world giveth, give I unto you...

15:2 Every branch in me that beareth not fruit, he taketh away: and every branch that beareth fruit, he purgeth it, that it may bring forth more fruit

15:5 ...for without me ye can do nothing

15:7 If ye abide in me, and my words abide in you, ye shall ask what ye will, and it shall be done unto you

15:8 Herein is my Father glorified, that ye bear much fruit; so shall ye be my disciples

15:10 If ye keep my commandments, ye shall abide in my love; even as I have kept my Father's commandments, and abide in his love

15:11 These things have I spoken unto you, that my joy might remain in you, and that your joy may be full

15:13 Greater love hath no man than this, that a man lay down his life for his friends
15:14 Ye are my friends if ye do whatsoever I command you
15:23 He that hateth me hateth my Father also
16:2 ...the time cometh, that whosoever killeth you will think that he doeth God service
16:23 And in that day, ye shall ask me nothing. Verily, verily, I say unto you, Whatsoever ye shall ask in my name, he will give it you
16:24 Hitherto have ye asked nothing in my name: ask and ye shall receive, that your joy may be full
16:27 For the Father himself loveth you, because ye have loved me, and have believed that I came out from God
16:33 These things have I spoken unto you, that in me ye might have peace. In the world ye shall have tribulation: but be of good cheer; I have overcome the world
17:3 And this is life eternal, that they might know thee the only true God, and Jesus Christ, whom thou hast sent
17:17 Sanctify them through thy truth, thy word is truth
19:8 When Pilate heard that saying, he was the more afraid
21:16 ...lovest thou me... Feed my sheep

Acts
1:7 ...it is not for you to know the times or the seasons, which the Father hath put in his own power
1:8 But ye shall receive power after that the Holy Ghost is come upon you: and ye shall be witnesses unto me
2:4 And they were all filled with the Holy Ghost, and began to speak with other tongues, as the Spirit gave them utterance
2:38 ...Repent and be baptized every one of you in the name of Jesus Christ for the remission of sins, and ye shall receive the gift of the Holy Ghost
3:15 And killed the Prince of life, whom God hath raised from the dead whereof we are witnesses
3:19 Repent ye therefore, and be converted, that your sins may be blotted out, when the times of refreshing shall come from the Lord
4:12 Neither is there salvation in any other: for there is none other name under heaven given among men, whereby we must be saved
4:30 By stretching forth thine hand to heal; and that signs and wonders may be done by the name of thy holy child Jesus
5:16 ...and they were healed, everyone
5:29 ...We ought to obey God rather than men
5:41 ...rejoicing that they were counted worthy to suffer shame for his name
6:2 ...It is not reason that we should leave the word of God, and serve tables

6:4 But we will give ourselves continually to prayer and to the ministry of the word

6:10 And they were not able to resist the wisdom and spirit by which he spake

8:30 And Philip ran thither to him... Understandest thou what thou readest?

*8:37 And Philip said, if thou believest... And he answered and said, I believe that Jesus Christ is the son of God

9:4 And he fell to the earth, and heard a voice saying unto him, Saul, Saul, why persecutest thou me?

10:15 What God hath cleansed, that call not thou common

10:38 How God anointed Jesus of Nazareth with the Holy Ghost and with power: who went about doing good and healing all that were oppressed of the devil; for God was with him

11:9 ...What God hath cleansed, that call not thou common

12:5 Peter therefore was kept in prison: but prayer was made without ceasing of the church unto God for him

12:23 And immediately the angel of the Lord smote him, because he gave not God the glory...

14:9 ...Paul ...perceiving that he had faith to be healed

14:10 Said with a loud voice, Stand upright on thy feet. And he leaped and walked

15:29 That ye abstain from meats offered to idols, and from blood, and from things strangled, and from fornication...

16:5 And so were the churches established in the faith, and increased in number daily

17:5 ...they received the word with all readiness of mind...

17:26 And hath made of one blood all nations of men for to dwell on all the face of the earth...

17:28 For in him we live and move and have our being...

17:30 And the times of this ignorance God winked at; but now commandeth all men everywhere to repent

17:31 Because he hath appointed a day, in the which he will judge the world in righteousness by that man whom he hath ordained...

19:2 ...Have ye received the Holy Ghost since ye believed...

19:6 And when Paul had laid his hands upon them, the Holy Ghost came on them; and they spake with tongues, and prophesied

19:11 And God wrought special miracles by the hand of Paul

19:20 So mightily grew the word of God and prevailed

Romans

1:11 For I long to see you, that I may impart unto you some spiritual gift...

1:16 For I am not ashamed of the gospel of Christ: for it is the power of God unto salvation to everyone that believeth; to the Jew first, and also to the Greek

1:22 Professing themselves to be wise, they became fools

1:24 Wherefore God also gave them up unto uncleanness through the lusts of their own hearts, to dishonour their own bodies between themselves

1:26 For this cause God gave them up unto vile affections: for even their women did change the natural use into that which is against nature

1:27 And likewise also the men, leaving the natural use of the woman, burned in their lust one toward another...

1:28 And even as they did not like to retain God in their knowledge, God gave them over to a reprobate mind...

2:8 But unto them that are contentious, and do not obey the truth...

3:1 What advantage then hath the Jew? Or what profit is their of circumcision

3:2 Much every way: chiefly because that unto them were committed the oracles of God

3:4 God forbid: yea, let God be true, but every man a liar;

3:23 For all have sinned, and come short of the glory of God

3:24 Being justified freely by his grace through the redemption that is in Christ Jesus

4:18 Who against hope believed in hope, that he might become the father of many nations...

4:19 And being not weak in faith, he considered not his own body now dead

4:20 He staggered not at the promise of God through unbelief, but was strong in faith, giving glory to God

4:21 And being fully persuaded that what he had promised, he was able also to perform

5:6 For when we were yet without strength, in due time Christ died for the ungodly

5:8 But God commendeth his love toward us, in that, while we were yet sinners, Christ died for us

5:12 ...as by one man sin entered into the world, and death by sin; and so death passed upon all men...

6:6 Knowing this, that our old man is crucified with him, that the body of sin might be destroyed...

6:11 Likewise, reckon ye also yourselves to be dead unto sin, but alive unto God through Jesus Christ our Lord

6:12 Let not sin therefore reign in your mortal body, that ye should obey it in the lusts thereof

6:14 For sin shall not have dominion over you: for ye are not under the law, but under grace

6:23 For the wages of sin is death; but the gift of God is eternal life through Jesus Christ our Lord
7:21 I find then a law, that, when I would do good, evil is present with me
8:1 There is therefore now no condemnation to them which are in Christ Jesus, who walk not after the flesh, but after the Spirit
8:2 For the law of the Spirit of life in Christ Jesus hath made me free from the law of sin and death
8:5 For they that are after the flesh do mind the things of the flesh; but they that are after the Spirit the things of the Spirit
8:6 For to be carnally minded is death; but to be spiritually minded is life and peace
8:8 So then they that are in the flesh cannot please God
8:9 But ye are not in the flesh, but in the Spirit, if so be that the Spirit of God dwell in you...
8:10 And if Christ be in you, the body is dead because of sin, but the Spirit is life because of righteousness
8:11 But if the Spirit of him that raised up Jesus from the dead dwell in you, he that raised up Christ from the dead shall also quicken your mortal bodies by his Spirit that dwelleth in you
8:12 Therefore, brethren, we are debtors, not to the flesh, to live after the flesh
8:13 For if ye live after the flesh, ye shall die: but if ye through the Spirit do mortify the deeds of the body, ye shall live
8:14 For as many as are led by the Spirit of God, they are the sons of God
8:19 For the earnest expectation of the creature waiteth for the manifestations of the sons of God
8:26 Likewise the Spirit also helpeth our infirmities: for we know not what we should pray for as we ought: but the Spirit itself maketh intercession for us with groanings which cannot be uttered
8:27 And he that searcheth the hearts knoweth what is the mind of the Spirit, because he maketh intercession for the saints according to the will of God
8:28 And we know that all things walk together for good to them that love God, to them who are the called according to his purpose
8:32 He that spared not his own Son, but delivered him up for us all, how shall he not with him also freely give us all things?
8:35 Who shall separate us from the love of Christ? Shall tribulation, or distress, or persecution, or famine, or nakedness, or peril, or sword?
8:37 Nay, in all these things we are more than conquerors through him that loved us
8:38 For I am persuaded that neither death, nor life, nor angels, nor principalities, nor powers, nor things present, nor things to come,

8:39 Nor height, nor depth, nor any other creature, shall be able to separate us from the love of God, which is in Christ Jesus our Lord

10:4 For Christ is the end of the law for righteousness to everyone that believeth

10:9 That if thou shalt confess with thy mouth the Lord Jesus, and shalt believe in thine heart that God hath raised him from the dead, thou shalt be saved

10:10 For with the heart man believeth unto righteousness; and with the mouth confession is made unto salvation

10:13 For whosoever shall call upon the name of the Lord shall be saved

10:17 So then faith cometh by hearing, and hearing by the word of God

11:29 For the gifts and calling of God are without repentance

11:33 O the depth of the riches both of the wisdom and knowledge of God! How unsearchable are his judgements, and his ways past finding out

11:34 For who hath known the mind of the Lord? Or who hath been his counselor?

11:36 For of him, and through him, and to him, are all things: to whom be glory for ever. Amen.

12:1 I beseech you therefore, brethren, by the mercies of God, that ye present your bodies a living sacrifice, holy, acceptable unto God, which is your reasonable service

12:2 And be not conformed to this world: but be ye transformed by the renewing of your mind, that ye might prove what is that good, and acceptable and perfect will of God

12:9 Let love be without dissimulation. Abhor that which is evil; cleave to that which is good

12:10 Be kindly affectioned one to another with brotherly love; in honour preferring one another

12:11 Not slothful in business; fervent in spirit; serving the Lord

12:14 Bless them which persecute you: bless them and curse not

12:18 If it be possible, as much as lieth in you, live peaceably with all men

12:20 Therefore if thine enemy hunger, feed him; if he thirst, give him drink: for in so doing thou shalt heap coals of fire on his head

12:21 Be not overcome of evil, but overcome evil with good

13:7 Render therefore to all their dues: tribute to whom tribute is due; custom to whom custom; fear to whom fear; honour to whom honour

13:10 Love worketh no ill to his neighbour: therefore love is the fulfilling of the law

14:23 ...for whatsoever is not of faith is sin

15:1 We then that are strong ought to bear the infirmities of the weak, and not to please ourselves

*16:24 The grace of our Lord Jesus Christ be with you all. Amen

I Corinthians

1:5 That in every thing ye are enriched by him, in all utterance, and in all knowledge
1:21 For after that in the wisdom of God, the world by wisdom knew not God, it pleased God by the foolishness of preaching to save them that believe
1:25 Because the foolishness of God is wiser than men; and the weakness of God is stronger than man
2:4 And my speech and my preaching was not with enticing words of man's wisdom, but in demonstration of the Spirit and of power
2:5 That your faith should not stand in the wisdom of men, but in the power of God
2:9 But as it is written, Eye hath not see, nor ear heard, neither have entered into the heart of man, the things which God hath prepared for them that love him
3:6 I have planted, Apollos watered; but God gave the increase
3:11 For other foundation can no man lay than that is laid, which is Jesus Christ
3:23 And ye are Christ's; and Christ is God's
4:1 Let a man so account of us, as of the ministers of Christ, and stewards of the mysteries of God
4:5 Therefore judge nothing before the time, until the Lord come...
4:7 ...what hast thou that thou didst not receive...
4:20 For the kingdom of God is not in word, but in power
6:18 Flee fornication. Every sin that a man doeth is without the body; but he that committeth fornication sinneth against his own body
6:20 For ye are bought with a price: therefore glorify God in your body, and in your spirit, which are God's
7:2 Nevertheless, to avoid fornication, let every man have his own wife, and let every woman have her own husband
9:16 ...woe is unto me if I preach not the gospel
9:22 To the weak became I as weak, that I might gain the weak...
9:27 But I keep under my body, and bring it into subjection: lest that by any means, when I have preached to others, I myself should be a castaway
10:12 Wherefore let him that thinketh he standeth take heed lest he fall
10:13 There hath no temptation taken you but such as is common to man: but God is faithful, who will not suffer you to be tempted above that ye are able; but will with the temptation also make a way to escape, that ye may be able to bear it
10:20 ...the things which the Gentiles sacrifice, they sacrifice to devils, and not to God: and I would not that ye should have fellowship with devils
10:23 All things are lawful for me, but not all things are expedient...

11:1 Be ye followers of me, even as I also am of Christ
11:4 Every man praying or prophesying, having his head covered, dishonoureth his head
11:5 But every woman that prayeth or prophesieth with her head uncovered dishonoureth her head; for that is even all one as if she were shaven
11:10 For this cause ought the woman to have power on her head because of the angels
12:3 ...and that no man can say that Jesus is the Lord, but by the Holy Ghost
12:7 But the manifestation of the Spirit is given to every man to profit withal
12:8 For to one is given by the Spirit the word of wisdom; to another the word of knowledge by the same Spirit
12:9 To another faith by the same Spirit; to another the gifts of healing by the same Spirit;
12:10 To another the working of miracles; to another prophecy; to another discerning of spirits; to another divers kinds of tongues; to another the interpretation of tongues
12:13 For by one Spirit are we all baptized into one body, whether we be Jew or Gentiles, whether we be bond or free; and have been all made to drink into one Spirit
12:21 And the eye cannot say unto the hand, I have no need of thee: nor again the head to the feet, I have no need of you
12:28 And God hath set some in the church, first apostles, secondarily prophets, thirdly teachers, after that miracles, then gifts of healings, helps, governments, diversities of tongues
13:1 Though I speak with the tongues of men and of angels, and have not charity, I am become as sounding brass...
13:4 Charity suffereth long, and is kind; charity envieth not; charity vaunteth not itself, is not puffed up
13:5 Doth not behave itself unseemly, seeketh not her own, is not easily provoked, thinketh no evil;
13:6 Rejoiceth not in iniquity, but rejoiceth in the truth;
13:7 Beareth all things, believeth all things, hopeth all things, endureth all things
13:8 Charity never faileth: but whether there be prophecies, they shall cease...
14:1 Follow after charity, and desire spiritual gifts, but rather that ye may prophesy
14:2 For he that speaketh in an unknown tongue speaketh not unto men, but unto God...
14:4 He that speaketh in an unknown tongue edifieth himself; but he that prophesieth edifieth the church
14:8 For if the trumpet give an uncertain sound, who shall prepare himself to the battle?

14:13 Wherefore let him that speaketh in an unknown tongue pray that he may interpret
14:20 Brethren, be not children in understanding: howbeit in malice be ye children, but in understanding be men
14:33 For God is not the author of confusion, but of peace, as in all churches of the saints
14:37 If any man think himself a prophet, or spiritual, let him acknowledge that the things that I write unto you are the commandments of the Lord
14:38 But if any man be ignorant, let him be ignorant
14:39 …covet to prophesy, and forbid not to speak with tongues
14:40 Let all things be done decently and in order
15:22 For as in Adam all die, even so in Christ shall all be made alive
15:33 Be not deceived, evil communications corrupt good manners
15:45 …The first Adam was made a living soul; the last Adam was made a quickening spirit
15:50 …flesh and blood cannot inherit the kingdom of God; neither doth corruption inherit incorruption
15:51 Behold, I shew you a mystery, we shall not all sleep, but we shall all be changed
15:53 For this corruptible must put on incorruption, and this mortal must put on immortality
16:13 Watch ye, stand fast in the faith, quit ye like men, be strong

II Corinthians

2:11 Lest Satan should get an advantage of us: for we are not ignorant of his devices
2:17 For we are not as many which corrupt the word of God…
3:17 …where the Spirit of the Lord is, there is liberty
4:3 But if our gospel be hid, it is hid to them that are lost
4:7 But we have this treasure in earthen vessels, that the excellency of the power may be of God, and not of us
5:7 For we walk by faith, not by sight
5:17 Therefore if any man be in Christ, he is a new creature: old things are passed away, behold, all things are become new
7:10 For Godly sorrow worketh repentance not to be repented of: but the sorrow of the world worketh death
8:9 For ye know the grace of our Lord Jesus Christ, that though he was rich, yet for your sakes he became poor, that ye through his poverty might be rich
9:6 But this I say, he which soweth sparingly shall reap also sparingly; and he which soweth bountifully shall reap also bountifully
9:8 And God is able to make all grace abound toward you; that ye, always having all sufficiency in all things, may abound to every good work

9:11 Being enriched in every thing to all bountifulness, which causeth through us thanksgiving to God
10:3 For though we walk in the flesh, we do not war after the flesh
10:4 For the weapons of our warfare are not carnal, but mighty through God to the pulling down of strong holds
10:5 Casting down imaginations and every high thing that exalteth itself against the knowledge of God, and bringing into captivity every thought to the obedience of Christ
11:14 And no marvel; for Satan himself is transformed into an angel of light
12:9 My grace is sufficient for thee: for my strength is made perfect in weakness
13:8 For we can do nothing against the truth, but for the truth

Galatians

2:20 I am crucified with Christ: nevertheless I live; yet not I, but Christ liveth in me: and the life which I now live in the flesh I live by the faith of the Son of God, who loved me and gave himself for me
2:21 I do not frustrate the grace of God
3:11 But that no man is justified by the law in the sight of God it is evident: for the just shall live by faith
3:13 Christ hath redeemed us from the curse of the law, being made a curse for us...
4:6 And because ye are sons, God hath sent forth the Spirit of his Son into your hearts, crying, Abba, Father
5:1 Stand fast therefore in the liberty wherewith Christ hath made us free, and be not entangled again with the yoke of bondage
5:16 This I say then, Walk in the Spirit, and ye shall not fulfill the lust of the flesh
5:17 For the flesh lusteth against the Spirit, and the Spirit against the flesh: and these are contrary the one to the other; so that ye cannot do the things that ye would
5:18 But if ye be led of the Spirit, ye are not under the law
5:19 Now the works of the flesh are manifest, which are these; adultery, fornication, uncleanness, lasciviousness, variance, emulations, wrath, strife, seditions, heresies,
5:20 Envyings, murders, drunkenness, revellings, and such like... they which do such things shall not inherit the kingdom of God
5:22 But the fruit of the Spirit is love, joy, peace, long suffering, gentleness, goodness, faith
5:23 Meekness, Temperance: against such there is no law
5:24 And they that are Christ's have crucified the flesh with the affections and lusts
5:26 Let us not be desirous of vain glory...

6:1...If a man be overtaken in a fault, ye which are spiritual, restore such an one in the spirit of meekness...
6:6 Let him that is taught in the word communicate unto him that teacheth in all good things
6:7 Be not deceived; God is not mocked: for whatsoever a man soweth, that shall he also reap

Ephesians

1:3 Blessed be the God and Father of our Lord Jesus Christ, who hath blessed us with all spiritual blessings in heavenly places in Christ
1:17 That the God of our Lord Jesus Christ, the Father of glory, may give unto you the spirit of wisdom and revelation in the knowledge of him
1:18 The eyes of your understanding being enlightened; that ye may know what is the hope of his calling, and what the riches of the glory of his inheritance in the saints
1:19 And what is the exceeding greatness of his power to usward who believe, according to the working of his mighty power
1:20 Which he wrought in Christ, when he raised him from the dead, and set him at his own right hand in the heavenly places
1:21 Far above all principality, and power, and might, and dominion, and every name that is named, not only in this world, but also in that which is to come
1:22 And hath put all things under his feet, and gave him to be the head over all things to the church
2:1 And you hath he quickened, who were dead in trespasses and sins
2:6 And hath raised us up together, and made us sit together in heavenly places in Christ Jesus
2:8 For by grace are ye saved through faith...
2:18 For through him we both have access by one Spirit unto the Father
3:9 And to make all men see what is the fellowship of the mystery, which from the beginning of the world hath been hid in God, who created all things by Jesus Christ
3:16 That he would grant you, according to the riches of his glory, to be strengthened with might by his Spirit in the inner man
3:17 That Christ may dwell in your hearts by faith; that ye, being rooted and grounded in love
3:18 May be able to comprehend with all saints what is the breadth, and length, and depth, and height
3:19 And to know the love of Christ, which passeth knowledge, that ye might be filled with all the fullness of God
3:20 Now unto him that is able to do exceeding abundantly above all that we ask or think, according to the power that worketh in us

3:21 Unto him be glory in the church by Christ Jesus throughout all ages, world without end, amen
4:23 And be renewed in the spirit of your mind
4:26 Be ye angry, and sin not: let not the sun go down upon your wrath
4:27 Neither give place to the devil
4:28 Let him that stole steal no more...
4:29 Let no corrupt communication proceed out of your mouth, but that which is good to the use of edifying, that it may minister grace unto the hearers
4:30 And grieve not the holy Spirit of God whereby ye are sealed unto the day of redemption
4:31 Let all bitterness, and wrath, and anger, and clamour, and evil speaking, be put away from you with all malice
5:3 But fornication, and all uncleanness, or covetousness, let it not be once named among you, as becometh saints
5:4 Neither filthiness, nor foolish talking, nor jesting...
5:5 For this ye know, that no whoremonger, nor unclean person, nor covetous man, who is an idolater, hath any inheritance in the kingdom of Christ and of God
5:6 Let no man deceive you with vain words: for because of these things...
5:7 Be not ye therefore partakers with them
5:14 Awake thou that sleepest, and arise from the dead, and Christ shall give thee light
5:15 See then that ye walk circumspectly, not as fools, but as wise
5:16 Redeeming the time, because the days are evil
5:18 And be not drunk with wine... but be filled with the Spirit
5:19 Speaking to yourselves in psalms and hymns and...
5:21 Submitting yourselves one to another in the fear of the Lord
5:22 Wives submit yourselves unto your own husbands, as unto the Lord
6:2 Honour thy father and mother; which is the first commandment with promise
6:3 That it may be well with thee, and thou mayest live long on the earth
6:4 And, ye fathers, provoke not your children to wrath: but bring them up in the nurture and admonition of the Lord.
6:10 Finally my brethren, be strong in the Lord, and in the power of his might
6:11 Put on the whole armour of God, that ye may be able to stand against the wiles of the devil
6:12 For we wrestle not against flesh and blood, but against principalities, against powers, against the rulers of the darkness of this world, against spiritual wickedness in high places

6:13 Wherefore take unto you the whole armour of God, that ye may be able to withstand in the evil day, and having done all to stand
6:14 Stand therefore, having your loins girt about with truth, and having on the breastplate of righteousness
6:15 And your feet shod with the preparation of the gospel of peace
6:16 Above all, taking the shield of faith wherewith ye shall be able to quench all the fiery darts of the wicked
6:17 And take the helmet of salvation, and the sword of the Spirit, which is the Word of God
6:18 Praying always with all prayer and supplication in the Spirit, and watching there unto with all perseverance and supplication for all saints

Philippians

1:6 Being confident of this very thing, that he which hath begun a good work in you will perform it until the day of Jesus Christ
1:29 For unto you it is given in the behalf of Christ, not only to believe on him, but also to suffer for his sake
2:9 Wherefore God also hath highly exalted him, and given him a name which is above every name
2:10 That at the name of Jesus every knee should bow, of things in heaven, and things in earth, and things under the earth
2:11 And that every tongue should confess that Jesus Christ is Lord, to the glory of God the Father
2:12 ...work out your own salvation with fear and trembling
2:13 For it is God which worketh in you both to will and to do of his good pleasure
3:3 For we are the circumcision, which worship God in the spirit, and rejoice in Christ Jesus, and have no confidence in the flesh
3:10 That I may know him, and the power of his resurrection, and the fellowship of his sufferings, being made comformable unto his death
3:13 ...but this one thing I do, forgetting those things which are behind, and reaching forth unto those things which are before
3:14 I press toward the mark for the prize of the high calling of God in Christ Jesus
4:1 ...stand fast in the Lord, my dearly beloved
4:4 Rejoice in the Lord always: again I say rejoice
4:6 Be careful for nothing; but in everything by prayer and supplication with thanksgiving let your requests be made known unto God
4:7 And the peace of God, which passeth all understanding, shall keep your hearts and minds through Christ Jesus
4:8 Finally brethren, whatsoever things are true, whatsoever things are honest, whatsoever things are just, whatsoever things are pure,

whatsoever things are lovely, whatsoever things are of good report; if there be any virtue, and if there be any praise, think on these things
4:13 I can do all things through Christ which strengtheneth me
4:19 But my God shall supply all your need according to his riches in glory by Christ Jesus
4:20 Now unto God and our Father be glory for ever and ever. Amen

Colossians

1:11 Strengthened with all might, according to his glorious power, unto all patience and longsuffering with joyfulness
1:13 Who hath delivered us from the power of darkness and hath translated us into the kingdom of his dear Son
1:16 For by him were all things created, that are in heaven, and that are in earth, visible and invisible...
1:18 And he is the head of the body, the church...
2:6 As ye have therefore received Christ Jesus the Lord, so walk ye in him
2:7 Rooted and built up in him, and established in the faith, as ye have been taught, abounding therein with thanksgiving
2:9 For in him dwelleth the fullness of the Godhead bodily,
2:10 And ye are complete in him, which is the head of all principality and power
3:2 Set your affection on things above, not on things on the earth
3:3 For ye are dead, and your life is hid with Christ in God
3:5 Mortify therefore your members which are upon the earth...
3:8 But now ye also put off all these; anger, wrath, malice, blasphemy, filthy communication out of your mouth
3:9 Lie one not to another, seeing that ye have put off the old man with his deeds;
3:10 And have put on the new man which is renewed in knowledge after the image of him that created him
3:12 Put on therefore, as the elect of God holy and beloved, bowels of mercies, kindness, humbleness of mind, meekness, longsuffering
3:13 Forbearing one another, and forgiving one another...
3:14 And above all these things, put on charity, which is the bond of perfectness
3:15 And let the peace of God rule in your hearts...
3:16 Let the word of Christ dwell in you richly in all wisdom...
3:18 Wives submit yourselves unto your own husbands, as it is fit in the Lord
3:19 Husbands, love your wives, and be not bitter against them
3:20 Children, obey your parents in all things...
3:21 Fathers, provoke not your children to anger...
3:23 And whatsoever ye do, do it heartily, as to the Lord, and not unto men

4:6 Let your speech be always with grace, seasoned with salt, that ye may know how ye ought to answer every man
4:17 ...Take heed to the ministry which thou hast received in the Lord, that thou fulfill it

I Thessalonians

1:9 ...and how ye turned to God from idols to serve the living and true God
1:10 And to wait for his Son from heaven...
4:4 That every one of you should know how to possess his vessel in sanctification and honour
4:7 For God hath not called us unto uncleanness, but unto holiness
4:11 And that ye study to be quiet, and to do your own business, and to work with your own hands
4:16 For the Lord himself shall descend from heaven with a shout, with the voice of the archangel, and with the trump...
4:17 Then we which are alive and remain shall be caught up...
5:6 Therefore let us not sleep as do others; but let us watch and be sober
5:16 Rejoice evermore
5:17 Pray without ceasing
5:18 In every thing give thanks: for this is the will of God in Christ Jesus concerning you
5:19 Quench not the Spirit
5:20 Despise not prophesyings
5:21 Prove all things; hold fast that which is good
5:22 Abstain from all appearance of evil
5:23 And the very God of peace sanctify you wholly; and I pray God your whole spirit, soul and body be preserved blameless unto the coming of our Lord Jesus Christ

II Thessalonians

1:6 Seeing it is a righteous thing with God to recompense tribulation to those that trouble you
2:17 Comfort your hearts, and stablish you in every good word and work
3:1 Finally, brethren, pray for us, that the word of the Lord may have free course
3:10 ...that if any would not work, neither should he eat

I Timothy

1:5 Now the end of the commandment is charity out of a pure heart, and of a good conscience, and of faith unfeigned
1:20 ...and Alexander; whom I have delivered unto Satan...

2:1 I exhort therefore, that, first of all, supplications, prayers, intercessions, and giving of thanks, be made for all men
2:2 For kings, and for all that are in authority; that we may lead a quiet and peaceable life in all godliness and honesty
2:3 For this is good and acceptable in the sight of God our Savior
2:4 Who will have all men to be saved, and to come to the knowledge of the truth
2:5 For there is one God, and one mediator between God and men, the man Christ Jesus
2:14 And Adam was not deceived, but the woman being deceived was in the transgression
3:2 A bishop then must be blameless, the husband of one wife...
3:3 Not given to wine, no striker, not greedy...
3:4 One that ruleth well his own house...
4:7 But refuse profane and old wives' fables and exercise thyself rather unto godliness
4:8 For bodily exercise profiteth little: but Godliness is profitable unto all things, having promise of the life that now is, and of that which is to come
4:12 ...be thou an example of the believers, in word, in conversation, in charity, in spirit, in faith, in purity
4:14 Neglect not the gift that is in thee...
4:15 Meditate upon these things; give thyself wholly to them; that thy profiting may appear to all
5:17 Let the elders that rule well be counted worthy of double honour
5:20 Them that sin rebuke before all, that others also may fear
5:22 Lay hands suddenly on no man...
6:6 But Godliness with contentment is great gain
6:7 For we brought nothing into this world, and it is certain we can carry nothing out
6:10 For the love of money is the root of all evil

II Timothy

1:7 For God hath not given us the spirit of fear; but of power, and of love, and of a sound mind
2:1 Thou therefore, my son, be strong in the grace that is in Christ Jesus
2:3 Thou therefore endure hardness as a good soldier of Christ
2:4 No man that warreth entangleth himself with the affairs of this life; that he may please him who hath chosen him to be a soldier
*2:15 Study to show thyself approved unto God, a workman that needeth not to be ashamed, rightly dividing the word of truth
2:16 But shun profane and vain babblings: for they will increase unto more ungodliness

2:19 Nevertheless the foundation of God standeth sure, having this seal
2:22 ...Flee also youthful lusts: but follow righteousness, faith, charity, peace with them that call on the Lord out of a pure heart
3:5 Having a form of godliness, but denying the power thereof, from such turn away
3:12 Yea, and all that will live godly in Christ Jesus shall suffer persecution
3:16 All scripture is given by the inspiration of God, and is profitable for doctrine, for reproof, for correction, for instruction in righteousness
3:17 That the man of God may be perfect, thoroughly furnished unto all good works
4:5 But watch thou in all things, endure afflictions, do the work of an evangelist, make full proof of thy ministry

Titus

1:8 But a lover of hospitality, a lover of good men, sober, just, holy, temperate
2:1 But speak thou the things which become sound doctrine
2:2 That the aged men be sober, grave, temperate, sound in faith, in charity, in patience
2:3 The aged women likewise, that they be in behaviour as becometh holiness, not false accusers...
2:4 That they may teach the young women to be sober, to love their husbands, to love their children
2:5 To be discreet, chaste, keepers at home, good, obedient to their own husbands, that the word of God not be blasphemed
2:7 In all things shewing thyself a pattern of good works: in doctrine shewing uncorruptness, gravity, sincerity...
3:9 but avoid foolish questions and genealogies

Philemon

1:4 I thank my God, making mention of thee always in my prayers
1:5 Hearing of thy love and faith, which thou hast toward the Lord Jesus, and toward all saints

Hebrews

1:1 God, who at sundry times and in diverse manners spake in time past unto the fathers by the prophets
1:2 Hath in these last days spoken unto us by his Son, whom he hath appointed heir of all things, by whom also he made the worlds
1:3 Who being the brightness of his glory, and the express image of his person, and upholding all things by the word of his power, when

he had by himself purged our sins, sat down on the right hand of the Majesty on high

1:4 Being made so much better than the angels, as he hath by inheritance obtained a more excellent name than they

1:7 And of the angels, he saith, Who maketh his angels spirits, and his ministers a flame of fire

2:1 Therefore we ought to give the more earnest heed to the things which we have heard, lest at any time we should let them slip

2:9 ...that he by the grace of God should taste death for every man

2:14 ...that through death he might destroy him that hath the power of death, that is, the devil

3:4 For every house is builded by some man; but he that built all things is God

4:2 For unto us was the gospel preached, as well as unto them: but the word preached did not profit them, not being mixed with faith in them that heard it

4:12 For the word of God is quick, and powerful, and sharper than any twoedged sword, piercing even to the dividing asunder of soul and spirit, and of the joints and marrow, and is a discerner of the thoughts and intents of the heart

4:16 Let us therefore come boldly unto the throne of grace, that we may obtain mercy, and find grace to help in time of need

5:13 For everyone that useth milk is unskillful in the word of righteousness: for he is a babe

5:14 But strong meat belongeth to them that are full of age, even those who by reason of use have their senses exercised to discern both good and evil

6:1 Therefore leaving the principles of the doctrine of Christ, let us go on unto perfection

6:4 For it is impossible for those who were once enlightened, and have tasted of the heavenly gift, and were made partakers of the Holy Ghost

6:5 And have tasted the good word of God, and the powers of the world to come

6:6 If they shall fall away, to renew them again unto repentance; seeing they crucify to themselves the Son of God afresh, and put him to an open shame

6:12 That ye be not slothful, but followers of them who through faith and patience inherit the promises

7:16 Who is made not after the law of a carnal commandment, but after the power of an endless life

7:18 That by two immutable things, in which it was impossible for God to lie, we might have a strong consolation, who have fled for refuge to lay hold upon the hope set before us

7:19 Which hope we have as an anchor of the soul, both sure and steadfast, and which entereth into that within the veil

7:25 Wherefore he is able also to save them to the uttermost that come unto God by him, seeing he ever liveth to make intercession for them
8:12 For I will be merciful to their unrighteousness, and their sins and their iniquities will I remember no more
9:22 And almost all things are by the law purged with blood; and without shedding of blood is no remission.
9:27 And as it is appointed unto men once to die, but after this the judgement
10:4 For it is not possible that the blood of bulls and goats should take away sins
10:16 This is the covenant that I will make with them after those days, saith the Lord, I will put my laws into their hearts, and in their minds will I write them
10:17 And their sins and iniquities will I remember no more
10:19 Having therefore, brethren, boldness to enter into the holiest by the blood of Jesus
10:22 Let us draw near with a true heart in full assurance of faith, having our hearts sprinkled from an evil conscience, and our bodies washed with pure water
10:23 Let us hold fast the profession of our faith without wavering…
10:25 Not forsaking the assembling of ourselves together…
10:35 Cast not away therefore your confidence, which hath great recompense of reward
11:1 Now faith is the substance of things hoped for, the evidence of things not seen
11:3 Through faith we understand that the worlds were framed by the word of God, so that things which are seen were not made of things which do appear
11:6 But without faith it is impossible to please him: for he that cometh to God must believe that he is, and that he is a rewarder of them that diligently seek him
11:10 For he looketh for a city which hath foundations, whose builder and maker is God
12:1 Wherefore, seeing we also are compassed about with so great a cloud of witnesses, let us lay aside every weight, and the sin which doth so easily beset us, and let us run the race with patience
12:2 Looking unto Jesus, the author and finisher of our faith; who for the joy that was set before him endured the cross, despising the shame, and is set down at the right hand of the throne of God
12:4 Ye have not yet resisted unto blood, striving against sin
12:12 Therefore lift up the hands that hang down, and the feeble knees
12:14 Follow peace with all men, and holiness, without which no man shall see the Lord
12:29 For our God is a consuming fire
13:1 Let brotherly love continue

13:2 Be not forgetful to entertain strangers, for thereby some have entertained angels unawares
13:4 Marriage is honorable in all, and the bed undefiled
13:8 Jesus Christ the same yesterday, and today, and forever
13:16 But to do good, and to communicate forget not: for with such sacrifices God is well pleased
13:20 Now the God of peace, that brought again from the dead our Lord Jesus, that great shepherd of the sheep, through the blood of the everlasting covenant
13:21 Make you perfect in every good work to do his will, working in you that which is well-pleasing in his sight, through Jesus Christ: to whom be glory for ever and ever, Amen

James

1:2 My brethren, count it all joy when ye fall into diverse temptations
1:3 Knowing this, that the trying of your faith worketh patience
1:4 But let patience have her perfect work, that ye may be perfect and entire, wanting nothing
1:5 If any of you lack wisdom, let him ask of God, that giveth to all men liberally, and upbraideth not; and it shall be given him
1:6 But let him ask in faith, nothing wavering. For he that wavereth is like a wave of the sea driven with the wind and tossed
1:7 For let not that man think that he shall receive anything from the Lord
1:8 A double minded man is unstable in all his ways
1:12 Blessed is the man that endureth temptation: for when he is tried, he shall receive the crown of life
1:17 Every good gift and every perfect gift is from above, and cometh down from the Father of lights
1:19 ...let every man be swift to hear, slow to speak, slow to wrath
1:20 For the wrath of man worketh not the righteousness of God
1:21 Wherefore lay apart all filthiness and superfluity of naughtiness, and receive with meekness the engrafted word, which is able to save your soul
1:22 But be ye doers of the word, and not hearers only, deceiving your own selves
1:25 But whoso looketh into the perfect law of liberty, and continueth therein, he being not a forgetful hearer, but a doer of the word, this man shall be blessed in his deed
1:26 If any man among you seem to be religious, and bridleth not his tongue, but deceiveth his own heart, this man's religion is vain
2:10 For whosoever shall keep the whole law, and yet offend in one point, he is guilty of all
2:19 Thou believest that there is one God; thou doest well: the devils also believe, and tremble

2:26 For as the body without the spirit is dead, so faith without works is dead also
3:2 ...If any man offend not in word, the same is a perfect man...
3:6 And the tongue is a fire, a world of iniquity...
3:8 But the tongue can no man tame; it is an unruly evil, full of deadly poison
3:9 Therewith bless we God, even the Father, and therewith curse we men, which are made after the similitude of God
3:17 But the wisdom that is from above is first pure, then peaceable, gentle, and easy to be entreated, full of mercy...
4:1 From whence come wars and fightings among you? come not they hence, even of your lusts that war in your members?
4:3 Ye ask, and ye receive not because ye ask amiss, that ye may consume it upon your lusts
4:4 Ye adulterers and adulteresses, know ye not that the friendship of the world is enmity with God? whosoever therefore will be a friend of the world is the enemy of God
4:7 Submit yourselves therefore to God, resist the devil and he will flee from you
4:8 Draw nigh to God and he will draw nigh to you. Cleanse your hands ye sinners, and purify your hearts ye double-minded
4:10 Humble yourself in the sight of the Lord, and he shall lift you up
4:17 Therefore to him that knoweth to do good, and doeth it not, to him it is sin
5:14 Is any sick among you? Let him call for the elders of the church; and let them pray over him, anointing him with oil in the name of the Lord
5:15 And the prayer of faith shall save the sick, and the Lord shall raise him up...
5:16 ...The effectual fervent prayer of a righteous man availeth much
5:17 Elias was a man subject to like passions as we are; and he prayed earnestly that it might not rain: and it rained not...

I Peter

1:2 Elect according to the foreknowledge of God the Father, through sanctification of the Spirit, unto obedience and sprinkling of the blood of Jesus Christ: Grace unto you, and peace, be multiplied
1:3 Blessed be the God and Father of our Lord Jesus Christ, which according to his abundant mercy hath begotten us again unto a lively hope by the resurrection of Jesus Christ from the dead
1:4 To an inheritance incorruptible, and undefiled, and that fadeth not away, reserved in heaven for you
1:5 Who are kept by the power of God through faith unto salvation ready to be revealed in the last time

1:7 That the trying of your faith, being much more precious than of gold that perisheth, though it be tried with fire, might be found unto praise and honour and glory at the appearing of Jesus Christ
1:8 Whom having not seen, ye love; in whom, though now ye see him not, yet believing, ye rejoice…
1:9 Receiving the end of your faith, even the salvation of your souls
1:13 Wherefore gird up the loins of your mind, be sober, and hope to the end…
1:15 But as he which hath called you is holy, so be ye holy in all manner of conversation
1:20 Who verily was foreordained before the foundation of the world…
1:22 Seeing ye have purified your souls in obeying the truth through the Spirit unto unfeigned love of the brethren…
1:23 Being born again, not of corruptible, but of incorruptible, by the word of God, which liveth and abideth forever
2:1 Wherefore laying aside all malice, and all guile, and hypocrisies, and envies, and all evil speaking
2:2 As newborn babes, desire the sincere milk of the word that ye may grow thereby
2:3 If so be ye have tasted that the Lord is gracious
2:5 Ye also, as lively stones, are built up a spiritual house, an holy priesthood, to offer up spiritual sacrifices, acceptable to God, by Jesus Christ
2:7 Unto you therefore which believe he is precious: but unto the disobedient, the stone which the builders disallowed, the same is made the head of the corner
2:9 But ye are a chosen generation, a royal priesthood, an holy nation, a peculiar people, that ye should show forth the praises of him who hath called you out of darkness into his marvelous and glorious light
2:11 Dearly beloved, I beseech you as strangers and pilgrims, abstain from fleshly lusts which war against the soul
2:13 Submit yourself to every ordinance of man for the Lord's sake…
2:16 As free, and not using your liberty for a cloke of maliciousness, but as the servants of God
2:17 Honour all men. Love the brotherhood. Fear God. Honour the King
2:18 Servants, be subject to your masters with all fear; not only to the good and gentle, but also to the froward
2:23 Who when he was reviled, reviled not again; when he suffered, he threatened not; but committed himself to him that judgeth righteously
2:24 Who his own self bare our sins in his own body on the tree, that we, being dead to sins, should live unto righteousness: by whose stripes ye were healed

2:25 For ye were as sheep going astray; but are now returned to the Shepherd and Bishop of your souls.

3:1 Likewise, ye wives, be in subjection to your own husbands; that, if any obey not the word, they also may without the word be won by the conversation of the wives

3:3 Whose adorning let it not be that outward adorning of plaiting the hair, and of wearing of gold, or of putting on of apparel

3:4 But let it be the hidden man of the heart, in that which is not corruptible, even the ornament of a meek and quiet spirit, which is in the sight of God of great price

3:7 Likewise, ye husbands, dwell with them according to knowledge, giving honour unto the wife, as unto the weaker vessel, and as being heirs together of the grace of life; that your prayers be not hindered

3:8 Finally, be ye all of one mind, having compassion, one of another, love as brethren, be pitiful, be courteous

3:10 For he that will love life and see good days, let him refrain his tongue from evil, and his lips that they speak no guile

3:15 But sanctify the Lord God in your hearts; and be ready always to give an answer to every man that asketh you a reason of the hope that is in you with meekness and fear

3:22 Who is gone into heaven, and is on the right hand of God; angels and authorities and powers being made subject unto him

4:1 Forasmuch then as Christ hath suffered for us in the flesh, arm yourselves likewise with the same mind…

4:6 For this cause also was the gospel preached to them that are dead…

5:2 Feed the flock of God which is among you…

5:5 Likewise, ye younger, submit yourselves unto the elder. Yea, all of you be subject one to another, and be clothed with humility…

5:6 Humble yourselves therefore under the mighty hand of God, that he may exalt you in due time

5:7 Casting all your care upon him; for he careth for you

5:8 Be sober, be vigilant; because your adversary the devil, as a roaring lion, walketh about, seeking whom he may devour

5:9 Whom resist steadfast in the faith…

5:10 But the God of all grace, who hath called us unto his eternal glory by Christ Jesus, after that ye have suffered a while, make you perfect, stablish, strengthen, settle you

5:11 To him be glory and dominion for ever and ever. Amen

II Peter

1:2 Grace and peace be multiplied unto you through the knowledge of God, and of Jesus our Lord

1:3 According as his divine power hath given unto us all things that pertain unto life and godliness, through the knowledge of him that hath called us to glory and virtue

1:4 Whereby are given unto us exceeding great and precious promises: that by these ye might be partakers of the divine nature, having escaped the corruption that is in the world through lust

1:5 And beside this, giving all diligence, add to your faith virtue; and to virtue knowledge

1:6 And to knowledge temperance; and to temperance patience; and to patience godliness

1:7 And to godliness brotherly kindness; and to brotherly kindness charity

1:8 For if these things be in you and abound, they make you that ye shall neither be barren nor unfruitful in the knowledge of our Lord Jesus Christ

1:9 But he that lacketh these things is blind, and cannot see afar off, and hath forgotten that he was purged from his old sins

1:10 Wherefore the rather brethren, give diligence to make your calling and election sure: for if ye do these things, ye shall never fall

1:11 For so an entrance shall be ministered unto you abundantly into the everlasting kingdom of our Lord and Saviour Jesus Christ

1:12 But these, as natural brutes and beasts, made to be taken and destroyed, speak evil of the things they understand not

1:14 Having eyes full of adultery, and cannot cease from sin; beguiling unstable souls... cursed children

1:15 Which have forsaken the right way, and are gone astray, following the way of Balaam the son of Bo'sor, who loved the wages of unrighteousness

1:17 These are wells without water, clouds that are carried with a tempest

1:20 Knowing this first, that no prophecy of the scripture is of any private interpretation

1:21 For the prophecy came not in old time by the will of man: but holy men of God spake as they were moved by the Holy Ghost

2:2 And many shall follow their pernicious ways; by reason of whom the way of truth shall be evil spoken of

2:3 And through covetousness shall they with feigned words make merchandise of you...

2:9 The Lord knoweth how to deliver the godly out of temptations, and to reserve the unjust unto the day of judgment to be punished

2:19 While they promise them liberty, they themselves are the servants of corruption: for of whom a man is overcome, of the same is he brought in bondage

2:20 For if after they have escaped the pollutions of the world through the knowledge of the Lord and Saviour Jesus Christ, they are again

entangled therein, and overcome, the latter end is worse with them than the beginning
2:21 For it had been better for them not to have known the way of righteousness, than after they have known it, to turn from the holy commandment delivered unto them
3:3 Knowing this first, that there shall come in the last days scoffers, walking after their own lusts
3:9 The Lord is not slack concerning his promise, as some men count slackness; but is longsuffering to us-ward, not willing that anyone should perish, but that all should come to repentance
3:10 But the day of the Lord will come as a thief in the night...
3:13 Nevertheless we, according to his promise, look for new heavens and a new earth, wherein dwelleth righteousness
3:18 But grow in grace, and in the knowledge of our Lord and Saviour Jesus Christ. To him be glory both now and for ever. Amen.

I John

1:8 If we say that we have no sin, we deceive ourselves, and the truth is not in us
1:9 If we confess our sins, he is faithful and just to forgive us and to cleanse us of all unrighteousness
2:15 Love not the world, neither the things that are in the world. If any man love the world, the love of the Father is not in him.
3:14 We know that we have passed from death unto life, because we love the brethren. He that loveth not his brother abideth in death
3:15 Whosoever hateth his brother is a murderer: and ye know...
4:4 Ye are of God little children, and have overcome them; because greater is he that is in you, than he that is in the world
4:18 There is no fear in love; but perfect love casteth out fear: because fear hath torment. He that feareth is not made perfect in love
5:1 Whosoever believeth that Jesus is the Christ is born of God: and every one that loveth him that begat loveth him also that is begotten
5:3 For this is the love of God, that we keep his commandments: and his commandments are not grievous
5:4 For whatsoever is born of God overcometh the world: and this is the victory that overcometh the world, even our faith
5:5 Who is he that overcometh the world, but he that believeth that Jesus is the Son of God
*5:7 For there are three that bear record in heaven, the Father, the Word, and the Holy Ghost: and these three are one
5:11 And this is the record, that God hath given to us eternal life, and this life is in his Son
5:12 He that hath the son hath life; and he that hath not the Son of God hath not life

*5:13 These things have I written unto you that believe on the name of the Son of God; that ye may know that ye have eternal life, and that ye may believe on the name of the Son of God
5:14 And this is the confidence that we have in him, that if we ask any thing according to his will, he heareth us
5:15 And if we know that he hear us, whatsoever we ask, we know that we have the petitions that we desired of him
5:21 Little children, keep yourselves from idols. Amen

II John
3 Grace be with you, mercy, and peace, from God the Father, and from the Lord Jesus Christ, the Son of the Father, in truth and love
7 For many deceivers are entered into the world, who confess not that Jesus Christ is come in the flesh. This is a deceiver and an antichrist
10 If there come any unto you and bring not this doctrine, receive him not into your house, neither bid him God speed
11 For he that biddeth him God speed is partaker of his evil deeds

III John 2
Beloved, I wish above all things that thou mayest prosper and be in health, even as thy soul prospereth

Jude
20 But ye, beloved, building up yourselves on your most holy faith, praying in the Holy Ghost
24 Now unto him that is able to keep you from falling, and to present you faultless before the presence of his glory with exceeding joy
25 To the only wise God our Saviour be glory and majesty, dominion and power, both now and ever. Amen

Revelation
1:6 And hath made us kings and priests unto God and his Father; to him be glory and dominion for ever and ever
1:8 I am Alpha and Omega, the beginning and the ending
1:11 ...I am Alpha and Omega, the first, and the last...
2:4 Nevertheless I have somewhat against thee, because thou hast left thy first love
2:25 But that which ye have already, hold fast till I come
3:2 Be watchful, and strengthen the things which remain, that are ready to die: for I have not found thy works perfect before me
3:6 He that hath an ear, let him hear what the Spirit saith unto the churches
3:20 Behold, I stand at the door and knock: if any man hear my voice, and open the door, I will come in to him, and will sup with him, and he with me

3:22 To him that overcometh will I grant to sit with me in my throne, even as I also overcame, and am set down with my Father in his throne
4:11 Thou art worthy, O Lord, to receive glory and honour and…
12:11 And they overcame him by the blood of the Lamb, and by the word of their testimony; and they loved not their lives unto the death
13:8 And all that dwell upon the earth shall worship him, whose names are not written in the book of life of the Lamb slain from the foundation of the world
13:16 And he causeth all, both small and great, rich and poor, free and bond, to receive a mark in their right hand, or in their foreheads:
13:17 And that no man might be able to buy or sell, save he that had the mark, or the name of the beast, or the number of his name
13:18 …and his number is Six hundred three score and six
16:2 And the first went, and poured out his vial upon the earth, and there fell a noisome and grievous sore upon the men which had the mark of the beast, and upon them which worshipped his image
18:2 …Babylon the great is fallen, and is become the habitation of devils, and the hold of every foul spirit, and a cage of every unclean and hateful bird
19:7 Let us be glad and rejoice, and give honour to him: for the marriage of the Lamb is come, and his wife hath made herself ready
20:2 And he laid hold on the dragon, that old serpent, which is the Devil, and Satan, and bound him a thousand years
20:7 And when the thousand years are expired, Satan shall be loosed out of his prison
20:10 And the devil that deceived them was cast into the lake of fire and brimstone…
20:15 And whosoever was not found written in the book of life was cast into the lake of fire
21:8 But the fearful, and unbelieving, and the abominable, and murderers, and whoremongers, and sorcerers, and idolators, and all liars, shall have their part in the lake which burneth with fire and brimstone…
22:5 And there shall be no night there; and they need no candle, neither light of the sun; for the Lord God giveth them light: and they shall reign for ever and ever
22:18 …If any man shall add unto these things, God shall add unto him the plagues that are written in this book
22:19 And if any man shall take away from the words of the book of this prophecy, God shall take away his part out of the book of life, and out of the holy city…

*Verses marked * in the New Testament have been deleted from many controversial bible versions described in the next section. Make sure your bible has these verses.*

Chapter 4

The Bible Changes Your Heart

The bible is designed to address every human condition and virtually everything that plagues the human heart. It addresses the rich and the poor, the depressed and the hyper-aroused manic, the drunk and the sober, the fearful and the reckless, the wicked and the righteous, the ungodly and the hyper-spiritual, the impulsive and the temperate, the gluttonous and the anorexic, the workaholic as well as the presumptuous oversleeping lazy underachiever. Of all these, the one thing bibles are well-known for globally are their comforting words. While the bible warns us about the dangers of hellfire and ungodly living, it does provide immense comfort, hope, strength and healing to the fearful, lonely, oppressed, rejected, depressed, disappointed and the broken-hearted. Unknown to many however, the bible also provides mental, emotional, and spiritual nourishment and direction in times of great prosperity. The words of the bible, regardless of where you are in your life's journey, can uplift your soul and empower your spirit. This is because the bible contains tremendous hidden power. When the power in the written words of the Bible touch your soul and spirit, a change, what I love to refer to as divine alchemy, can take place in your heart, and drastically change your life. If you know anyone that has changed drastically as a result of the bible's influence despite the odds against such a change, you'll understand the hidden transforming power in the bible. This power can only be experienced; it cannot be described with words. Again, it is from the bible, that you'll learn of God's great love for you and all mankind.

> *For God so loved the world that he gave his only begotten Son, that whosoever believeth in him should not perish but have everlasting life.*
> *John 3:16*

Only the bible teaches that God is constantly knocking on the door of your heart, hoping you'll let him in.

> *Behold, I stand at the door, and knock: if any man hear my voice, and open the door, I will come in to him, and will sup with him, and he with me. Revelations 3:20*

Perhaps someone once invited you to a church or bible study and you felt a gentle but definite tug on your heart to open up. Or a close friend or family member that hated God in time past has now accepted Jesus into their hearts. You know they care about you and that they want you to have the same joy and assurance they now have. But instead of opening your heart and receiving God's love, you cut off any interaction with them or even worse, punish or humiliate them. You ought to open the door of your heart but you've refused. God will still keep knocking till you take your last breath. You have to however be careful not to turn your heart into stone, unable to hear God or feel the pain you'll be causing others through your hardness of heart. As the writer of Hebrew said

> *While it is said, To day if ye will hear his voice, harden not your hearts, as in the provocation. Hebrews 3:15*

You may have lived your life thus far believing some godless atheistic babble that there is no God. But deep down in your heart, at the very core of your being, you sense there is a God while wondering what might happen to you when you die. Should you continue to pretend that there is no God, or should you yield your heart to him? I think it's better to yield your heart to God and let him give you a beautiful new heart. A beautiful heart is the most valuable thing any human can possess and it comes from just one source, the Almighty God. A beautiful human heart is of such great value to God, he specializes in making hearts beautiful. God promised everyone that desires such a heart they will have one:

> *A new heart also will I give you, and a new spirit will I put within you: and I will take away the stony heart out of your flesh, and I will give you an heart of flesh. Ezekiel 36:26*

The heart in this verse is a metaphorical heart, not your physical heart. This metaphorical heart is that part of you that colors your perceptions with a unique flavor and gives life and meaning to the real you. Your heart makes you an original! Your metaphorical heart represents the seat of your emotions, governs your actions, drives your deepest desires and pushes you to take action consistently. Your metaphorical heart gives fire to your soul. This fire could be the size of a matchstick, candlestick or a volcano. We've all met individuals with so much passion and fire in their hearts, practicing their craft with meticulous attention, dedication and compassion to produce mind-boggling results. If you've heard of Martin Luther King Jr., Mother Theresa, Les Brown, Anthony Robbins, Steve Jobs, Bill Gates, Elon Musk, Oprah Winfrey, Bishop TD Jakes, Serena Williams or Hussein Bolt, you'll understand what it means to have fire in your soul! Your metaphorical heart is quite different from your physical heart. If your physical heart stops beating, you're dead. When your metaphorical heart dies on the other hand, you can still live for days or decades, like the walking dead, living a doped, depressing sad life, that may unfortunately end in suicide or sudden death.

> *But it came to pass in the morning, when the wine was gone out of Nabal, and his wife had told him these things, that his heart died within him, and he became as a stone. And it came to pass about ten days after, that the Lord smote Nabal, that he died. I Samuel 25:37,38*

Nabal's metaphorical heart, the part that gave meaning to his soul, died, right after he received the bad news from Abigail, his wife. Though he remained alive physically for another ten days, he became a dead man mentally, emotionally, and perhaps spiritually, the moment he received the news. As a physician, I've seen stroke and heart attack patients who die days later in the same manner. When your metaphorical heart dies, it loses its fire, and life can cease to be passionate or meaningful. This can result in stagnation, sadness, addiction, depression, suicide and death, no matter how much you've accomplished in life.

Getting Through Life's Tragedies

We will all experience tragedies and great loss as we journey through life. So will you. The words of the Bible, believe it or not, will greatly prepare you for such times. When tragedy strikes, you'll need strength and sometimes, great faith to face challenges, recover losses and rekindle your passion for winning, in the game of life. You'll greatly increase your chances for recovery following a tragedy, if you put your trust in God and have a new heart. Having friends to help you in your time of need is great but only few have such friendships. Sadly, what most of us call friendships are fake ships. So in times of tragedy all you have left is often God and yourself. God can give you all the strength you need to win the battles of your life, but only if you trust Him. If you have no friends, no faith and no reserves of strength, you may give up on life. Even those who have lots of wonderful friends and family do give up. God never fails those who trust in him and giving up on life is not an option if you have children or others depending on you. In other words, if you're a responsible adult, giving up and killing yourself should not be an option. Tricked into a marriage by a psycho who started laughing that she had me trapped within an hour after the wedding reception was one of the greatest tragedies in my life. So was the death of my first son months before he could go off to college. An only child, my mother died when I was just thirteen. Losing my mother was one of the worst things that could ever happen to me. But I could not give up on life. That's why you now have this book in your hands. Each of these events created gaping wounds that hurt like hell. Yet I thank God for giving me the strength to trust him for even better endings. God's strength comes from reading, understanding and meditating on the Bible.

Resuming Life's Journey With a Stronger Heart

Let's say you're going through a bad time in life. You're not a Christian, but unlike the atheist whom the Bible calls a fool, you know there is a God up there. You just do not believe in him or trust him. If all you have left to help you right now is God, will you choose Him? If you are a responsible adult on whom others can depend, I think you should! The best way to dial up into heaven and ask for God's help is to give your life to him. By giving your life to God, you'll start developing a deep connection to him. This connection, like that between a husband and wife, gives you an opportunity to share your most intimate troubles with God. Sharing your burdens with God based on a close relationship with him lightens the load in your life significantly. But this sharing can only take place effectively if you have an agreement with God to share such things with him. You establish this agreement through an exchange of vows between you and God. You agree to accept him into your life, and he in turn, agrees to carry you through all of life's storms, forgive you of your sins, give you a new heart, and help you when no one else will. If you feed this new heart a healthy spiritual diet regularly, it might even make you successful and wealthy.

With a new heart, you'll have direct access to God through which he can communicate with, comfort, guide and heal you. You build this direct line through prayer and memorizing and meditating on bible verses daily. As you do so, you'll develop a better understanding of God's ways and his will for your life. Meditation is akin to laying down railroad tracks, while memorization is like building roads. Fasting and prayer are methods of transporting blessings and information between heaven and earth on the railroad tracks and roads you have established through meditation and memorization. The new heart God gives you is like a language app to help you understand God's language, a foreign language that most of us do not understand. This "app" can also help you understand some of the hidden mysteries in the Holy Bible. A new heart is the only channel through which God will reignite your passion for life when things are stagnant or going downhill.

The Holy Spirit's Power: Your Backup Power Source

But ye shall receive power after that the Holy Ghost is come upon you…
Acts 1:8

If you have a new heart from God and are going through difficult times, particularly emotionally, you might discover another source of fire powering your life. It's like having a backup generator kicking in to give you electricity following a power outage after a hurricane. This is the power of the Holy Spirit, doing what he does best, working on your heart. The Holy Spirit will work on your heart to bring you to the place where you recognize your need for a divine heart transplant. If you let Him, the Holy Spirit will replace your ugly, deceitful and desperately wicked old heart of sin with a brand new heart filled with love, joy, peace and power.

Life will always find the right challenge for you if you don't find it first. Without a biblical view of life in general, you may develop depression and confusion when life hits you hard. Such depression is like an "infection of the soul". An untreated bladder infection can cause symptoms such as fever any pain. If the fever is treated with Tylenol but the infection causing the fever is ignored, overwhelming infection, septic shock and death can occur. The fever is just a symptom and while treating it with Tylenol is okay, it will be negligent to treat just the fever and not treat the infection causing the fever. An untreated "infection of the soul" (depression) can equally lead to severe and life-threatening "depressive shock" and death by suicide. Suicide could therefore be likened to an untreated severe infection that ends in death. The only way to prevent septic shock and death from a bacterial infection is to treat the original infection. While there are several antibiotics that can effectively treat most bacterial infections, there is not one pill known that can effectively treat any condition of the human soul! No one dare argue or submit a claim to the Food and Drug Administration that they have a pill that addresses the condition of the human soul. Depression is a condition of the human soul and is caused by multiple factors. As you'll see in the next chapter, no pill can cure depression if the primary cause is not first addressed. Failure to address this cause can lead to suicide.

Chapter 5

Why The Rich Commit Suicide

Suicide, the 10th leading cause of death in the United States according to the Center for Disease Control (CDC), took about 45,000 lives in 2016 in the United States and about 800,000 worldwide. It was the second leading cause of death between the ages of 15 and 34 in 2015 in the US and costs over $60 billion annually in combined medical and work loss costs. Suicide victims kill themselves when they feel completely hopeless. Anyone can feel hopeless, but should the rich and famous people also feel the hopelessness that drives a poor dejected divorced or dying desperate individual to take their life? The simple answer is yes. Despite their possessions or fame, the rich and the poor alike have a soul in need of salvation, healing and deliverance. If the rich and famous don't get these needs met, they could take their lives. Even those who are not rich and famous have more possessions than our predecessors could ever dream of having and more drugs for treating the most common trigger for suicide, depression. But most of these interventions don't work as well as they should. And that's why between 1999 and 2016, suicide rates increased by more than 30% in half of the US while 54% of these suicide victims did not have a known mental health condition. The rich and affluent, Robin Williams, Kate Spade and many more are killing themselves, while even far more are thinking about suicide. In 2014, according to the CDC, for every suicide committed, there were 27 reported suicide attempts and over 227 seriously considering suicide, among adults 18 or older. The CDC has one of the most comprehensive suicide prevention programs in the world. However, in its comprehensive *Technical Package on Suicide Prevention*, no mention is made about the role of hope, religion, faith or the word of God in suicide prevention. This is faulty thinking at best or a dangerous intentional atheistic omission. As you're about to see, excluding God, religion and faith from any comprehensive suicide prevention program nullifies the word "comprehensive". Such a program is destined for failure from its inception. Perhaps that's why in spite of the billions of dollars spent on antidepressants (AD) annually, the suicide rates have kept rising.

Between 1999 and 2014, the use of antidepressants increased by 65% according to the CDC with a corresponding rise in suicide rates during the same period. Annual sales of antidepressants globally are over $13 billion. This means more money is spent on ineffective therapies for suicide prevention than on less expensive and equally effective ones such as exercise and religious practices, the latter been a major source of hope for hopeless and suicidal individuals. In a collaborative meta-analysis done by Vanderbilt University and Shandong University School of Public Health in China for example, religion was shown to be protective against suicide. This analysis showed that the absence of religion increased an individual's risk of suicide by 2.5 to 5.6 times. The conclusion of these experts is simply:

> "Therefore public health professionals need to strongly consider the current and social atmosphere of a given population when designing suicide prevention strategies." *Wu A, Wang J-Y, Jia C-X(2015). Religion and Completed Suicide: A Meta-Analysis. PLoS ONE 10(6): e0131715/journal.pone. 0131715*

In a *Nurse's Health Study* article by Harvard Professor Tyler VanderWeele and colleagues published in the August 2016 issue of the *Journal of The American Medical Association (JAMA)*, women attending a religious service once a week or more had a rate of suicide 5 times lower than that of women that don't attend religious services. In another 2016 article published in the *Archives of Suicide Research* by Drs. Lawrence, Oquendo and Stanley, religious service attendance was shown to protect from suicide attempts, but not against suicide ideation. Religious people experience the ups and downs of life like everyone else and should be expected to have suicidal thoughts. But they won't kill themselves either because the religion forbids suicide, or it offers something called hope. But religion and the strong anchor of hope it offers potential suicide victims is directly or indirectly ignored completely in the CDC's *Technical Package on Suicide Prevention*. Hope is cheaper than any drug on the market and is addictive and safe. It can be found in God's word but it is not in the CDC *Technical Package*.

The majority of suicide victims, share one predominant emotion, hopelessness, and the only real cure for hopelessness is hope. Yet hope is the last thing that most psychiatrists will offer to suicidal patients, if at all. I wonder how many psychiatrists today have read Dr. Norman Vincent Peale's bestseller, *The Power of Positive Thinking* or recommend it to their patients. Instead many patients will get a bunch of pills, typically, an antidepressant, a mood stabilizer and an anxiolytic. Hope cannot be found in a pill, it can only be found in God, the Bible, religion, faith or all combined. Hope is a state of the soul, an awakening deep within the human consciousness that enables you to accept present painful realities as a passing phase on your way to a better future. Therefore prescribing an antidepressant as if it were a magic bullet to anyone contemplating suicide without adding the essential ingredient called hope is questionable, particularly with the currently available evidence. One question to be answered before looking at this available evidence is

How Effective Are Antidepressants?

Antidepressants (AD) are a major tool, the most expensive one, in the psychiatrist's toolbox. But how effective are antidepressants by themselves, and how effective are they when compared with other therapies for depression? First, antidepressants may not be as effective as touted – they may worsen the duration and intensity of depression and increase the risk of suicide. A French study of over 35,000 patients showed that taking antidepressants for more than one month increased the risk of relapse back into depression. Secondly, at the University of Louisville School of Medicine's Dr. El Mallakh and colleagues have identified Chronic Resistant Depression as a newly recognized side-effect of antidepressants and called it tardive dysphoria, parallel to tardive dyskinesia, a well known side-effect of psychotropic drugs. Dr Mallakh and colleagues showed that 80% of patients maintained on antidepressants suffered relapses and that when treatment was continued in those with a poor response to the drug, they are at greater risk of developing treatment-resistant depression. So what kind of data did the drug companies submit to the *FDA (Food and Drug Administration)* to obtain approval for such ineffective drugs? At George Washington University School of Public Health, Dr. Thomas Moore and University of Connecticut's Dr. Irvin Kirsch and colleagues reviewed the data submitted by drug companies to the FDA for six of the most widely prescribed antidepressants in the US: Celexa(citalopram), Effexor(Venlafexine) Paxil(Paroxetine) Prozac(fluoxetine), Serzone(nefazodone) and Zoloft(sertraline). In their article published in the July 15, 2002 issue of *Prevention & Treatment*, they found that 80% of the response to antidepressants was duplicated in the placebo group. In addition, the mean difference between those given the drug and those given a placebo was only 2 points on the 21-item or 17-item Hamilton Depression scales (HDS). The 17-item HDS consists of 17 items with 50 points while the 21-item HDS consists of 21 items with 62 points. A score of less than 7 means no depression (or cured depression) while a score of 25 or more on either scale means there is severe depression. A difference of only 2 points between a drug and placebo on this scale means there is really not much difference between drug or placebo.

To answer the second question, that is, are there comparable or better treatments than antidepressants, we must look at the meaning of better treatments. Better treatment would mean, cheaper, no side effects, and easy to administer. Keep in mind that I have not delved into the commoner and sometimes intolerable or dangerous side effects of the antidepressants. There are several effective and better alternatives to AD, some of them costing little or nothing. One of such cost-effective treatments is exercise, that is, besides hope therapy. In the *British Medical Journal of Clinical Research* landmark review article by DS Lawler and SW Hopkin published in 2001 for example, exercise was shown to reduce symptoms of depression as measured on the Beck Depression Inventory (BDI). BDI is another commonly used screening tool for depression. It consists of 21 items each with a score from 0 to 3 with a score of 13 or less indicating minimal depression and a score of 29 to 63 indicating severe depression. Exercise in this study reduced BDI score by an average of -7.31 points. While, several studies have observed the positive effects of exercise on depression, only a few have compared exercise side-by-side with antidepressants. The Duke University SMILE *(Standard Medical Intervention vs. Long-term Exercise)* study by Dr. Blumenthal and colleagues was one of such few studies. SMILE compared aerobic exercise with AD in the treatment of depression. A total of 156 adults were split into three groups. One group received the antidepressant Sertraline (S), another group aerobic exercise (X) only, and the third group received both antidepressants and exercise (X+S). After 16 weeks of treatment with either aerobic exercise (X), 50 to 200mg of Sertraline (S) or a combination of both treatments (X+S), no differences were found between the three different groups. Even more importantly, 10 months after the study was completed, the "exercise only" group (X) showed lower rates of relapse compared to the antidepressant (S) or antidepressant + aerobic exercise (X+S) group. This simply meant that exercise alone was "better" at lifting the veil of depression than either antidepressants or a combination of both antidepressant and exercise. The dose of exercise required to reduce symptoms of depression was found to be 30 minutes, 3 times a week for 3 months, according to Ochsner New Orleans cardiologists, Dr. Richard Milani and Dr. Carl Lavie. *(Am J Med 2007;120(9): 799-806.* So how many psychiatrists routinely prescribe exercise to depressed or suicidal patients?

Another puzzling question to ask is if 50 to 70 percent of suicide victims have an underlying depression that has not responded to antidepressants, why did antidepressants fail them? The answer can be found in psychiatry Professor Emeritus Aaron Beck's work on depression. Called *Beck's Cognitive Triad* (different from the *cardiology Beck's triad*), Professor Beck described the depressed individual has having an irrational and pessimistic view of three areas: **themselves**, their **world** and the **future**. These aberrant perceptions can be changed by talking with and training the depressed or suicidal patient to think differently and show them how to do so, but it is delusional to expect a pill not designed for brainwashing to change the depressed individual's believe system. Add hopelessness to the depressed person's irrational pessimistic view of themselves, their world and their future and you'll get a depressed and suicidal individual. With the current standard treatment, antidepressants, with or without psychotherapy, this individual is at greater risk of killing themselves. Since hopelessness is a universal trait in most suicide victims, you can infer that hope is the most important thing suicidal patients need. Physicians, psychiatrists and psychologists and those who care for suicidal and depressed patients should all be trained to provide hope therapy. Hope comes in many forms and several studies have shown that the biggest source of hope is from organized religious services. But will hope therapy work for depressed and suicidal patients? One way to answer this question is to look at a group that does not believe in God, has no moral restraint against suicide and shares no hope about life beyond the grave. Then see how they fare with respect to suicide. Such a group would include atheists and other irreligious groups. Staks Rosch, a vocal atheist and progressive humanist in his online December 8, 2017 *Huffington Post* article *Atheism Has a Suicide Problem*, admits that depression, the number one precursor to suicide, is a serious problem amongst atheists. He however blames the high suicide rate amongst atheists on religious people. Yet he admits that atheists are disagreeable (pessimistic, irrational) not just with the world around them but also with themselves. He is admitting that atheists are already infected with two of Professor Beck's Cognitive Triad for depression. Put "three atheists in a room and it won't be long before some issue divides them", Staks admits in the article. This in itself suggests that atheists have a pessimistic worldview, a trait that increases their risk for depression and therefore suicide. Atheists also have a greater tendency toward hopelessness because they deny the greatest source of hope, the almighty God. Yet this atheist blames Christians for their high suicide risk!

> *Now the God of hope fill you with all joy and peace in believing, that ye may abound in hope, through the power of the Holy Ghost.*
> *Romans 15:13*

Christians believe in something and someone bigger than and outside of themselves and draw hope from their knowledge of God and faith in him. Atheists on the other hand believe in nothing other than themselves. Romans 15:13 states clearly that hope comes from God. He that denies the God of hope will end hopeless. Atheists, by denying God, deny themselves hope. Atheists will therefore continue to struggle against hope and God until hopelessness sets in and takes over their lives. Once they reach this point, suicidal thoughts easily creep in. The atheist can either surrender to God or continue to fight against the waves of hopelessness until in frustration they take their own lives.

Someone should have told Mr. Staks that we will all go through difficulties in life. When we do, those who believe in someone or something bigger and outside of themselves find hope in whatever they believe. If you believe nothing, your hope level will be nothing, and this means you are without hope or basically hopeless. Hopeless people are far more likely to be depressed and to commit suicide than those who have an anchor of hope in God. Those who have placed their hope in riches and fame will find out that those things do not provide them true hope or fill the void of emptiness or feelings of hopelessness. Nor can alcohol, awards, clubs, cults, drugs, marriage, parties or sex fill this void of emptiness that often precedes hopelessness. Only the truth of knowing God and the Savior Jesus Christ can set people free from suicide and suicidal tendencies.

If the Son therefore shall make you free, ye shall be free indeed. John 8:36

That's why Christians are relatively immune to suicide while people and nations with high numbers of atheists and hopelessness have very high suicide rates. The presence of God and religion would explain the relatively low suicide rates in places like Afghanistan (5.5 suicides per 100,000 people), Iraq (3/100,000). Nigeria has a suicide rate of 9.5/100,000, while the United States, Russia, Belgium, China, Japan and Ghana have 15.3, 31, 20.7, 9.7, 18.5 and 5.4 suicides per 100,000 people respectively. (www.worldpopulationreview.com). In times of trouble and sometimes in the face of challenges, the godless and therefore hopeless, will take their own lives rather than be thankful. The first major goal of suicide prevention should therefore be to instill hope into the potential suicide victim.

Why art thou cast down, O my soul? and why art thou disquieted within me? hope thou in God... Psalm 42:11

Real hope must extend beyond our life on planet earth otherwise,

If in this life only we have hope in Christ, we are of all men most miserable. I Corinthians 15:19

If after we die we have nothing else to look forward to, then life on earth would be meaningless. We know that when we die or if Jesus Christ returns before we die, our present bacteria-infested, sick, dying, diseased and weak physical bodies will be transformed into immortal, strong, perfect, bodies free of sickness, sorrow, pain or oppression:

> *In a moment, in the twinkling of an eye, at the last trump: for the trumpet shall sound, and the dead shall be raised incorruptible, and we shall be changed. I Corinthians 15:52*

Having such hope is not only healthy, it is worth having if it keeps millions from jumping out of windows, hanging themselves, overdosing on drugs or blowing out their brains. Yet atheists call this hope a delusion. A delusion strong enough to instill hope to the hopeless individual and keep millions of people from attempting or committing suicide is a delusion worth having and sharing with the world. If someone you loved has committed suicide, someone whose memory still brings tears, pain and burdens of sadness to your soul, I'm sure you would rather have them alive with this "delusion" than to be dead and gone. This "delusion" is the hope of eternal life that helps Christians see beyond their present circumstances and live joyfully with hope, no matter what they're going through. If you will receive Christ into your life, you will receive this "delusion" of hope called eternal life. Accepting your need for such hope might at first seem embarrassing, but you will be glad you made the decision afterwards. It is the most important key to preventing suicides on a global scale.

> *And this is the record, that God hath given to us eternal life, and this life is in his Son. I John 5:11*

Faith in Jesus Christ brings God and eternal hope into your life as well as an infusion of power, faith, love, joy and peace. You would not want to kill yourself once you receive eternal life.

> *For God so loved the world, that he gave his only begotten Son, that whosoever believeth in him should not perish, but have everlasting life. John 3:16*

Death cannot take away this hope of eternal life as our lives become woven with God's own life through his eternal Holy Spirit dwelling in us when we receive Jesus Christ. That's what gives so much hope to even persecuted Christians. The Holy Spirit instills the will to live in us and helps us to be more than conquerors in the face of challenges or tragedies. If that hope is called delusion, so be it. The more we strive to remove God from our schools, colleges, courts, businesses and even churches, the more hopelessness we will find in society and the higher our suicide rates will climb. As the world system continues to pull down ancient landmarks of godliness in the land and replace it with humanistic ungodly laws, policies, and God-haters, hopelessness will rise and so will suicide even among the rich.

Hope therapy is the only way to curb rising suicide in any society and it can only come from believing and trusting in God and His word.

Are there any other therapies that could be compared with AD? Not touted in mainstream medicine and clinical practice, meditation and mindfulness-based cognitive therapy (MBCT) have actually been shown to be effective in the treatment of depression. In a systematic review of 47 randomized clinical trials by Dr. Madhav Goyal and colleagues at Johns Hopkins University published in the March 2014 issue of the *Journal of The American Medical Association (JAMA)*, meditation was shown to reduce the negative aspects of psychological stress. However, they concluded that meditation was "not better" than any active treatment (drugs, exercise, behavioral therapy). What's surprising was their use of the phrase "not better" rather than "almost as good as". MBCT was almost as good as antidepressants at reducing the negative symptoms of depression such as lack of motivation or lack of energy. In another study of 160 patients in Toronto, Canada, published by Dr. Zindel Segal and colleagues in the December 6, 2010 issue of the *Archives of General Psychiatry*, MBCT was found to protect against relapses or recurrence of depression just as effectively as antidepressant therapies. Again, the PREVENT study, published in the July 2015 issue of *The Lancet* by Dr. William Kuyken and colleagues at Oxford University similarly showed that MBCT helped prevent depression recurrence as effectively as maintenance antidepressant medications. *(PREVENT study = Prevention of Recurrent Episodes of Depression with Venlafexine for Two Years).*

In his book *Theory and Practice of Psychiatry*, Professor Bruce Cohen of Virginia University stated that a sense of hopelessness is one of the strongest predictors of suicide. It is the most important thing to look for in depressed patients. It's also my firm believe that all psychiatrists, psychologists and suicide care teams should be trained on how to instill hope into every potential suicide victim and not just identify hopelessness. It's quite clear at this point that hope is a factor that exceeds what the current healthcare system can offer victims of impending suicide from the CDC's *Technical Package on Suicide Prevention.*

The Heart of a Suicide Victim
The suicide victim has a heart overwhelmed by their circumstances or their perception of it. They feel hopeless and the immediate crisis intervention for an impending suicide victim should be to give them hope. Hope is not a pill nor can it be found in a pill. Virtually every depressed and suicidal individual is suffering from wounds of the soul. Fresh or old, these wounds can only heal with tender care of the soul, never through pills. There is no drug that can offer hope to a

suicidal or depressed patient. To desire to stay alive when faced with problems, the suicide victim needs something or someone bigger than themselves or their problems. They need God, faith or religion, something bigger than their perceived problem, something they can hold on to. Hope is that thing!

Five dominant or overwhelming emotions that accompany or precede suicide are loss, guilt, blame, control and anger. The suicide victim usually has lost something (deceased family member, marriage, prestige, job, relationship, money or dignity), feels angry, guilty, or has lost control, while seeking someone to blame for the emotional state or loss. The victim may feel the need to take the blame for the loss as a means of controlling what cannot otherwise be controlled. How do you control the death of a loved one who dies from cancer for example? You can't. But the suicide victim, whether or not they have a diagnosed mental illness, may want to punish whoever they feel is responsible, including themselves. If it means killing themselves, so be it. They may feel whatever they have lost, dignity, money, position, relationship, is far more important than their own lives. The suicide victim is angered by their inability to control everything in their life. So many people find themselves in hopeless situations without having a medical diagnosis or condition. They just feel hopeless as life hits them and they may attempt suicide. Once a hopeless situation arises, community responders should be available to evaluate suicide risk. They should be in California right now checking out wildfire victims to identify those at risk of suicide. Any one can be trained to look for hopelessness or to screen using the Beck Hopelessness Scale or similar tool. You don't need a medical diagnosis or degree in order to identify someone at high risk for suicide. The idea of requiring a medical diagnosis as a prerequisite to suicide prevention is a major reason for the rise in suicides. The exclusion of God in suicide prevention strategies further compounds this problem. Most of the suicide prevention programs forget that God is a contender in the central issue of suicide. Suicide victims may be angry towards God for their problems and may blame him for not bailing them out.

Whether the five dominant emotions in those committing suicide do have some justification or not, everyone loses when a suicide occurs. We must therefore do all in our power to cut that risk down to zero.

Suicide and The Guilty Noose of Sin
Suicide victims can be weighed down into severe depression by the burden of their own sins far more than by the burden of their imagined problems. Sin can strangle mental and emotional freedom and rational thinking and lead to impulsive acts including suicide. Sin

must be dealt with by asking God for forgiveness. If you don't ask God to forgive you, whether or not you believe in God,

> ...be sure your sin will find you out. Numbers 32:23

If you sin, that sin may hinder the flow of God's love and blessings and prevent you from thinking rationally. That's how men hooked on pornography loose their jobs, marriage and home. God wants to forgive you of your sins but you must ask for it.

> *If we say that we have no sin, we deceive ourselves, and the truth is not in us. If we confess our sins, he is faithful and just to forgive us our sins, and to cleanse us from all unrighteousness. If we say we have not sinned, we make him a liar, and his word is not in us.*
> I John 1:8-10

The sooner you ask God for forgiveness and turn away from the sin, the quicker you'll probably be in recovering from the compounding negative effects of your sin. If you let sin run its natural course unchecked, it turns to evil, wickedness, destruction and death. Sin destroys everything in its path:

> *For the wages of sin is death; but the gift of God is eternal life through Jesus Christ our Lord. Romans 6:23*

Sin creates an invisible baggage on the soul that could lead to depression and suicide. That's why you must repent when you sin.

> *Sherry and Shannon are in their late forties. Both women are sinners and commit the same exact sins everyday. Sherry admits that for the last 20 years, she always asked God for forgiveness every night before going to bed, particularly when things get rough at work. Shannon on the other hand commits the same sins as Sherry but doesn't believe there is God. Let's presume that both women commit one sin per hour during their 16 waking hours. That's 16 sins per day.*

For the sake of illustration, let's presume that each sin weighs 1 ounce and is carried on the soul of the sinner until he or she asks God for forgiveness. How much sin would each lady have in one year? At the end of each day, each lady has 16 ounces of sin hanging on her neck. Since Sherry asks for forgiveness every night and receives forgiveness and cleansing that same night, she wakes up everyday free of the burden of her sins. In one year she will only be carrying the burden of one day's sins, 16 ounces, or one pound. Shannon on the other hand goes to bed every night with the weight of her sins hanging on her soul plus that of the previous days, months or years. In one year, Shannon will have 5,840 ounces or 365 pounds of sin hanging on her neck in contrast to Sherry's 16 ounces or one pound. Why this much difference? Why is Sherry carrying a lower burden of sin than Shannon? It's pretty simple. The Bible says

> For I will be merciful to their unrighteousness, and their sins and their iniquities will I remember no more. (Hebrews 8:12)

The difference between the burden of sin each woman is carrying is that God forgives those who ask for forgiveness (I John 1:9) and forgets the sin. Sherry's sins have been forgiven. Shannon doesn't believe there is God so she never asks for forgiveness. But denial won't take away her sins. At 365 pounds per year, in twenty years, Shannon will be carrying 7300 pounds of sin! The Chevrolet Suburban weighs about 5800 pounds, the E 350 Mercedes Benz, 3,825 pounds. So imagine Shannon dragging an invisible Chevy suburban and some extra weight around her neck everywhere she goes! That much weight will eventually wear anyone out regardless of whether you are rich or famous. When both women get off work on Friday, Sherry goes home, while Shannon boards the train downtown to see her therapist. If you're carrying a heavy load in your soul that's weighing you down, this is what the bible recommends:

> Come unto me, all ye that labour and are heavy laden, and I will give you rest. Mathew 13:28

Suppose like Shannon, you've been carrying a heavy load of sin from years or decades of not asking God for forgiveness. This load of sin may be proportional to the severity of your depression and suicidal thoughts. The only way to get rid of your burden of sin is by asking God for forgiveness. God loves you, knows what sin could do to you and wants to help you get rid of this heavy weight of sin on your soul:

> Casting all your cares upon him, for he careth for you. I Peter 5:7.

The last two bible verses are saying you should hand over your worries, fears, burdens and sins to God. Some suicide victims enjoy struggling and arguing against the existence of God until the weight of their sins eventually strangles them to do the unthinkable but predictable suicide. They feel the heavy burden of sin, fail to understand that sin is the reason they feel depressed and suicidal, and they try every other means to eliminate this burden unsuccessfully. And some preachers don't make it any easier as they are determined to avoid preaching about sin. After months or years of failed antidepressants and psychotherapy, such individuals finally realize their wealth, fame or success or the psychiatrist from the Ivy League medical school cannot help them. That's when they start considering suicide. They realize something is still there that's weighing them down, like a noose around their necks. They had placed all their hopes in doctors who felt antidepressants would work. But how many doctors know about the antidotes for sin or hopelessness? Very few do. According to the 11th edition of *Kaplan & Saddock's Synopsis of Psychiatry*, physicians have a higher suicide rate than the rest of the United States population; about 400 physicians commit suicide every year, and psychiatrists followed by ophthalmologists and anesthesiologists have the greatest risk. Psychiatrists who ought to be providing hope to their patients may themselves be battling with high levels of hopelessness. That's perhaps why many depressed and suicidal victims feel they have to kill themselves. The medical board will probably suspend a psychiatrist's license for telling suicidal patients that their sins are a possible source of depression or suicidal ideation. Sin, doing wrong in the eyes of God, can only be eliminated by God's forgiveness and by surrendering to the cleansing power of the blood of Jesus Christ. If sin is the cause of hopelessness and depression there is only one cure:

> ...and the blood of Jesus Christ his Son cleanseth us from all sin. I John 1:7

The only thing that will wash away your sins and the burden they have created on your soul is the blood of Jesus Christ. This basic truth, understood by some kindergarten children, remains unknown to many rich and famous folk.

> *And ye shall know the truth, and the truth shall make you free.*
> *John. 8:32*

How do you free yourself from over 7300 pounds of invisible but real sin hanging around your neck over a twenty-year period? What about those who commit 5 sins an hour instead of one? The average America Brown cow weighs just over 1500 pounds. So 7300 pounds of sin around your neck is about 5 invisible cows around your neck! Imagine going to work everyday or to a party on weekends with 5 cows latched tightly to your neck! If you want to get rid of this feeling of heaviness, you'd have to do it God's way. I suggest you experiment with this prayer and see if God will set you free from your burden of sins and contact me if you experience freedom by doing so:

> *God in heaven, if you are out there and can hear me, if you consider me a sinner but you still love me, if Jesus is the only way to be set free from this pressing weight of sin over me, then I ask for your forgiveness and that the blood of Jesus wash away my sins in Jesus*

name. *Come into my heart today and help me start a new life with you in my life. Set me free in the name of Jesus. Amen.*

There is enough information in the medical literature to inform suicide prevention practitioners to incorporate Christian services and religious practices such as meditation into their program. For example, Harvard neuroscientist Dr. Sara Lazar reported a decrease in grey matter density in the amygdala of stressed but otherwise healthy patients after 8 weeks of mindfulness-based stress reduction (MBSR) training, that is, meditation. The greater the density of grey matter and the greater the activity in the amygdala, the greater the stress a person will be experiencing in real time. Dr. Lazar suggests that through MBSR, patients can develop better emotional responses to stress, the very thing we wish suicidal and depressed patients would develop.

Some suicide victims are ungrateful for what they have. Among this group are those that are truly successful, don't realize they are blessed, encounter some challenges along the way, and hang, shoot or poison themselves while the world continues to admire them for the very things they ought to be thankful for. Here is what one of my pastors says of those who fail to offer their best to God while they can:

> *The burden of success will sink you if you never offer it. The burden to perform will exhaust you if you never offer it. The burden to produce will leave you empty if you never offer it.*
> **- Pastor Jessie Prince, Grace Outreach Center, Plano, TX**

Whenever you hear that a celebrity or someone successful has committed suicide, think of these three statements. Many celebrity suicide victims get to a crossroad in life where they must admit they've been living a lie, accept God's forgiveness and love, and be thankful for what they already have. Instead, they fight God off, hoping their success will be a good antidote for their emptiness, exhaustion or sinking depression. That's a recipe for suicide. If you've denied the existence of God based on past disappointments for not protecting you or a loved one, get real. It's time to accept that you can't control everything in your life, no matter how hard you try or how good you think you are. Life happens to everyone including you. That means good times and bad times. Grow up and suck it up. Accept God's love and understand that there are millions of people out there that would gladly trade places with you. The two hands with which you intend to hang yourself, someone else wish they had even one. You see yourself as ugly when you look in the mirror, whereas your peers or neighbors wish they were as attractive as you. You think you don't have enough and want to end your life while someone with less than a tenth of what you have in the same zip code was in church last Sunday testifying of God's goodness. The severely depressed man or woman that has denied God's gentle knocking on their heart may secretly hope to win a mental tug of war against God. He or she hopes to do so by wresting control of their soul away from God. They move into self-destructive mode by insisting that God will not have their soul and rather than surrender their life, destroy it by committing suicide. It's as if the suicide victim is saying

> "God, I see I can't control what happens in my life, but I won't let you either. I'll kill myself. That way, if I can't have control of what's going on in my life, you won't have my life either. I win by killing myself".

Messed up isn't it? Killing oneself is always a messed-up deal. I am yet to find anyone who felt that a suicide was justified. It takes a little more than severe mental illness to take your own life. Sometimes it requires the highest form of selfishness, indulgent self-pity, ugly pride and zero concern for those you're leaving behind. It takes an ugly heart to casually take another life and only the ugliest heart will take its own life. Suicide is often the result of a power struggle between two individuals, God, and man. It requires the person completely refusing to surrender to God. *"I win by killing myself"*, the suicide victim may believe. I lost my mother when I was thirteen years old with no siblings and a distant father. As bad as life could sometimes get for me, suicide wasn't an option. I did get depressed and really didn't have much social support to work through my grief, but believed I was capable of accomplishing whatever goals I set for my life. As a teenager, one of my greatest sources of encouragement came from Dr. Norman Vincent Peale's *The Power of Positive Thinking*. If I felt really down, I'd cry a little, hit the books, study even harder and prepare for a better future.

Suicide Is So Wrong and You Shouldn't Have To Commit It
Don't get me wrong at all. Things may go terribly wrong in your life that you feel like killing yourself. When that happens, you must immediately brush off thoughts or feelings about killing yourself before they fix themselves firmly into your subconscious mind and become difficult to shrug off. Instead, make a list of things that you have or have accomplished, count your blessings. Be thankful, no matter what. Put your life into God's hands and secede control. Help someone in worse shape than you are. There are many less fortunate souls out there that would benefit from your wisdom, talent, kindness, experience and generosity. Things you no longer use may be extremely valuable to others. Go down to the soup kitchen and volunteer. But don't kill yourself. Try to put a smile on some dying

child's face in the leukemia ward, or send a word of encouragement to someone that has lost a loved one. You'll see a change in your own mood. While the thought of ending your life may be a normal reaction to serious life challenges, the act of killing yourself is not normal. If you plan to kill yourself, something evil has taken over your mind, and your heart has definitely turned ugly. Don't allow such ugliness to ruin your best years.

When a rich and famous person commits suicide, it's because they want to control life itself. No one can control life; both the righteous and the ungodly will have their share of tragedies. Work through your challenges, learn from them, and you'll become a much better person. If you find things are out of your control and influence, it's still no excuse for attempting suicide. Only God has the kind of control you're seeking and you're going to frustrate yourself trying to get such control. No amount of success should delude you into thinking you can control whatever life brings. Hoping to be in control of every situation you encounter in life is commoner amongst suicide victims, particularly in the United States. Suicide in conclusion, is often about blame, loss, anger, guilt, sin, and control. Blaming God, blaming yourself, blaming others and trying to be in control of whatever life brings you, losing something you can't live without, deeply seated anger, guilt and un-confessed accumulated sin combined without irrational pessimistic thinking mixed with hopelessness can make anyone suicidal.

Those that have given God a permanent place in their hearts never follow a suicide path even when they are depressed. They have weapons that are mighty enough to cast down any imagination or thoughts of suicide. They give everything to God based on their knowledge of the words in the bible and the guidance of the Holy Spirit. Those without God may recognize people with such a heart. They must respond either positively or negatively to such individuals. It will eat them up to be neutral to such an individual. For example, when the Apostle Paul was without such a heart, he persecuted and killed Christians. But once he encountered Jesus and received Him, he gladly faced persecution and death for the one he previously persecuted. Throughout history, religious individuals with an ugly heart have always sought ways to persecute those with a beautiful heart. That's why Cain slew Abel and that's why you may have seen Christians beheaded or slaughtered like cattle in the news. This degree of evil is on an upward trend around the world, with people preferring to kill those with a golden heart, or commit suicide themselves, rather than surrender their weary souls to God. If you're broke, broken, weary, rich, poor, obscure or famous, God is knocking at the door of your heart. Welcome him in. Receive him into your heart. He will uplift your soul and empower your spirit. All your accomplishments are nothing compared to an uplifted soul with a regenerated spirit. And it is only when you have a new heart that you can find rest for your weary soul. A significant amount of mental illness, sense of constant despair, emptiness, drug addiction, particularly depression and suicides amongst the affluent, can often be tied to their struggle against the soul's need to surrender to God. Not only must the heart of everyone, rich or poor, famous or obscure, be submitted to God, each of us must read the bible and know what God demands of us.

God expects us to use the power in His word to confront and overcome challenges, not to avoid them. While you may feel you are unprepared for these character-building tests, they will enable you to grow spiritually and mature emotionally. So rest assured that as long as you are alive, you will face challenges that will test your endurance and character and alter how you view life. How you handle these life challenges depends on your social support, how much of God's word dwells in you, and whether or not you've received a new heart from God. If you don't have enough of God's word in you and do not believe in or trust God to help you through life, your human social support or success may eventually prove inadequate. As I mentioned earlier, I lost my mother months after I turned thirteen. For an only child, that wasn't easy, and in addition, I wasn't a Christian. Yet intuitively, I still trusted God to protect and lead me. He didn't fail. Nine years later, I gave my life to Jesus Christ. So can you.

Over a year ago, my first son, rather than go off to college, passed away. That was a great loss from which I can't say I've recovered or will ever fully recover. In all, within the last three years alone, I have lost a grandmother, a father, and a son. How am I holding it together? The Bible as well as prayer and intimate fellowship with Jesus Christ have been my source of strength. There'll never be enough words to describe my wife's love and unwavering support too. While surrounded by friends I can call on, none of them can comfort me where I need it the most, deep within my soul and spirit. Only God can do that and I'm glad he has given me a new heart to recognize his presence and comfort. How about you? Do you have a new heart? Can you recognize his voice, or his presence? Have you opened your heart to him? Are you willing to open your heart to him so he can take the heavy load off your soul? Have you experienced such great loss that you need God's comforting presence right now in order not to breakdown or hurt yourself? Do you want to feel the comforting presence of God and know he is there for you right now? Would you like to have a new heart and a new spirit just like Ezekiel 36:26-27 says? If the answer is yes, then pray this prayer:

Heavenly Father, I acknowledge that I am a sinner with an ugly heart full of sin. I repent of all the sins I have committed and ask for your forgiveness. Wash me completely clean with the precious blood of Jesus and give me a new heart and a new spirit. Lord Jesus, come into my heart today fill me with your Holy Spirit. Help me to turn completely away from my sinful wicked ways and begin a new life with you. Thank you for saving me, in Jesus' name. Amen.

If you're grieving a loss, you can hand your grief over to God in prayer. Let the bible guide you through your journey. While virtually every man struggles with lust and virtually every woman with submission, the real battles of life must be won with rich deposits of the word of God in our hearts. In Ephesians 6:17, the bible tells us that the word of God is the sword of the spirit. The more bible verses you have memorized and can recall when faced with challenges, the bigger your sword. Jesus clearly demonstrated this in Matthew 4:4 when Satan came to tempt him. He defeated the devil by speaking God's words to him. There is power in the bible verses and they are activated through reading, memorization, meditating, studying, trusting and obeying. A part of your soul is coupled to the words as you study and memorize them. The changes they create mentally, emotionally and at the molecular level are unparalleled. Hope is restored and your faith is gradually built up. As you meditate on the bible verses, your spirit and your soul merge with the hidden power in the bible verses and power is released or stored to help you now or later. The more words you have, the more power is released or stored waiting for release. That power is God's power, not yours, and it can work whenever it is released through your lips. Releasing God's word is called prophesying and powerful things can happen when we prophesy to one another based on God's word. That's why the Apostle Paul said

Wherefore, brethren, covet to prophesy, and forbid not to speak in tongues. I Corinthians 14:39

Those that have accepted Jesus Christ as Lord and Savior are the most effective at prophesying because they have access to God through His eternal Holy Spirit. The word of God has hidden power that manifests in your life in varying degrees depending on your faith and the extent to which the Holy Spirit has access to your will. You, provide that access. God cannot force you to yield. For the word of God to have its fullest expression in your life however, you must yield your heart completely to God. If you'd like to do so, first, ask God to forgive you of all your sins, and for Jesus to wash your sins away with his blood. He will give you a new life. By new life I mean he will give you a new heart and a new spirit according to Ezekiel 36:26. You need this new spirit to tap fully into the hidden power of the words in the bible. Many of us have thought or done terrible things in life that we feel dirty and guilty about when we look up to heaven. But Jesus knows this and that's why he died for us. It doesn't matter what you've done. Give your heart and life to God, confess your sins to him and receive the gift of his Son's sacrifice. Jesus Christ is the only one who died so you can be free from the filth you're experiencing deep down in your soul. He will clean out the filth that makes you puff, inhale and exhale cigarettes, hoping to eliminate the irritability in your soul. Once you receive Christ, set aside some time daily to cling your soul to God's word, and to pray and memorize some bible verses. This habit will set your life on a path you've never before imagined possible. There will be a joy, peace, beauty, holiness and power permeating your life that will amaze you. The only ones that will hate you for this transformation are those who hate God but appear religious. Friends and family you thought were very religious may start showing hostility towards you. Jesus is still available to them. God gave all things to his Son, Jesus Christ and he wants everyone to come to him, but only through his Son, Jesus Christ. (John 14:6) If you reject this relationship protocol of heaven, you may never experience the fullest extent of God's love for you.

> *Whoseoever denieth the Son, the same hath not the Father: but he that acknowledgeth the Son hath the Father. (I John 2:23)*

If you don't accept God's terms and you die, the only thing you'll know about God, which you won't like at all, is his wrath and judgment. (Revelation 20:15) It doesn't have to be that way, but you have a choice to either accept Jesus Christ as Savior or deny him.

For the Depressed Person
- No one is exempt from mental and emotional hardship
- You have to be smart enough to not like your life the way it is
- You have so much more value alive than dead. Don't kill you
- If you're hearing voices telling you to kill yourself, tell them to shut up in Jesus' name
- Ask God to forgive you of your sins and to lift your burdens
- Call a friend or find someone you can help and help them
- Nullify any blood covenant you made with the devil with the blood of Jesus Christ by accepting Jesus into your heart now
- God Loves you and wants to help you one-on-one
- Pray for hope, courage, strength
- Call 1-800-273-8255 in the US or your suicide help line

Chapter 6

How The Bible Got Me My Dream Job

If you're a Christian, there are two things you can do with the bible. You can tap into its power or interpret it. I have seen the power of God flow from His word into circumstances and homes when spoken, believed and acted upon. My conclusion as a lover of God's word is that you too can tap into this source of supernatural power even without understanding the theological context or interpretation of the verse releasing power into your life. Does a newborn baby know what Vitamin D is? No! But the baby drinks milk and gets Vitamin D anyway! To tap into the power in God's word, all you need is to hear the word and act on it. Tapping into this source of divine power is one of God's intentions for having the Bible written. Interpreting the Bible is much harder than tapping into its hidden power. The bible is the power of God clothed with the words of men mysteriously awaiting the heart of faith to reveal its hidden power and treasure. In theory, tapping into this secret power source called the bible may appear to be even more demanding than interpreting it. With the right teacher or resources, you can understand the meaning of a bible verse while thinking it's much harder to experience its hidden power. But in practice, tapping the hidden power of the bible is actually much easier than interpreting it. So even if you don't have any idea of the writer's intentions, and are therefore unable to fully understand or interpret a particular verse of the bible, that verse still has hidden power and treasure that you can tap into and enjoy. All you do is memorize, meditate, apply it and trust it. The bible is not just an advanced scientific document it is also the most powerful spiritual document in existence. It is without a doubt written by men, yet the words of these men seem to contain an undeniable wisdom, a mysterious power as well as God's plan of salvation. If you've read the preceding sections and memorized some of the verses, you may already have experienced some powerful changes such as a quickening of your mind and spirit, particularly if you are born again. If you can pierce through the words in the bible with your regenerated spirit and renewed mind for revelation through memorization, meditation and confession, you might experience a dose of this divine power. A verse or portions of the bible could suddenly come alive in your heart during moments of quiet reflection. Sometimes hearing an individual filled with God's presence and power (anointing) speak bible verses can ignite what's already in your heart. The words in the bible also have the power to lead sinners to salvation through Jesus Christ, and to draw us away from sin and hell.

The Bible is declared as the inspired word of God with life-giving properties (John 6:63) and irrefutable power (Hebrews 4:12). Our attempts to understand the message of the bible cannot be undertaken as a solo journey. If we do so, we will at best, understand only one aspect, leaving us blindsided. That's why we are told in the book of Hebrews not to forsake the assembling of ourselves together (Hebrews 10:25). We should get together with other believers regularly, share the word in fellowship and prophesy into each other's lives based on God's words in the Bible. It's not enough to go to a church that has an awesome music band or a great speaker for a pastor; the words of God need to be prophesied directly into your life on a fairly regular basis. Many churches by virtue of their structured sermons and organized religion may not be able to do this vital prophesying. No wonder so many Christians are on antidepressants! Prophesying lifts the soul and spirit and is the best antidote for depression. Attending a church where the word of God is not spoken directly into your life from the pulpit or through a smaller fellowship group regularly may lead to depression. Such a church or fellowship may not create the mental and spiritual atmosphere and growth that you need for effectively transforming your life. (Romans 12:2)

While theologians have helped us understand how to interpret the Bible, there are still many puzzling questions about the bible they cannot explain. For example, if EVERY word of God is pure and powerful, can you take any bible verse, meditate on it, and experience the power of God hidden in it? Also, can you experience the power of God in a verse even if you cannot interpret the verse? Common Christian sense would suggest yes, but theologians may say no. Theologians may recommend you not waste your precious time meditating on a verse that bears no relevance to you today. If you follow this approach by theologians however, you may cheat yourself of so many blessings hidden in the bible. Every word in the bible, whether from the Old or New Testament, clothes and hides God's power. While some theologians may disagree with me on this, you can hang your faith on this very truth and transform your life powerfully. The following true story might help you understand how the power hidden in God's word may be released in your own life.

> One Sunday in September 1997, I arrived at a friend's apartment in Brooklyn, New York, following instructions of the Holy Spirit to go and meet with the Chairman of Medicine at that Hospital and request for an interview and a job. I called to make an appointment

first thing Monday morning and was given a Friday appointment. On Tuesday morning, while meditating on these four words...

... I have given you... Genesis 1:29

My mind narrowed its focus to these four words with such intensity it felt as if they were burning tracks into my soul. That's when the phone rang in the apartment. It was the Chairman's secretary. I thought she wanted to shift the appointment closer when she asked to speak with Dr. Caxton Opere. As soon as I let her know she had me on the line, she told me my Friday appointment with the Chairman had been cancelled. And this was just Tuesday!

Pay close attention to what happened next as you may discover the hidden key to a rare opportunity that may change your life forever.

I thanked her, dropped the phone, and the words "I HAVE GIVEN YOU" instantly came alive, nudging me to action. I showered, shaved and in minutes was in my best suit on my way for a job interview at the Internal Medicine Department. Those words in me gave me no other option and strangely enough, I was enjoying the moment. The hospital was less than a block away from the apartment. As I walked into the Medicine Department I saw the chairman himself carrying some papers in his hands. He seemed caught a little off guard but smiled and said, "Hi, Caxton, you look great," Thanks, I replied, smiling at him. I immediately told him, "I know you have a job for me here". He looked at me, smiled again, and invited me into his office. After exchanging pleasantries, and speaking for a few more minutes, he called in three other physicians: the Residency Program Director, the Head of the Medical staff, and one other attending physician. They were all excited to see and interview me. I got the job and it changed my life!

The Context of A Verse

You should understand that in Genesis 1:29, God was speaking to a sinless perfectly created being, Adam, thousand of years ago, in the Garden of Eden. God wasn't speaking to sinful, flawed Caxton, in Brooklyn. Moreover, the world Adam lived in back then was entirely different from the one I lived in as of September 1997 when God said "go to Brooklyn". Yet I was able to tap into the power of four words spoken to a sinless perfect Adam. So can you. There is a spiritual power hiding in the words in the Bible. From a theologian's standpoint, this verse should have no relevance to me in 1997. And by the way, some theologians do not believe God can speak to you, some don't believe in the baptism of the Holy Spirit and some don't believe in hell. When that appointment (Yes, that was my story) was cancelled, I could have blamed God for sending me on a futile journey to New York. Instead, I took responsibility for the word that was already given to me, and it forcefully rejected the cancelled appointment, and neutralized the negative effects of the phone call on my spirit. I had a secret revealed to me that God's word could not return back to God without accomplishing its purpose (Isaiah 55:11). That verse was not fiction but fact for my soul. And with the power hidden in the four simple words, *"I have given you"* burning like fire (Jeremiah 20:9) deep in my soul and spirit, I walked confidently into an unplanned interview and got the job that permanently transformed my life. So can you if you walk by faith that comes from loading your mind up with rich deposits of bible verses.

The words in the bible have a powerful driving force of their own. That force can be activated in you also. Words written by men but clothed with God's power, printed in the Bible, can cause such changes. Meditation is one of the ways to unlock this divinely hidden power in the scriptures. That was why Paul instructed Timothy to

> *Meditate upon these things, give thyself wholly to them, that thy profiting may appear to all. (I Tim 4:15)*

Paul was telling Timothy to meditate and give himself completely to the scriptures in order for his success in ministry, business, family life or all three, to become visible to all observers. So should you.

When Paul was writing the words in I Timothy 4:15 to Timothy, he was sending power to Timothy. While it was written almost two thousand years ago, that power is still available to you today. So make sure you do not limit yourself to seeking the mere context of the words in a verse if you are a child of God. The same words can work in your favor even without a complete understanding of their context. If we limit ourselves to contextual interpretations of the Bible, then we'd say Paul was giving some "good advice" to Timothy, and that Paul wasn't speaking to us directly. We could go even further and say that since we don't have a relationship with Paul, his words were meant only for Timothy and not for us. But that would contradict the Bible's instruction that

> *ALL SCRIPTURE is given by the inspiration of God, and is profitable for doctrine, for reproof, for correction, for instruction in righteousness. II Timothy 3:16*

I hope you can immediately see the error of an undying theological loyalty to context as it may negate the whole point of reading and believing the bible and then applying it to yourself! If you want to interpret the bible as a student of theology, it's important that you understand the context of the verse, chapter or section in question: who, where, what, when, why and perhaps how. But as you've seen from my story, context was not in the picture as I sat down to meditate on the four words in Genesis 1:29. You may never be able to tap into the power in God's word if you rely only on context instead of tapping into its power. Using II Timothy 3:16 as an example, you may not be able to apply the verse to yourself if you insist on context. You really would have to take the verse out of context if you want to get the most out of this verse and admit that perhaps it wasn't really Paul, but God, speaking through Paul, to Timothy. This makes more sense theologically. Contextually, we do not have a relationship with Paul, yet the verse must surely apply to us. Does the instruction Paul gave to Timothy back then apply to us today? You bet! While Paul was instructing Timothy back then, God is still instructing every believer through Paul's words today. Context or not, the bible contains instructions and hidden power waiting to be released. Miss this point, that is, the bible containing hidden power waiting to be released, and you might miss the single most important fact about the bible; the bible contains the power of God clothed with the words of men.

The words of the Bible are like indestructible stem cells, with no limits to their potential. Several years ago, I had a medical colleague dealing with a decade of infertility. The Lord said I should tell her she would have a son and specifically told me to speak Isaiah 54:1 to her. About two years later she delivered a baby boy. Another colleague spoke to me in confidence about childlessness and I said next time you sleep with your wife, speak the word of God to your loins and ask God to open her womb. The only child they have came from that instruction. At 3am one morning in Baton Rouge, a lady was brought in by ambulance with her father and her daughter. She recognized me immediately but I didn't. While still puzzled as to why she would bring her daughter on that ambulance ride, she introduced herself. This was her only daughter. I had spoken God's word to her eleven years ago. Therefore, our best approach to life should be to always have God's word in our hearts for all aspects of life. We should align ourselves internally to whatever God says in his word. This internal alignment with God's word is the key to living our fullest lives.

Chapter 7

Jesus, Hidden as בְּרֵאשִׁית in Genesis 1:1

From all indications, the bible is a book inspired by a superior intelligent being with clear intentions, astonishing accuracy and an awareness of future scientific inventions. This being has complex mathematical abilities as well as an understanding of future scientific advances. For example, the book of Revelation mentions the idea of a microchip in the arm or forehead almost two thousand years ago:

> *And he causeth all, both small and great, rich and poor, free and bond, to receive a mark in their right hand, or in their foreheads: And that no man might buy or sell, save he that had the mark, or the name of the beast, or the number of his name.*
> Revelations 13:16,17

Microchips implanted under the skin for everyone are coming! The bible was not the idea of mere mortals. Some verses, words or even letters contain unfathomable layers of information that once deciphered, clearly could not have been written by any ordinary human being with finite intelligence. You'll see in this and subsequent chapters that the men that wrote the bible must have had plenty of help from a superior being with scientifically advanced thoughts.

The 1st Word in Genesis is בְּרֵאשִׁית

The first word in the Hebrew Torah in Genesis 1:1 consists of 6 letters and is pronounced *B'reshit* and looks like this -

בְּרֵאשִׁית

This Hebrew word בְּרֵאשִׁית means *"In The Beginning"*. Some scholars say that b'reshit means "In a beginning" while others say it means "In beginning". But whether "in a beginning", "at the beginning" or "in His beginning", all Hebrew scholars agree this first word is talking about some beginning.

Each Hebrew letter has a unique number and a symbol. The unique number is called its Hebrew Numerical Value or HNV. For example, the first letter of the Hebrew alphabet א, pronounced 'alef', has a value of 1. The last letter of the Hebrew alphabet, ת, pronounced 'tau', has a value of 400. All the other Hebrew alphabets have HNV values between 1 and 400. Also, Hebrew words, unlike English words, are read from right to left not from left to right. So the first letter in the word b'reshit, בְּרֵאשִׁית, is בְּ and not ת while the last letter is ת and not בְּ. Each Hebrew letter also has one or more symbols. So each Hebrew letter has both an HNV and a symbol. Let's now look at each letter in the first word in Genesis more closely.

בְּרֵאשִׁית
= In the Beginning

בְּ = 2

The first letter in the first word is pronounced 'Bet'. Its two symbols are tent and house. A tent is a temporary structure while a house is a permanent structure. The HNV (Hebrew numerical value) for 'bet' is 2. The tent is a temporary structure and represents the church of which Christ is head. The church is on earth temporarily and will eventually be raptured to heaven (I Thessalonians 4:16).

רֵ = 200

The second letter is 'Resh'. Its symbol is a male head and its numerical value is two hundred. The male head is Jesus, and he is the head of the tent above. When the first letter בְּ (bet) is combined with the second letter רֵ (resh), the word formed, רַבּ is pronounced as (Bar) in Hebrew. Bar in Hebrew means son.

א = 1

Alef, אthe third letter in the word b'reshit, is the first Hebrew alphabet. Its HNV is 1 and its symbol is an ox head. Ox head means strength or God's power. The bible says Jesus is the power of God. (Romans 16:25). Alef therefore represents the Son of God with power.

שׁ = 300

The fourth letter is שׁ, 'shin'. Its symbol is teeth. Teeth are for biting and chewing and the symbol represents destruction. The numerical value for 'Shin' is 300, which is also the number for priesthood. שׁ represents the destruction or complete elimination of the role of the priesthood. (Hebrews 7:12) Jesus came to eliminate the daily sacrifices for the sins of the people. שׁ also represents Jesus' death on the cross, the destruction of his mortal body (Hebrews 10:5) in order to fulfill divine prophecy.

י = 10

The fifth letter is 'Yod' and its symbols are hand and arm. Its HNV is 10. Both hand and arm represent work (John 4:34), perhaps the work Jesus would do on our behalf. The symbol may also imply that Jesus, by the work of his own *hands*, would die on the cross. That's not all. Jesus died by having his *hands* nailed to the cross. And remember that his *arms* were also stretched out on that cross. Don't forget he had to *carry* that cross (John 19:17) with his *hands* until Simon of Cyrene had to help him. He told his disciples he was going to l*ay down* his own life (John 10:15) and *take it back* again (John 10:17-18). All this, happening around one word, *hand*! You lay something down with your *hands*, and pick it up again, with the same *hands*.

ת = 400

The last letter in the first word in Genesis is 'Tau' and its symbol is the cross. Tau is also the last letter in the Hebrew alphabet. This was quite a surprise to me since we were told the Romans invented crucifixion when in fact it was always part of the Aramaic ancient Hebrew predating the Romans by thousands of years. The cross, the symbol for the last alphabet, "tau", is also the symbol for the last thing God needed to do in order to restore man back to himself. Amazing!

With the above in mind, here is a table with all the 6 letters of the first word, b'rashet, בְּרֵאשִׁית. Each letter is placed with its HNV and corresponding symbol, as well as one or more meanings of the symbol. Even if you hate tables because of math, this shouldn't be that intimidating. To make it much easier to understand the hidden message encrypted into the letters בְּרֵאשִׁית, the six Hebrew letters, have been rearranged in the table below to read from left to right in the English form rather than right to left in the original Hebrew form.

Study the table below closely. See if you can decode the encrypted message God put in the very first word in the bible. The best way to do this is to try and form just one sentence using all the words in the last two rows (Meaning 1, Meaning 2). Once you form your first sentence, see how many other sentences you can create as you go from left to right.

רֵאשִׁיתבְּ = B'rashet = In the beginning (Genesis 1:1)

Hebrew	בְּ	ר	א	שׁ	י	ת
Say it	Bet	Resh	Alef	Shin	Yod	Tau
English	B	R	A	SH	E	T
HNV	2	200	1	300	10	400
Aramaic Symbol						
Meaning 1	Tent	Head	Ox, strength	Teeth	Hand, arm	Cross
Meaning 2	House	Son	God	Destruction	Work	Cross

HNV = Hebrew Numerical Value

If you're good with puzzles, you might end up with a sentence like this:

> The head ר of the tent בּ, the Son, God's strength א, destroyed שׁ by the hand י on a cross ת.

Another version could be:

> The tent בּ head, God's א Son ר, destroyed שׁ by his hands י on the cross ת

Or another version could say:

> The head of the tent, the Son of God, the power of God, Christ, will be destroyed by the work of his own hand on the cross.

Still another version could read:

> "The head of the church, the Son and power of God, will destroy the priesthood by the work of his own hands on the cross."

> "The tent's head, the Son of God, in his own strength and by the work of his own hands, will stretch out his hands on the cross and, and change the priesthood through the sacrifice he has made on the cross."

Either way you look at it, Jesus' death on the cross was encrypted into the very first word of the Torah, b'rashet, even before Adam sinned in the Garden of Eden. (Revelation 13:8).

The very first word in the Torah contains the Gospel of Jesus Christ and the entire message of the New Testament. Amazing!

Chapter 8

Mathematical Symmetry in Genesis 1:1

Just as the first word in the Bible makes an astounding statement, the entire first sentence in Genesis packs its own punch. Genesis 1:1 in the King James Version (KJV) has ten words and reads

In the beginning God created the heaven and the earth.

But in Hebrew there are seven words not ten:

בְּרֵאשִׁית בָּרָא אֱלֹהִים אֵת הַשָּׁמַיִם וְאֵת הָאָרֶץ׃

When transliterated, the above sentence would read as:

B'rashet bara Elohim et hashamayim v'et ha'aretz

I have created a similar table to the one in the previous chapter, so you can easily track each word. Remember I do not know any Hebrew myself. I can't even say good morning in Hebrew. So if I can learn this, so can you.

Word	7th	6th	5th	4th	3rd	2nd	1st
Hebrew word	הָאָרֶץ׃	וְאֵת	הַשָּׁמַיִם	אֵת	אֱלֹהִים	בָּרָא	בְּרֵאשִׁית
Voiced	Ha'aretz	V'et	Hashamayim	?	Elohim	Bara	B'rashet
English word	Earth	And	Heaven	-	God	Created	In the beginning
HNV	90+200+1+5	400+1+6	40+10+40+300+5	400+1	40+10+5+30+1	1+2+200	400+10+300+1+200+2
Total = 2,701	296	407	395	401	86	203	913

Each Hebrew letter, word or sentence has its own number value called HNV. But it isn't just letters that have HNV's, words also have HNV's. The HNV of a word is obtained by adding up the HNV's for the individual letters that make up that word. For example, the HNV for B'rashet is 913. Take a look at the table to see how I obtained this number. Genesis 1:1 also has its own HNV. You can calculate the HNV for Genesis 1:1 by adding up the HNV's of each word. The

HNV for Genesis 1:1 is obtained by adding up the HNV's for each word:

$$913+203+86+401+395+407+296$$
$$= 2701$$

The HNV for all the words in Genesis 1:1 is therefore 2701.

At first, this number doesn't appear unique. The number 2701 is 37 multiplied by 73 and there is a beauty in the symmetry you're about to see with this number. Either way you look at 2701, it equals 37x73 or 73x37. Can you see that the two numbers 37 and 73 multiplied to get 2701, are mirror images of each other?

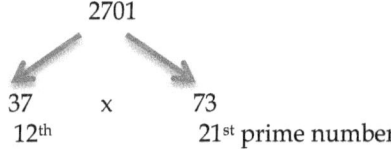

37   x   73
12th   21st prime number

There is another type of symmetry that can be observed from 2701 based on the two numbers 37, and 73. Both are prime numbers; 37 is the 12th prime number and 73 is the 21st prime number. Notice anything about numbers 12 and 21? Both 12 and 21, like 37 and 73, are mirror images of each other. This is a unique form of positional symmetry for 37 and 73, the 12th and 21st prime numbers

37...73 : 73...37
12...21 : 21...12

There are no two prime numbers that share this double symmetry besides 37 and 73. Take the prime numbers 13 and 31 for example. The number 13 is the 6th prime number and 31, the 11th prime number. No double symmetry. How about 17, the 7th prime number, and 71 the 20th prime number? Still no double symmetry! If you go to the higher numbers, you will get lost. You can perform a Google search using "is 311 the 65th prime number". All sorts of websites will pop up and you might find what you're looking for. A good website is www.primefan.tripod.com if it's still up and running. It has a table with the first 500 prime numbers. There are no two numbers on that table that share this unique double symmetry seen between the 12th prime number, 37, and the 21st prime number, 73. So why do the HNV's for the first sentence in the bible add up to 2701, a number so unique that it can only be obtained by multiplying two prime numbers that are themselves mirror images of each other and also occupy symmetrical positions on the prime number listing? Is an intelligently superior being, using an intelligently designed system of numbers to tell us something? I think so. But that's not all. Let's merge numbers 37 and 73 to make the number 3773. The symmetry is obvious, isn't it? Still not impressed? Then watch what happens next when the number 3773 is broken to its factors?

3773
=
7x77x7

Mirror symmetry again. It's as if God is trying to communicate with us by saying, "Hi, it's me" while waving at us from the Bible. Hopefully, we're paying attention. Next, I'd like you to participate in some simple exercises by adding up some HNV's.

In the first exercise, I'd like you to add up the HNV's for the 1st and 3rd words in the Torah. The 1st word is B'rashet and the 3rd word is Elohim with HNV's of 913 and 86 respectively

1. Add HNV's for the 1st and 3rd words in Genesis 1:1
    = In the beginning + God
    = B'rashet + Elohim
    = בְּרֵאשִׁית + אֱלֹהִים =
    = 913 + 86
    = **999**
    = **37x3x3x3**

In the next three exercises, we will add HNV's for three different words in Genesis 1:1

2. The 2nd, 4th and 5th words
    = Created + Untranslatable word + Heaven
    = הַשָּׁמַיִם + בָּרָא + אֵת =
    = 203 + 401 + 395
    = **999**
    = **37 x 3 x 3 x 3**
    Coincidence? I doubt it. Let's do the third exercise.

3. The 3rd, 5th and 6th words
    = הַשָּׁמַיִם + וְאֵת + אֱלֹהִים =
    = God   + And + Heaven

154

$$= 86 \quad + 407 \quad + 395$$
$$= \mathbf{888}$$
$$= 37 \times 3 \times 8 \ (8=2\times2\times2).\ 8 \text{ is two multiplied three times!}$$

4. The 3rd, 5th and 7th words
   = הָאָרֶץ + הַשָּׁמַיִם + אֱלֹהִים
   = God + Heaven + Earth
   = 86 + 395 + 296
   = **777**
   = **37x7x3** (3773 symmetry!)

$$999 = 37\times3\times9 = \mathbf{111}\times9$$
$$888 = 37\times3\times8 = \mathbf{111}\times8$$
$$777 = 37\times3\times7 = \mathbf{111}\times7$$

Notice that the four answers 999, 999, 888 and 777 all have 37x3 in common. This number is called the highest common factor for these three numbers. It is an interesting number. Multiply 37 and 3 and you get
$$37\times3 = 111$$

If you lay out this number for symmetry you'll have 3...7...3! Only God could have arranged this phenomenon with such mathematical precision and symmetry! Next, if you add the two prime numbers 37 and 73:
$$37 + 73 = 110$$
$$110 = 11 \times 10$$
$$11 + 10 = 21 = 3 \times 7.$$
Again the numbers 3 and 7 show up!

That's not all. There are seven words in Genesis 1:1, each with a different number of letters.

בְּרֵאשִׁית	בָּרָא	אֱלֹהִים	אֵת	הַשָּׁמַיִם	וְאֵת	הָאָרֶץ:
6	3	5	2	5	3	4

⬅

When the number of letters in each word is placed under the corresponding word, and you add them up, you'll have
$$4+3+5+2+5+3+6 = 28$$

Break down 28 to its prime numbers and you'll have a symmetry repeating itself: 28 = 2x7x2, that is, 2...7...2. According to Don Kistler, several different authors on bible numbers, as well as the website www.bbclandrum.com, 28, is the number for eternal life. A coincidence? Probably not! So in the very first verse in Genesis 1, made up of 28 letters, God is already hinting us about eternal life! There are exactly 28 Hebrew letters in the first sentence in the Bible and the entire Bible is written so we can have eternal life through Jesus Christ!

> *But these are written, that ye might believe that Jesus is the Christ, the Son of God; and that believing ye might have life through his name. John 20:31*

Let's look at another occurrence of symmetry with the seven words in Genesis 1:1. The first word in Genesis 1:1 has 6 letters and the seventh word 4 letters respectively. The 2nd and 6th words each have 3 letters while the 3rd and 5th words both have 5 letters each. A triangle can be created using the number of letters for each of these seven words. To create this triangle, place all the seven numbers in their exact order on one row. Create the next row underneath the first row by deleting the first and last numbers. The first row will have 4,3,5,2,5,3,6, the second row 3,5,2,5,3, the third row, 5,2,5 and the last row 2.

As you take away the first and last numbers in the first row, mirror symmetry emerges. As you keep removing numbers from both ends to create a new row, this symmetry persists, and you'll get a triangle that looks like this:

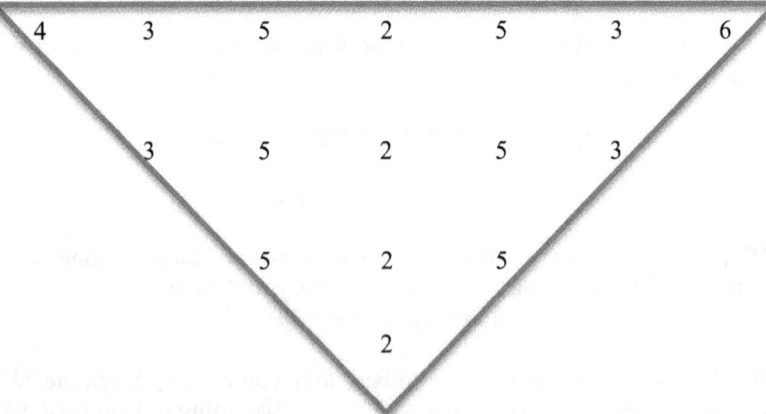

As you create all four rows, a triangle of numbers is formed from the seven numbers (2,3,3,4,5,5,6). But don't forget that there are only five numbers (2,3,4,5,6).

Add these numbers together: 2+3+4+5+6 = 20

The number 20 is the biblical number for redemption. If you add up all the numbers in the triangle, you'll get 60. The easiest way to do this is to see the triangle as having four horizontal rows. Add up all the numbers in each of the four rows of the triangle:

Row 1: 4+3+5+2+5+3+6 = 28
Row 2: 3+5+2+5+3 = 18
Row 3: 5+2+5 = 12
Row 4: =2

28+18+12+2 = 60

The number 60 is the HNV for the 15th letter of the Hebrew alphabet, samekh, ס. The root meaning of the word samekh is to support or uphold. Jesus is the one who supports or upholds the earth and the heavens by the word of his power (Hebrews 1:3). Just as the first verse in Genesis showed us, The Alpha and Omega created, supports and upholds the earth and the heavens. Now 60 = 20 x 3. The number 20 is the Hebrew number for redemption while 3 is the number for resurrection. Three also represents Trinity and the three things that make up a man: spirit, soul, and body. There are 3 things belonging to man that need to be redeemed: spirit, soul and body. (I Thess 5:23). The redemption of man (20) can only take place through death. The number 23 is the biblical number for death and it equals 20 + 3. The numbers are speaking here. What the numbers are saying are that in order for the 3 things that make up a man (spirit, soul and body), made in the image of God to be redeemed (20), death (23) must occur. So Jesus died on the cross and rose again the third day (3) to complete the divine mathematical equation linking death (23) to the redemption (20) of the spirit, soul and body of man (3). As far as Jesus is concerned, Death (23) equals Redemption (20) plus Resurrection (3). This latter point is the most potent mathematical concept Christians can draw strength from when facing difficulties in life. Jesus also emphasized that some things in our lives must die before we can live meaningful, powerful and successful lives.

Verily, verily, I say unto you, Except a corn of wheat fall into the ground and die, it abideth alone: but if it die, it bringeth forth much fruit. John 12:24

Most of our fears and phobias are related to a fear of dying or our unwillingness to die to self. We must give up these fears and phobias by applying the death principle. It may not be easy, but no one promised us an easy life and we must die to whatever weaknesses we have, confront death, and beat it. We must be willing to do what Queen Esther did when her people were threatened with annihilation:

> *Go gather together all the Jews that are present in Shushan, and fast ye for me, and neither eat nor drink three days, night or day: I also and my maidens will fast likewise; and so will I go unto the king, which is not according to the law: and **if I perish, I perish**. Esther 4:16*

Today, Esther's words still resonate through history as one of the most powerful words ever spoken!

Most bible scholars agree that the number 7 stands for perfection and the number 4 for creation. Genesis is about the creation (4) of heaven and earth by a perfect (7) being as stated in Genesis 1:1. It should therefore not surprise you that the creation (4) of the heaven and the earth by a perfect being (7) God is summarized in Genesis 1:1 using 28 letters, that is, 7 x 4 letters!

At the end of Genesis 1 in verse 31, the Bible says

> *And God saw everything that he had made, and, behold, it was **very good**. (Genesis 1:31)*

Doesn't it seem odd that after creating the heaven and the earth with all its beauty and splendor, God still described all of creation as "very good" rather than "perfect"? Any serious Bible student knows that God uses words very precisely. So why do you think God used the phrase "very good" rather than "perfect" even at the beginning? Was Genesis 1:31 written to show us that God had a much grander plan for both heaven and the earth? The answer can be found in three different bible verses. Isaiah prophesied about this plan:

> *For, behold, I create new heavens and a new earth: and the former shall not be remembered, nor come into mind. Isaiah 65:17*

The Apostle Peter hoped for it:

> *Nevertheless we, according to his promise, look for new heavens and a new earth, wherein dwelleth righteousness. 2 Peter 3:13*

The Apostle John saw it in a vision,

> *And I saw a new heaven and a new earth: for the first heaven and the first earth were passed away; and there was no more sea. Revelations 21:1*

God already knew in Genesis 1:1 while creating the earth that he would create another heaven and earth. So he called this first earth very good but not perfect.

In conclusion, Genesis 1:1 deals with the creation, Jesus as the Son of God, redemption, resurrection, death, the cross, perfection, in addition to so many other truths about an awesome God's carefully thought out intentions. Throughout the entire bible, there are specific verses where God uses numbers to communicate eternal truths to us. Genesis 1:1 is one of these verses. As you can see, eternal life, death, resurrection, the cross, the Son of God, redemption and so many others have been hidden in God's word for centuries. Ours is a journey of discovering what seems hidden but which God intends to be known to his children. No other book ever written on the subject of God or religion could have been so meticulously crafted with scientific data thousands of years ahead of its time as the Holy Bible.

Chapter 9

אֵת, The Untranslatable Word

אֵת

Of the seven Hebrew words in Genesis 1:1, the fourth word, the middle one, is quite intriguing. This fourth word is made up of two letters, aleph(א) and tau(ת) to form the word אֵת. This two-letter "word" has baffled Hebrew scholars for centuries because it is not a real word in the Hebrew language. Yet it stands imposing right in the middle of the most powerful phenomenon in human history, the creation of heaven and earth. Why? Even its position in the seven-word verse, as the fourth word, is telling us something as 4 is the number for creation. Unlike the authors of the different controversial bible versions that irreverently deleted bible verses they do not understand, Jewish scholars have had the mental discipline and reverence for God's word to just leave אֵת alone in Genesis 1:1. Thank God they did. As you've seen so far with the uniqueness of the HNV's in previous sections, removing this fourth "word" would have been catastrophic. The two letters אֵת don't form any Hebrew word, yet from all indications, they weren't placed there by accident. Most Hebrew scholars just call the two letters אֵת "untranslatable". So, what are these combined but "untranslatable" two letters trying to tell us?

The אֵת letter combination does have great significance. There are twenty-two letters in the original Hebrew alphabet. The first alphabet is א (aleph) and the last alphabet is ת (tau) and the message both letters are communicating in the middle of the first sentence in the Torah is the identity of Jesus Christ. Jesus Christ is the Beginning and the End, the one by whom all things were created and without whom anything would have been created. (John 1:3: Colossians 1:16). Let's look a little closer.

In Revelations 1:8, Jesus said to the Apostle John,

I am Alpha and Omega, the beginning and the ending... Revelation 1:8

The book of Revelation was written in Greek. There are 24 letters in the Greek alphabet. The first letter of the Greek alphabet is Alpha and the last letter Omega. But when Jesus appeared to John he was not speaking Greek but Aramaic, which John then translated into Greek. This means that Jesus would have said to John

I am the א *"Aleph" and the* ת *"Tau"*

John would then have written this in Greek as "Alpha" and "Omega". So the fourth word את in the seven-word sentence of Genesis 1:1, the "untranslatable word", is referring to Jesus the Alpha and the Omega or the Aleph and the Tau, את. These two letters were placed by God to point to Jesus Christ as the Alpha and Omega. He made all things and without him was not anything made that was made. The את was inserted into the middle of the verse of creation right before the heaven was mentioned in Genesis 1:1. It is impossible for humans and all of creation to be perfect without את, Jesus. Without the את, there would only be 6 words, and 6, is the number for Satan. Without Christ, we face the same fate as Satan in the lake of fire but we are made perfect and complete (7) in him. (Colossians 2:10)

As you have seen in a previous chapter, the untranslatable את placed in the center of the seven words in Genesis 1:1 also results in an amazing mathematical symmetry of words and numbers that would not have been otherwise possible to reproduce. So Genesis 1:1 could be written as

In the beginning created God Aleph and Tau, the heaven and the earth

Before closing this chapter, let me remind you again, that I don't know any Hebrew at all. I can't even say a single sentence in Hebrew. I cannot say I'm hungry in Hebrew and if you dropped me off in Jerusalem right now, I might just starve to death without the help of a Good Samaritan!

Chapter 10

God's Favorite Numbers

Numbers are a unique way of communicating fixed principles or unchangeable realities. I hope that by now, you've also seen that the Bible is much more than the words of some cranky religious fanatics. There are several books written about numbers in the Bible, some tethering on the mystic, esoteric and even the occult. In this chapter, I want you to get a taste, not a full course, of how numbers help establish some biblical principles and realities in the bible. You will have a greater appreciation of the grander design and wisdom of God in the writing of the Bible. I have chosen some numbers to illustrate specific biblical truths you'll find interesting if not amazing. I started learning much of what I'm about to share with you about thirty years ago from a book written by Don Kistler called *The Arithmetic of God*. It's an awesome book to start with if you're interested in learning more about numbers in the Bible. There is another book my wife recommended to me at the time of writing this book called *Numbers That Preach* by Troy Brewer.

3
Resurrection

The number 3 stands for resurrection. Three people were raised from the dead in the Old Testament. Elijah raised one, Elisha two. Jesus raised three people from the dead in the New Testament. Jesus himself rose from the dead on the third day and was tried in three different courts; Sanhedrin, Herod and Pilate's. Peter denied Jesus three times. Three people were executed on Calvary, Jesus and two thieves. Jesus told his disciples he would be killed and raised on the third day.

The Son of man must suffer many things, and be rejected of the elders and chief priests and scribes, and be slain, and be raised the third day. Luke 9:22

Passover was specified by God to take place on the 14th day of the Jewish first month.

In the fourteenth day of the first month at even is the Lord's Passover. Leviticus 23:5

Passover was also the day Jesus was crucified. While there is a lot of unnecessary controversy about what day Jesus was killed or when he rose, the Bible is quite clear about when these things happened. At least clear enough for us to understand what God is trying to communicate to us through his only begotten, Jesus Christ.

> And it was the preparation of the Passover, and about the sixth hour: and he saith unto the Jews, Behold your King! But they cried out, Away with him, crucify him. Pilate saith unto them, Shall I crucify your King? The chief priests answered, We have no king but Caesar. Then delivered he him therefore unto them to be crucified. And they took Jesus, and led him away. And he bearing his cross went forth into a place called the place of a skull, which is called in the Hebrew Golgotha: Where they crucified him, and two other with him, on either side one, and Jesus in the midst. (John 19:14-18)

Jesus was crucified on the 14th day of the first month, the day of Passover sacrifice. He rose from the dead three days later:

> For as Jonas was three days and three nights in the whale's belly; so shall the Son of man be three days and three nights in the heart of the earth. Matthew 12:40

Jesus predicted his own death and spent three days and three nights in the heart of the earth. Some scholars say he was crucified on the 14th day, some, the 15th. There is a mathematical concept hidden in the events of Jesus' death and resurrection that gives us a better idea of exactly when he was crucified and when he rose from the grave. Let's look at it.

The third time Jesus appeared to his disciples after his resurrection, the disciples had just gone fishing. The number of fish they caught is an important mathematical clue to the day of the month Jesus rose from the grave and therefore to the day he died. Let's look at the bible verses that give us a clue.

> Simon Peter went up, and drew the net to land full of great fishes, an hundred and fifty and three: and for all there were so many, yet **was not the net broken**. Jesus saith unto them, Come and dine. And none of the disciples durst ask him, Who art thou? knowing that it was the Lord. Jesus then cometh, and taketh bread, and giveth them, and fish likewise. This is now the third time that Jesus shewed himself to his disciples, after that he was risen from the dead. John 21:11-14

The first important clue is 153, the number of fish caught. According to the scriptures, Jesus was crucified on the 14th day of the month. He rose on the 17th day of the month, after spending three days and three nights in the heart of the earth. Jesus is our Passover lamb, slain for the sins of the world. If the Passover lamb is killed on the 14th day of the month, it follows from all bible principles that Jesus would have been crucified on the 14th day of the month also. He is our Passover lamb and God is a God of order so why would Jesus have been crucified on any day other than the 14th? Jesus rose on Sunday, the first day of the week.

Now when Jesus was risen early the first day of the week, he appeared first to Mary Magdalene, out of whom he had cast out seven devils.
Mark 16:9

He rose on the first day of the week for sure. But did he die the day he was crucified? The bible says so:

Then came the soldiers, and brake the legs of the first, and of the other which was crucified with him. But when they came to Jesus, and saw that he was dead already, they brake not his legs. John 19:32

Now we have more than one way to figure out using the bible's own accounts of when Jesus was crucified. He was crucified on the 14th day of the month following which he spent 3 days and 3 nights in the heart of the earth. The first night he spent in the heart of the earth, aka hell, would be the 14th and the third night would be the 16th. The bible says he rose on the first day of the week. That would be on a Sunday, early in the morning or perhaps just after midnight. So he spent Thursday night the 14th, Friday night the 15th, and Saturday night the 16th, in the heart of the earth. That's a total of three nights and Jesus never lies or deceives. He wasn't crucified on Good Friday! At the ninth hour on the same day he was crucified, Jesus died on the cross.

And it was about the sixth hour, and there was darkness over all the earth until the ninth hour. And the sun was darkened, and the veil of the temple was rent in the midst. And when Jesus had cried with a loud voice, he said, Father, into thy hands I commend my spirit: and having said thus, he gave up the ghost. Luke 23:44-46

Stating the obvious by merging all the verses regarding Jesus' death and resurrection into one sentence, we would have:

> The 3rd time Jesus appeared to his disciples following his resurrection from the grave on the 17th day of the month, exactly **3** days after he was crucified, Simon Peter caught exactly **153** fish and not one fish escaped.

If you put all the numbers in the conclusive statement above side by side, you'll have

$$3, 17, 3, 153.$$

The first number, **3**, is the third time Jesus appeared to his disciples in John 21:14. The second number, **17**, is the day of the month he rose from the grave and the third number, **3** is the number of days he spent in the heart of the earth as he had promised. The last number, **153**, is the exact number of fish Simon Peter caught.

There is a mathematical formula hidden in this passage just like the one in Genesis 1:1. Can you see it? There are probably many more but I'll give you just two examples.

In the first example, multiply all the first three numbers, 3, 17 and 3.

$$3 \times 17 \times 3$$

$$= 153$$

The total number of fish Simon Peter caught!

At first, it might seem odd that the writer of John placed emphasis on the number of fish caught, but the additional mention of the fact that the net was not broken is mathematically conclusive. God is speaking to us through the bible. It should therefore be clear why the number of fish had to be recorded as an exact number and that the net was not broken.

The Light Giver of The World
By adding up the numbers connected to *Peter and The Gang's* post-resurrection fishing event, that is, 3,17,3,153, you have

$$3+17+3+153$$
$$= 176$$

$$176 = 8 \times 22$$

It is accepted by Bible students and scholars alike that 8 is the number for a new beginning. The number 8=7+1 while the number 22=21+1= (7x3)+1. Watch the relationship between 8 and 22. If you subtract one from 8 and from 22, the one life Jesus sacrificed so we can be perfected through his sacrifice, you'll have, 7 and 21 respectively. 21 divided by 7 equals 3, the number for the resurrection and the Godhead! Jesus sacrificed his life (1), so we could have new life (8) and be complete (22). The number 22 is considered by some to be a Cipher or key from God.

As you already know, there are 22 Hebrew letters, the language used to write the original Torah with mathematical precision. In Brother Don Kistler's book, *The Arithmetic of God,* the number 22 was shown to be the biblical number for light. So what does the number 22 for light produce when combined with 8, the number for a new beginning? Follow me.

The 22 letters of the Hebrew alphabet are used by God to shed light on his purpose and kingdom by giving us knowledge. This knowledge and therefore light, is brought to us when these 22 letters are used to form words. So there is a very tight connection between 22, the number for light and also the number of original Hebrew alphabets, and 8, the number for new life.

> *Thy word is a lamp unto my feet, and a light unto my path.*
> *Psalm 119:105*

> *The entrance of thy words giveth light, it giveth understanding unto the simple. Psalm 119:130*

> *Born again, not of corruptible seed, but of incorruptible, by the word of God... I Peter 1:23*

Jesus said that once you are born again (8), you become the light (22) of the world.

> *Ye are the light of the world*
> *Matthew 5:14*

Jesus also told Nicodemus in John 3:3 that, except a man be born again(8), he cannot see (22) the kingdom of God. You need light (22) to see. Jesus is the Word that was made flesh (John 1:14). Jesus the Word called himself the light of the world.

> *As long as I am in the world, I am the light of the world.*
> *John 9:5*

The 22 letters of the Hebrew alphabet produce words that in turn bring light into the souls of men. There is an infinite and complex matrix of numbers and letters in the bible and the connections between number 8 and 22 seem to me to be one of the most exciting and complicated combinations. If you've ever seen an ignorant poor illiterate and look into their eyes, you'll see that the one thing missing in those eyes is light. When you look at another person filled with the

Holy Spirit or an educated, knowledgeable and smart individual, you'll probably see a shining light in their eyes. Knowledge, the result of absorbing different words formed from alphabets (22), brings light (22). The greatest source of knowledge is the knowledge of God. If you want to know him, you'll need his light in you. You'll receive knowledge, light, wisdom and salvation. You will be born again by his word. And your light will shine brighter within your soul.

One interesting example I found while writing this book was in Luke 7:21. Besides dying on the cross for our sins, Jesus had the most powerful healing ministry of all time. This powerful healing ministry is what separated him from many other prophets and false prophets. No one could heal like Jesus. To those in need of healing, whether deaf, dumb, blind, lame, sick, dying, bleeding, insane, septic or convulsing, the most important ministry work Jesus did on earth before he died was healing. It was a time when there were no plastic surgeons to fix cleft lips and palates, no cardiologist to put stents in narrowed arteries, and no orthopedic surgeons to replace worn out knees or shattered limbs. There was one unique day in Jesus' ministry that has gone unnoticed by most preachers. On this particular day, the sun rose from the East as usual. Everything started the same way and nothing seemed out of the ordinary. At least not until two well-meaning guys, both disciples of John the Baptist, came to confront Jesus face to face with the most powerful question ever asked of him. The question was very direct, appeared to be so simple, but demanded something no one had ever asked Jesus. What these men did was ask Jesus if he was the Messiah or should they look elsewhere.

When the men were come unto him, they said, John Baptist hath sent us unto thee, saying, Art thou he that should come? or look we for another?
Luke 7:20

At first, the question John's disciples asked Jesus seemed absurd and perhaps simple. But it was a very difficult question requiring a demonstration of Christ's very deity. Jesus was expected to provide sufficient proof that he was indeed God manifest in the flesh. They pleaded with Jesus, and he yielded. If John were to die at the hands of some tyrant ruler, at least he would have the satisfaction of knowing his cousin was truly the Messiah. Up until that moment, Jesus had healed by speaking, touching, affirming someone's faith or releasing virtue from himself. But on this particular day, Jesus did the most astonishing thing in order to heal–nothing! He didn't pray, speak, affirm or touch anyone and no one was prepared for what was about to happen next. Till today, this short record by Luke has never been duplicated by anyone in human history. To reassure John's disciples that he was indeed the Messiah, Jesus had to do something no one else but God could do. He did. So what exactly did Jesus do?

> *And in that same hour he cured many of their infirmities and plagues, and of evil spirits; and unto many that were blind he gave sight.*
> *Luke 7:21*

Within minutes, countless numbers of sick and possessed people were cured of all their diseases. Not healed but cured! In many other records of Jesus healing people, the bible differentiates between healing and cure. The following example should help you understand the difference between healing and a cure. If a gangrenous diabetic foot is amputated, the stump left behind will need some time to heal. The stump may heal but the foot does not grow back. But what if the gangrenous black foot is restored back to normal so it doesn't need to be amputated? What if after amputation, the foot grows back again? Miracles of this sort were what Jesus did when John's disciples showed up to ask who he was. Jesus did something so mind-boggling to affirm his deity by curing far more people than it was physically possible to heal in an hour. So many were cured within minutes so that any doubts cousin John's disciples had about Jesus being the Messiah disappeared. It was a great day for sick patients and for healthcare in Jerusalem. It was also one of the greatest days in Jesus' earthly healing ministry. It was quite effortless and would have gone unnoticed if not for the keen observation of the trained eye of one man, Luke the physician. Perhaps we might experience an encore of such a great healing moment in our ministries today, if we dare ask God for such a moment.

In all the four Gospels, the only person that recorded this hour of massive healing for the masses was Luke the physician. Some interesting numbers are also associated with this healing recorded in Luke 7:21. Luke is the 3rd book of the New Testament. Exactly where this healing is recorded in the 3rd book of the New Testament is also important in understanding the complex matrix of numbers in the Bible. To be cured means to bring back to perfection or made completely (7) whole. Since Luke was the only one that recorded this curing of the masses, you might guess that his record would be associated with the number 7. This is quite interesting because the greatest healing moment in Jesus' earthly ministry was actually recorded in the **21st** verse of the **7th** chapter of the **3rd** Gospel in the book of Luke.

$$21 = 7 \times 3$$
3rd book multiplied by the 7th chapter equals 21st verse.

Coincidence? Maybe. Maybe not! The latter seems more likely.

5
Grace

The 5th time Noah's name is mentioned in the Bible, it is associated with grace. By the law of precedence when anything shows up for the first time in the bible, you know it has to be important in the sequence it appears.

> *But Noah found grace in the eyes of the Lord. Genesis 6:8*

Presuming that the number 5 is connected to grace, there should be at least one other clue in the Bible to help us see the connection of the number 5 to grace. This example is taken from *Arithmetic of God*. When Jacob was returning from exile, he sent his servants and wives ahead of himself. Splitting the carriages into different groups for fear that his brother might kill him, Jacob said:

> *And I have **oxen**, and **asses**, **flocks**, and **menservants**, and **womenservants**: and I have sent to tell my Lord, that I may find **grace** in thy sight. Genesis 32:5.*

Jacob listed five things he had acquired. The fifth time Ruth's name was mentioned in the bible, guess what? It is connected to grace!

> *And Ruth the Moabitess said unto Naomi, Let me now go to the field, and glean ears of corn after him in whose sight I shall find **grace**. Ruth 2:2*

When David went out to meet Goliath, he took five smooth stones and gracefully dispatched this towering giant. Grace is a measure of smoothness and ease. Brother Don Kistler, author of *Arithmetic of God*, described these 5 stones David took as representing the grace with which a child of God overcomes the world. Perhaps even more important is the fact that we need grace to overcome and subdue the giants of this world.

7
Completion, Perfection

The number 7 represents perfection, completion. The 7th time Noah's name was found in the Bible, it was associated with perfection.

> *Noah was a just man and perfect in his generation (Genesis 6:9)*

There are 7 days in a week and seven musical notes, Do Re Mi Fa So La Ti. Music is one of the most powerful mediums on earth. Yet, no matter how brilliant the musician, all their music must be created from these 7 musical notes. Again, Jesus, perfect man, perfect sacrifice for our sins, spoke seven different times on the cross before he died. These are his words those seven times:

1st
Then Jesus said, Father, forgive them; for they know not what they do...
Luke 23:34

2nd
And Jesus said unto him, Verily I say unto thee,
To day shalt thou be with me in paradise.
Luke 23:43

3rd
... he saith unto his mother, Woman, behold thy son.
Then saith he to the disciple, Behold thy mother.
John 19:26-27

4th
My God, My God, why hast thou forsaken me? Mark 15:34

5th
I thirst. John 19:28

6th
It is finished. John 19:30

7th
Father, Into thy hands I commend my spirit:
Luke 23:46

After completing his work, God rested on the 7th day.

And on the seventh day God ended his work which he had made; and he rested on the seventh day from all his work which he had made. Genesis 2:2

8
New Birth

Eight is the number for new beginnings and the new birth. Eight people went into Noah's ark. These were Noah, Ham, Shem and Japheth and their wives. (I Pet 3:20; 2 Peter 2:5). David, a man after God's own heart from whose lineage Jesus would come, was the eighth son of Jesse. (I Samuel 17:12-14) Peter outlined eight qualities every Christian should have in order to be fruitful: faith, virtue, knowledge, temperance, patience, godliness, brotherly kindness and charity. (II Pet 1:4—7) The eighth time Noah's name was mentioned, the bible states Noah walked with God. (Genesis 6:9). The only ones that can walk with God are those that are born again. In John 3:3,5, Jesus told Nicodemus he had to be born again. Jesus used the word "born" eight times. The eighth time the word "born" was used in this chapter, Jesus said

> *Marvel not that I said unto thee, Ye must be born again. John 1:8*

The very first time Jesus used the word born in this chapter, it was used also used in the phrase born again:

> *Jesus answered and said unto him, Verily, verily, I say unto thee, Except a man be born again, he cannot see the kingdom of God.*
> *John 3:3*

8th occurrence x 1st occurrence = 8x1 = 8 = New birth

12
Authority

When Elijah, decided to prove the existence and authority of the one and only God of heaven to idol worshippers, he built an altar with twelve stones (I Kings 18:22-44), poured twelve barrels of water on it and asked for fire to come down from heaven on the waterlogged altar. There are several other examples of 12 as the number for authority. There are 12 hours to the day and 12 hours to the night, allotted by God and unchangeable. The sun rules the day for 12 hours while the moon rules the night for 12 hours, according to Genesis 1:16-18. There are 12 months in a year. At the age of 12, Jesus demonstrated his perfect understanding of his earthly purpose and God's laws with today's equivalent of theology and law professors in the synagogue (Luke 2:46-49). In Matthew 10:1, Jesus gave 12 disciples (including Judas) power to cast out demons, at the beginning of his outreach ministry:

> *And when he had called unto him his twelve disciples, he gave them power against unclean spirits, to cast them out, and to heal all manner of sickness and all manner of disease. Matthew 10:1.*

Jesus fed a large crowd with only five loaves of bread and two fish and there were 12 baskets left over:

And they did all eat, and were filled: and they took up of the fragments that remained twelve baskets full. Matthew 14:20.

17
Victory

In I Samuel 17:45, David confronted Goliath with divine authority (12) in the name of the Lord carrying 5 (Grace) smooth stones. When you add 12 for authority to 5 for grace, you get

$$12+5 = 17 = \text{Victory}$$

Despite Goliath's big mouth, little David obtained victory over him with a 12+5 strategy. Jesus conquered death and rose from the grave victoriously 3 days after the Passover using the 14+3 strategy. This Passover took place on the 14th day of the month. (Leviticus 23:5; John 19:14-16; I Corinthians 5:7) So Jesus rose on the 17th day of the month (I Corinthians 15:4), 3 days after he was crucified. In John 21:11, the disciples caught 153 fish. The number 153 equals 17 x 3 x 3 and represents the day of the month Jesus rose from the dead (17th) x the day he rose after he was crucified (3rd) x the 3rd time he appeared to his disciples after he rose from the grave. Notice they didn't catch 152 or 154 fish and the net was not broken.

$$17 \times 3 \times 3 = 153$$

Because the number 153 is tied to victory and the resurrection, the work Jesus did cannot be broken or undone, as the Bible says the net was not broken. The victory over sin and Satan that Jesus obtained for us on the cross through his suffering and death cannot be overturned.

23
Death

The number 23 represents death in the bible. As you saw in the previous chapter, Jesus redeemed (20) man's spirit-soul-body complex (3) by his death (23) on the cross and rose the 3rd day.

$$20 + 3 = 23$$

Our Passover Lamb, Jesus, died at the 9th hour, on the 14th day of the month.

$$9+14 = 23$$

The 23rd time some names were mentioned in the bible, death or the threat of it, can be found in the preceding corresponding or subsequent verse. The 23rd time Jacob's name was mentioned, Rebekah informed Jacob that his brother Esau planned to kill him.

(Genesis 27:42). The 23rd time Haman's name appears (Esther 5:14) he prepared the gallows, an instrument of death for Mordecai, Esther's uncle. On the 13th day of the twelfth month, (Esther 9:1) the 10 sons of Haman (Esther 9:10) were executed.

$$10+13 = 23$$

66

There are 66 books in the bible and Isaiah is considered to be the most important prophet in the Old Testament. There are 66 chapters in Isaiah. Isaiah was the only prophet with the largest number of prophecies concerning the birth, earthly ministry, suffering and death of our Lord Jesus Christ. Isaiah prophesied of the virgin birth of Jesus Christ accurately:

> *Therefore the Lord himself shall give you a sign; Behold, a virgin shall conceive, and bear a son, and shall call his name Immanuel. Isaiah 7:14*

On what would seem like the celebration of Jesus' birthday in heaven, Isaiah again declares the nature of Jesus' authority:

> *For unto us a child is born, unto us a son is given: and the government shall be upon his shoulder: and his name shall be called Wonderful, Counsellor, The mighty God, The everlasting Father, The Prince of Peace. Isaiah 9:6*

Isaiah prophesied about the Holy Spirit's anointing, and how this anointing would operate in Jesus' earthly ministry when he wrote:

> *The Spirit of the Lord God is upon me, because the Lord hath anointed me to preach good tidings unto the meek; he hath sent me to bind up the brokenhearted, to proclaim liberty to the captives, and the opening of the prison to them that are bound; To proclaim the acceptable year of the Lord, and the day of vengeance of our God; to comfort all that mourn; To appoint unto them that mourn in Zion, to give unto them beauty for ashes, the oil of joy for mourning, the garment of praise for the spirit of heaviness; that they might be called trees of righteousness, the planting of the Lord, that he might be glorified. Isaiah 61:1-3.*

Isaiah also prophesied the death of Jesus Christ including the purpose of his death with amazing precision:

> But he was wounded for our transgressions, and he was bruised for our iniquities, the chastisement of our peace was upon him, and with his stripes, we are healed. Isaiah 53:5

All these prophecies were recorded about seven hundred years before Jesus was born! Isaiah was one of the two prophets in the Old Testament that gave an excellent description of Satan's rebellion against God and his fall from heaven:

> How art thou fallen from heaven, O Lucifer, son of the morning! How art thou cut down to the ground, which didst weaken the nations. For thou hast said in thine heart, I will exalt my throne above the stars of God: I will sit also upon the mount of the congregation, in the sides of the north: I will ascend above the heights of the clouds; I will be like the most High. Yet thou shalt be brought down to hell, to the sides of the pit. Isaiah 14:12-15

My final example on numbers is from Abraham and his two sons. The bible tells us that Abraham was circumcised when he was 99 years old and Ishmael 13 (Genesis 17:23-24) while Isaac was circumcised (Genesis 21:4) when he was only 8 days old. What if someone walks up to you and claims that Abraham was circumcised when he turned 70, Ishmael at age 2, and Isaac at age 1? Did you know that there is a foolproof system built into the actual bible record to defeat such a claim? There is a mathematical formula linking the numbers for the circumcision of all three men, Abraham, Ishmael and Isaac. If you're really good in math, see if you can find the connection between the three numbers, 99, 13, and 8, for the circumcisions of Abraham, Ishmael and Isaac.

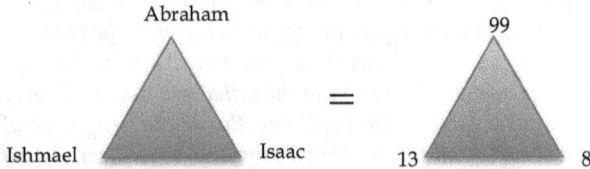

The clue to the puzzle lies in a Greek mathematical symbol $\sum$. This mathematical symbol helps us link all three numbers connected with Abraham and his boys. Wondering how? If you add up Ishmael's circumcision number, 13, to Isaac's, 8, you get 21 and no connection to Abraham's 99.

$$8 + 13 = 21$$

But if you apply the mathematical symbol Σ to Ishmael's circumcision number and repeat the calculation
$$8 + \Sigma 13 = 99$$

The mathematical symbol Σ means summation by addition. It is performed by adding up all the numbers, starting from 1, leading up to the number in front of the Σ sign. So $\Sigma 5$ equals $1+2+3+4+5 = 15$ which can also be obtained by adding 1 to 5 (the number in front of Σ), multiplying the answer by 5, and then divide that answer by 2.

$$(5+1) \times 5 \div 2$$
$$= 6 \times 5 \div 2$$
$$= 30 \div 2$$
$$15$$

At a very young age, Carl Gauss, the Prince of Mathematics, was told to add up all the numbers from 1 to 100. This is Gauss' formula:

$$\Sigma N = N \times (N+1) \text{ divided by } 2$$

Now let's compute **8 + Σ13** where N = 13. Let's see if the answer will have any connection to **99,** Abraham's circumcision number.

First we must find $\Sigma 13$

Step 1 (n+1): $13 + 1 = 14$

Step 2 (n+1) x n: $14 \times 13 = 182$

Step 3 (n+1) x n/2: $182/2 = 91$

$\Sigma 13 = 91$

$8 + \Sigma 13 = 8 + 91 = 99$

(Isaac's number 8) + (Ishmael's number $\Sigma 13$) = (Abraham's number 99)

That's God's way of confirming the circumcision numbers!

If God had a list of favorite numbers, I think both 3 and 7 would top that list!

Chapter 11

The Holy Bible or Perfect Bible?

The Holy Bible is the written medium through which the thoughts and plans of God for mankind are conveyed to us through a combination of narrative, law, history, genealogy, poems, and prophecy. While God is mysterious and the whole concept of a God, Trinity, heaven or hell, angels and demons remains an unending mystery, God has chosen the Bible as the medium through which he reveals enough about himself and his plans for those who care to know him or about him. The Bible shows how the earth was created, what sustains the earth and its inhabitants, why humans were created, and God's ultimate plans for the human race and planet earth. It reveals the nature of God and the contrasting nature of man. It shows us how to live a holy life pleasing to God, the nature of sin and its destructive consequences, the differences between heaven and hell, how to get to either destination, and how to deal with the ugliness of sin. The Bible provides instructions on our moral, societal, ethical, marital, spiritual and parental responsibilities to others and to our families and business relationships. The Bible also gives us a clear understanding of future events such as Armageddon, the coming of the Antichrist, the Mark of the Beast, 666, Implanted microchips, the Rapture, the Afterlife, and Judgment Day. The Bible contains words that have power to heal, defeat our #1 enemy (self), our #2 enemy (Satan), our #3 enemy (sin), our #4 enemy (the world), and is a source of encouragement and hope. The bible is the greatest instrument known for building mountain-moving faith, satisfying the spiritual hunger and thirst of all those genuinely seeking the truth about God, and developing intimacy with an otherwise mysterious God. If you diligently study, memorize and meditate on the words in the bible, your mind will begin to operate with greater speed and power. Finally, the Bible provides the best description of the greatest leader that ever walked the face of the earth in perfect love to die for our sins, Jesus Christ, the Son of God, Savior of all.

It isn't too surprising therefore, that the Bible remains the greatest bestselling book of all time. According to the frequently quoted *Bible Society* statistic, "2.5 billion copies of the Bible were printed between 1815 and 1975". More recent statistics by the *Gideons* put that number at 6 billion Bibles. These numbers show just how awesome a book the Bible is.

God's Word Forms a Brain Protein (WGp)

Imagine that you have memorized and can recall at will, ten verses of the bible ever since you were a little child. These verses are imbedded deeply in your long-term memory. Let's now say that you've read *Bible Vitamins* and have memorized twelve additional verses of the bible in your first week. You now know them so well, if I woke you up in the middle of the night, you'd recite them to me without missing a single word. Three months later you still remember these twelve verses effortlessly but in addition, you have now mastered an additional twenty new verses. Science has now shown that new pathways as well as new proteins must have been synthesized in your brain to create this long-term memory for bible verses. In the near future, these pathways may be detectable on brain scans either as an increase in gray matter, an increase in or new metabolic brain activity, or increased brain wave electrical activity. If this can be proven, it means proteins specific for the word of God have been synthesized in your brain. I'm certain that as scientists in general move away from the stone age believe that God doesn't exist to acknowledging God's existence, they might figure out how to measure the proteins formed as a result of memorizing these bible verses. They may also be able to identify what part(s) of the brain have the highest concentrations of these protein(s). I don't want to get too far ahead of myself but since I have come this far, I would like to call these proteins synthesized as a result of memory specific to the word of God, Word of God Protein, and represent them or it with the symbol WGp. WGp may be one protein in different quantities or conformations in the brain or a group of different proteins with the same conformation. Perhaps in the future, we would hear of WGp1, WGp2, WGp3, for the different types of WGp. You may also be able to classify Christians based on the concentration of WGp in their brains. It is also quite possible that the concentration of WGp in the brain and in other tissues of the body determines the level of confidence, faith and authority a Christian demonstrates in the real world. There could also be a slight possibility that while proteins for long-term memory for other learned material may be located solely in the brain and/or blood stream, WGp may be present not only in the brain and bloodstream, but in all the other tissues and organs of the body. That's perhaps how WGp dominates the actions of a truly saved and transformed Christian. Wouldn't you then wish you could measure the WGp of the woman that touched the hem of Jesus' garment and was made whole instantly? (Mark 5:28-34) These individuals are not just hearers or memory banks for WGp, but doers of the word. I believe that forming WGp will lead to greater peace of mind and self-control, lesser need for antidepressant therapy and fewer suicides or crimes against humanity. WGp may be the only physically quantifiable characteristic of faith that can be measured in advanced scientific laboratories of the future. WGp is a real entity formed by God's word, the faith as a mustard seed mentioned by Jesus in Matthew 17:20. It will eventually be shown to operate at the individual's anatomical, biochemical and physiological levels. The presence or absence of WGp and the actual amount may determine how much practically useful faith we have and can exercise and whether or not we get results even when we say we believe. It could also determine who gets healed when we pray. WGp may be completely absent in those who claim they believe even if everything else in their life contradicts what they claim. One thing should be clear regarding the DNA of God's word; any source for God's word that omits or changes words intentionally or otherwise in order to create information that no longer communicates the essence of a verse, cannot claim to be the word of God. If it's different from what was originally revealed and written, it is genetically inferior and can therefore not be called the word of God. It would not lead to formation of WGp.

The Perfect Bible

There is no such thing as a perfect bible. The brains of each individual function differently and even the same brain functions differently at different times based on mood, perception, environment and so many other factors. The whole point of having your own bible is so you can cozy up in a secluded spot, read, memorize and meditate and apply the words you have stored in your brain, and try to get the most instruction, information and inspiration from God's word. While you may be in the market to purchase a Bible or are already in possession of one, be aware of the different classes of Bibles available today. If you went to a bookstore to look for a perfect bible, you might not find one. That doesn't mean you won't find one that's perfect for you. It just won't be a perfect Bible. A perfect Bible is one that was written with the hands of God in only one language, arranged chapter and verse by God himself, printed in God's printing press in heaven by his holy angels and then distributed on earth exclusively through churches and can be understood by every one regardless of what language they speak. Such a bible does not exist. God doesn't write bibles, he inspired men to do so. Nor do angels print and send them to earth. Men moved by the Holy Spirit were given that task. So we should expect good bibles and bad ones because man is the middleman! A bad bible is one that removes or distorts essential truths about God including his plan of salvation, the identity of God's only begotten Son Jesus, or warnings about judgment and hell. A bad bible eliminates or obscures biblical truths either by deleting words, making simple words more complex, shorter verses longer and therefore more difficult to memorize, or eliminates the basic rhythm of a verse so it becomes difficult to understand or memorize. A good bible lies between the perfect and the bad. To find a good bible, you must have a checklist of bible verses that convey eternal truths. If they are missing, you've got a bad bible on your hands.

Which Bible Should You Read?

One of the questions many young believers ask is which Bible version is the best one to buy. To answer this question, you'd first have to decide whether your bible is a bad or controversial version. A controversial version of the bible is one that intentionally omits or completely changes verses and therefore the original intention of the author and then makes excuses to justify the change(s). Wise church leaders do not look favorably upon these versions even though the authors or publishers find their own ways to justify its printing. When you change or eliminate entire bible verses, you have eliminated far more than you think. Looking through the last few chapters of this book, you will agree that sometimes changing even a single letter can have such great implications. It's pointless getting into debates about which bible is bad as there seems to be a veil over the minds of most people today, in and outside the church. When you go to a bookstore, don't look for a perfect bible or a bad one. We are all created differently and the type of material you will find easy to read may be more difficult for me to read because our brains are wired differently. So you need to find a bible that enhances your ability to read, memorize and recall the verses in it. Just make sure you get a Bible that has not deleted any important bible verses, some of which may be keystone verses. A keystone verse is a verse that ties everything together on a particular topic so you can have a clear picture of what God is trying to convey through that topic. No matter what Bible version you choose, always remember that the fundamental reason for the existence of every verse in the bible is that God wants to communicate something to us through that verse or group of verses. Some have however had the audacity to remove obvious verses in order to suit their desires or philosophy. These are bad bibles and you can be sure they will not help you grow spiritually or mature confidently in Christ. If you want to have and demonstrate spiritual authority and not just scriptural familiarity, you'll need to have a good bible. Rather than debate what makes a bad bible, the following checklist will help you determine if the bible you're currently using or the one you're interested in is a good or bad one:

Matthew 17:21
Matthew 18:11
Mark 7:16
Mark 9:44 and 9:46
Mark 11:26 (Many are in hell because of this insane deletion!)
Luke 17:36
John 5:4
Acts 8:37
Romans 16:24
I John 5:7
I John 5:13
Revelations 1:11

If any of these twelve verses are missing in your Bible, you do have a bad bible. There are 31,102 verses in the bible and if any of these twelve verses are "accidentally" deleted from your bible, you can't be sure what else has been deleted. You may not even notice the deletions. These deletions are often based on an ulterior motive not scholastic excellence, archaeological findings, or godly spiritual discernment. Controversial bibles delete key verses intentionally in order to distort the meaning of scriptures or mislead Christians. The effect of these omissions is often to create a genetically deformed bible.

Only about 10 percent of professing Christians have read the entire bible. The remaining ninety percent move around with varying levels of ignorance. What this ninety percent know of God's word may vary between zero and 99.9% of what's in the bible. Until you've read the entire a bible a number of times, you may not understand the detrimental effects provided by the intentional deletions found in bad and controversial bibles. For example, one of the controversial bible versions has deleted the word "REPENT" 44 times, "LORD" 66 times, "HEAVEN" 50 times and "HELL" 22 times. The word "DAMNATION," found only in the New Testament eleven times and used by Jesus six times to warn us about hell, has been removed completely from some of these controversial bibles. Any bible that deletes warnings about the possibility of ending in hell if I keep doing wrong is a bad bible. It's extremely important that you understand the negative impact of such deletions on your soul.

To understand the significance of deleting keystone words or verses from the bible, think about your eyes. How would life be if both of your eyes were plucked out? Each eye weighs about 7.5 grams or about a quarter of an ounce and both eyes weigh 15 grams. If the weight of an average adult is 75kg, the combined weight of both eyes, 15 grams, would be 0.02 percent of an average adult's weight.

That's an extremely small portion of the adult's weight. Do you know anyone that would agree to have their eyes plucked out because they only weigh 0.02% of their total body weight? I doubt it. That would be insane! Yet that's what controversial and bad bibles are doing, removing the eyes of a topic or principle, blinding Christians to topics of importance, while saying it's just a small portion.

For example, fasting, described in Matthew 17:21 and Isaiah 58:6-9, opens the eyes of your soul, empowers your spirit, releases divine power, triggers the decent of holy angels from heaven, challenges the evil atmospheres and breaks down invisible barriers. That's why even occultists sometimes fast for forty days. Yet your bible version, as do many modern day controversial bibles, may not have this eye-opening verse. Whenever a key verse for a topic in the Bible is deleted, the eyes of that topic have literally been plucked out.

OCULECTOMY: Plucking out the eye or eyes.

Using fasting as an example, Matthew 17:21 says

Howbeit, this kind goeth not out but by prayer and fasting.

Since the word "FASTING" occurs 21 times in the entire Bible, deleting just one occurrence of fasting means deleting 4.8 percent of fasting. Deleting 0.02 percent of an average person's weight by plucking out both eyes turns that person blind so a 4.8 percent deletion, 240 times is huge. Ironically, if your eyes were plucked out and you lost 0.02 percent of your body weight, and then measured yourself on a scale, that loss may not even be picked up by the scale and yet, you'd still be blind! Fasting kills our old sinful nature (Ephesians 4:22), enables the new man to rise up (3) and perfects (7) this new man. Why would any well-meaning person delete it?

$$3 \times 7 = 21 \text{ times!}$$

In the four Gospels, Jesus used the word "fasting" four times and deleting just one of these four occurrences means deleting 25 percent of Jesus' views on fasting. Deleting 0.02 percent of a man can blind the man, so what can removing 25 percent of an important topic do to that topic? If you've ever fasted and enjoyed the many benefits of this spiritual discipline, you'll find it puzzling that the King James Version has this verse while many of the newer controversial versions don't. This verse on fasting is the eye of fasting for the entire topic of fasting in the New Testament. Take it out and you've rendered fasting for the New Testament believer blind and disabled. Such an omission is indefensible, even though you might see well-meaning politically correct theologians trying to defend it.

Controversial bibles have helped raise a generation of gluttons, Christians whose appetite switches have never been switched off, not even for a day of fasting since they were born or born again! If you've ever experienced the benefits of fasting, you wouldn't want to hide these benefits from others. Not if you love this person. But if you've never fasted and have never experienced the emotional, physical or spiritual benefits of fasting and therefore do not understand why people should fast, then fasting for you is just an intellectual debatable topic not a real thing. It wouldn't take you but a split second to remove it from your man-made pride-based version of the bible. We've been told by leading theologians that the KJV is not the best version available to a serious Christian, but in reality, what else is out there? Nothing else. Very few understand the intricate workings of our enemy, the devil, or his actions in these last days. Jesus warned us that the time is coming in the history of mankind when even the righteous ones will almost be deceived:

> *For false Christs and false prophets shall rise, and shall shew signs and wonders, to seduce, if it were possible, even the elect. Mark 13:22*

The Bible says that the tables will be turned so obnoxiously against what is right, holy and pure, that those who are living right will be labeled evildoers. Homosexuality is condemned by the bible. There was a recent video I saw of a man whose gay daughter committed suicide. Years after her death, her father, who had rightfully opposed her lifestyle, gave a speech, condemning himself. He said "I realize I was wrong and she was right". What deception! Right becoming wrong and wrong becoming right. As Jesus predicted, the time has come when those who kill the righteous will think they are doing God a favor:

> *They shall put you out of the synagogues: yea, the time cometh, that whosoever killeth you will think he doeth God service. John 16:2*

This deception is already affecting vast numbers of people from all walks of life. If you doubt this, go on Facebook and see how Christians are tearing each other apart. Unfortunately, many professing Christians are already caught in this web of deception. This deception seems to be coming from four main sources; the media, our schools, church pulpits and controversial bibles. You are probably fully aware of the first three, but the fourth, affecting the spirit of man through Bibles, is much more subtle.

Let's take a much closer look at a few of the deleted verses in the checklist I gave you earlier.

Matthew 17:21
Howbeit this kind goeth not out but by prayer and fasting.

Fasting is an important physical, mental, emotional and spiritual discipline all believers ought to engage in regularly. Fasting draws us away from our selfish carnal desires and breaks (Isaiah 58:6) invisible spiritual, mental, emotional, financial and physical barriers. It is one of the means through which the power of God is drawn into the souls of men and women of faith. When coupled with a quiet secluded time of contemplative meditation, prayer and the studying of God's word in an individual filled with the Holy Spirit, fasting can be a weapon of atomic proportions. Tampering with Jesus' use of the word fasting therefore makes no sense. As soon as John the Baptist introduces Jesus to us in Matthew 3:11 and baptized him, Jesus retreated into the wilderness for a forty-day fast. Based on practical experience, it appears that fasting transforms you into a clean vessel through which spiritual power can be stored for immediate or future release when required. Jesus undertook this period of fasting and it seemed sufficient to take him through the entire public ministry up till the time of his death. While it seems Jesus could have fasted for shorter periods and perhaps regularly during his time here on earth, no other mention is made of such besides the forty-day fast. It's a complete insult to the King of Glory to remove any of his words on fasting.

Matthew 18:11
For the Son of man is come to save that which was lost

This second verse has been similarly deleted from many bibles by authors who think they are equal with Jesus but want to claim they are Christians. The verse is telling us why Jesus came in his own words. Why would anyone want to delete this verse from the Bible unless he or she belongs to the devil? While I have delved deeper into the motives behind these types of deletions in another book, just note that if this verse is not in your Bible, it is a bad bible indeed. The surgical excision of these types of verses was carefully and masterfully carried out by two guys, Westcott and Hort (W-H), practicing Satanists who took hold of the Bible and over a twenty-eight year period, corrupted it. According to theologian Dean John Burgon, Westcott and Hort have "poisoned the River of life at its sacred source".

Mark 7:16
If any man have ears to hear, let him hear

The Bible has several warnings about burning in hell for all eternity. If there is a hell, the bible clearly tells us to avoid it at all costs. Why would anyone want to delete such eternal warnings unless they were in league with Satan himself? You can't twist or rewrite the Bible to accommodate your feelings except you're a spiritual felon. Yet there are bishops who don't believe there is a hell. The next two verses have similar warnings.

Mark 9:44 and 9:46
Where their worm dieth not, and the fire is not quenched

Check your bible to make sure they are there. Again you can see the intentional removal of warnings about hell. These warnings would make you cringe and soberly repent of your sinful ways and turn to God. Just because you don't believe in hell or an angry God does not mean you cannot end up there. Like every normal parent, God gets angry when his children do wicked things. Is that a crime? Please wake up!

Mark 11:26
But if ye do not forgive, neither will your Father which is in heaven forgive your trespasses.

This is a keystone verse that can save many from having a heart attack once they've learnt how to forgive. Removing this one is completely insane and many have gone on to hell because of this! This keystone verse transforms how we interact with people we don't like or dislike. Forgiveness is not an option. We must forgive "everyone", whether we like it or not, no matter what they did. You can identify a Christian with a bad Bible, if they ever read it, when you hear them say "I will never forgive Mr. X or Lady Y". If you don't forgive, you are going to hell. It doesn't matter what the person did to you. Forgive and let God heal you, even if you can't forget. The capacity to forgive may need to come from God. So ask!

Luke 17:36
Two men shall be in the field, the one shall be taken, and the other left

This is another keystone verse warning Christians and all who read the Bible of an upcoming event. It reminds us all to stay in shape spiritually and keep walking and working along a godly path. Why was it removed? To mislead and breed complacency in Christians! Sinister, isn't it? Such is the depravity of those who remove these warnings. To satisfy their own temporary selfish desires they place others at risk of losing everything for all eternity.

Acts 8:37
And Philip said, If thou believest with all thine heart, thou mayest. And he answered and said, I believe that Jesus Christ is the Son of God.

You can be sure that whoever deleted this one does not believe that Jesus Christ is the Son of God!

I John 5:7
For there are three that bear record in heaven, the Father, the Word, and the Holy Ghost: and these three are one.

This description of the trinity in the above verse has been deleted in many newer bible versions. Caught pants down, some of the publishers of these bad bibles have been reinserting the deletions. It doesn't matter if you understand or don't know how God can have a Son or Holy Spirit. Any Christian in their right mind would want to humbly pray to have some glimpse of this glorious description. But the spiritual felons, wolf in sheep clothing, have done it again, excising major truths about the relationship between Jesus and our heavenly Father. This verse was intentionally deleted by some folk that don't believe in the Deity of Jesus Christ. Why would you want to call yourself a Christian if you don't believe in the deity of Christ?

Revelations 1:11
Saying, I am Alpha and Omega, the first and the last...

This entire verse is deleted in those terrible Bibles which if you look carefully, may be the very one you have under your pillow.

The next verse is one of the most distorted Bible verses:

Study to show thyself approved unto God, a workman that needed not to be ashamed, rightly dividing the word of truth. II Tim 2:15

What does your Bible say? There are several problems with the distorted versions of II Timothy 2:15 in many bad bibles. First, the word "study" has been deleted in many bad bibles. "Study" is a keystone word, occurring only once in the Old Testament and twice in the New Testament. Deleting one means deleting roughly 33 percent. II Timothy 2:15 in bibles such as the NIV, ESV, NASB, CSB, CEV, ISV say:
Do your best to make yourself presentable to God...

Study should not have been deleted because people will stop studying. Replacing study with "Do your best" is wrong. Secondly, it is theological insanity to think you can do your best to present yourself to God. You may do your best to present yourself to Buddha or Allah, but you can't do your best to present yourself to God. How can your best be good enough when God says

> *But we are all as an unclean thing, and all our*
> *righteousness are as filthy rags...Isaiah 64:6*

Our righteousness is filthy so we cannot approach God by virtue of anything we do. Your best cannot make you presentable to God. You can only be presented to God through the cleansing blood of Jesus Christ:

> *But now in Christ Jesus ye who sometimes were far off*
> *are made nigh by the blood of Christ. Ephesians 2:13*

If presenting ourselves before God is mandatory, only the blood of Jesus can help us fulfill this mandate:

> *Having therefore, brethren, boldness to enter into*
> *the holiest by the blood of Jesus Hebrews 10:19*

The holiest place is where God dwells and we cannot get there by doing our best. We can't even "study" to get into the holiest place. Only the blood of Jesus can qualify us for the holiest place. That blood has been shed for us and is available to us. Check your bible.

Some people might accuse me of removing Bible verses in those places where I use a sic (...). I am not removing verses, just whetting your appetite for more. I hope you get hungry for more. Here is what the Bible says about making deletions and misleading additions:

> *For I testify unto every man that heareth the words of the prophecy*
> *of this book, If any man shall add unto these things, God shall add*
> *unto him the plagues that are written in this book. Revelation 22:18*

> *And if any man shall take away from the words of the book of this*
> *prophecy, God shall take away his part out of the book of life, and*
> *out of the holy city, and from the things which are written in this*
> *book. Revelation 22:19*

You have seen a few verses deleted from the bible and the potential for such omissions to mislead. Yet the fundamental question to ask such crooked scribes is how much of God's words do they have to delete before creating a terribly distorted version of the Bible? How much is too much? The answer may be found by looking at hemoglobin, a protein molecule that carries oxygen to every cell in our body, and keeps us all alive.

Chapter 12

God's Hemoglobin

Hemoglobin transports the oxygen in our blood to the cells to keep them alive. It also transports carbon dioxide back to the lungs. Without it, or with insufficient quantities, you may not be alive for long. No human being can survive without it. When people bleed to death, it's often because they lost too much hemoglobin. Hemoglobin is a protein molecule making up about 95 percent of the dry weight of each red blood cell. Each hemoglobin molecule has four chains: two alpha (α) and two beta (β) chains. Each α chain has 141 amino acids and each β chain, 146 amino acids. All the four chains making up the hemoglobin molecule have 574 amino acids. Don't be deceived by the large number of amino acids in this molecule to think you can change just one of them without dire consequences. Replacing just one amino acid, glutamic acid, with another one, valine, creates the sickle cell hemoglobin. This single change results in the lifelong suffering of sickle cell patients. Let's do some simple mathematics here that will help you understand bible deletions.

The hemoglobin molecule is a perfect molecule suited for life and till date, no scientific advance can replace it. As you might have figured by now, the number of amino acids in the hemoglobin molecule is a multiple of 7.

$$574 = 7 \times 2 \times 41$$

7 stands for perfection,
2 represents division
41 stands for deception

The abnormality in the hemoglobin molecule resulting in sickle cell disease can be used to help you understand the potential consequences of the deletions in many of the controversial bible versions. First, I'd like you to know a little bit about sickle cell disease (SCD). People with SCD often experience recurrent chronic and severe pain in the bones from shearing of the red blood cells during a sickle-cell crisis. They may suffer strokes at a younger age and usually have lost function of their spleen by the time they are teenagers. As a result they are very prone to certain infections. Sickle cell disease affects millions of people around the world and according to the

World Health Organization, in Africa, more than 200,000 babies are born every year with sickle cell disease and more than 70% of those with SCD live in Africa. SCD shortens the lifespan of those afflicted and patients rarely live past the age of thirty in West Africa. Things are much better for "sicklers" in Europe, the US and the Caribbean Islands where their life expectancy is between forty-five and fifty years. While I have been fortunate to treat some patients over sixty years old with sickle cell disease in the US and Caribbean Islands, very few patients make it past the fifty-year mark. The pain and suffering associated with this chronic severe pain and short life spans in these sickle cell patients is due to only a slight difference in the hemoglobin molecule. How slight is this difference? The answer will help you take the issue of bad bibles more seriously.

A sickle cell patient has 573 out of the 574 amino acids in their rightful place. Only one amino acid, glutamic acid is different in SCD. It has been replaced by valine. The SCD patient therefore has

$$573/574 \times 100 = 99.83 \text{ percent normal amino acids.}$$

So a sickle cell patient is 99.83 percent normal. A change of just 0.17 percent in something God created results in so much pain, suffering and early death. Just before publishing this book, I asked a few experienced nurses the following question about hemoglobin:

> *Assuming that a normal human being without sickle cell disease is 100% normal, what percentage of normal between 1 and 100% would you score a sickle cell patient who experiences bone pain and hemolytic crises regularly?*

Curt, an experienced emergency room nurse and a good friend of mine in Northern Louisiana, said that SCD patients were about 85 percent abnormal. A few weeks later while preaching at a church in Dallas, I asked two nurses and a physician, the same question. The first nurse said a sickler was 5 percent normal, the second nurse, 25 percent normal, while the physician said 7 percent normal. In reality, a sickler is 99.83 percent normal; only a slight genetic tweaking is responsible for all their pain and suffering. So when you see the drastic changes made in some of the controversial bible versions and all their unnecessary omissions, know that these bibles cannot deliver spiritual material at the same level as the non-controversial ones. Some of them may in fact lead you astray spiritually. If you would like to know more about how tampering with God's work even to the tune of 0.000001 percent, can result in major catastrophes, get a copy of Lee Strobel's *A Case for A Creator*.

Since there are 31,102 verses of the Bible, I don't see how you can detect a bad Bible or why you should spend so much energy trying to spot one. But if you would like to do so, use the verses I have listed above as a checklist. If these verses are missing, it is a controversial Bible. Dump it. The King James Version is not a controversial bible even if it is imperfect. Decide which bible to read and use the verses listed in the previous chapter as a quick checklist. Do I therefore endorse the King James Bible? Yes. That's because there is no controversy in it regarding spiritual truths or Christ's Deity.

The words of God can find their fullest expression through you in any circumstances. This expression of God's word and power in your life depends on your level of submission. The greater your submission, the greater will be the expression of God's word in your life. While you can pick and choose any word to meditate upon, remember that God is sovereign. He does things according to his own will. Just because you meditate on a verse in the bible does not automatically release its power into your life. The power is released according to God's will. Note also that the words we should desire to manifest in our situations, are God's words, not ours. So just because you've memorized some bible verses about the resurrection or wealth does not mean you can raise the dead or get rich. But in the same token, God can use you to raise the dead, heal the sick and bless you financially. It's his word, he created the world by that word, and all things are subject to him. So remain humble even as much as you ought to be thrilled about the power placed in your hands through the word of God.

Chapter 13

Cooking up Ancient Manuscripts

How come we have so many different versions of the Bible today and why do we have bad or controversial bibles? It all started in 1881, when two Cambridge University scholars, Brooke Foss Westcott (W) and Fenton John Antony Hort (H), published a book, The New Testament in The Original Greek (NTOG). They claimed that unlike the manuscripts used to collate and publish the 1611 King James Version, they were using much older manuscripts. They had spent 28 years writing this one book. As soon as the book was published, almost everyone jumped at it. Today, virtually all the modern bible versions such as the RSV, ASV, ESV, NIV, Good News and more, have used W-H's book to rewrite the New Testament. If you look carefully at the problems with these newer versions, a clear-cut pattern emerges. Verses pointing to the deity of Christ have been methodically deleted. W-H left enough evidence at the "crime scene" that reveal their true intentions. They deny the deity of Jesus. Why would anyone want to be called a Christian and at the same time deny the deity of Christ? Were both men simply pretending to be Christians? Did these men cook up their own ideas of the bible and if they did, why did they?

Westcott and Hort Lied About Mark 16

One of the arguments intelligently brought forth by Westcott and Hort (W-H) regarding the King James Version of the Bible relates to the last 12 verses of Mark 16. According to W-H, the last twelve verses of Mark, that is, Mark 16:9-20, were all later additions as they were not present in the Codex Vaticanus, (Codex B) a manuscript dated to be written around 325 AD and considered to be one of the most reliable copies of the Greek New Testament. This reliability was based solely on the age of the manuscript. It was in the Vatican library as early as 1481 but was not made available to scholars until the 19th century. Codex Vaticanus was later found to be a corrupted text. W-H relied significantly on the corrupted Codex Vaticanus in creating their New Testament in The Original Greek and therein lies a catastrophic flaw in all the newer versions. Almost all the "bad bibles" were written using Westcott and Hort's NTOG. Many of the deletions pointed out in previous chapters can be found in almost all the bad bibles. The intent of W-H may not have been clear to those publishing or printing these newer versions of the bible, but the deletions and omissions in them nevertheless give them away. W-H abused their titles as Cambridge scholars, or would one rather say, capitalized on their reputations as intellectuals, not as godly men at Cambridge, to claim that Mark 16:9-20 was not part of the original Gospels. Anyone filled with the Holy Spirit would readily disagree with these Cambridge scholars because these twelve verses in Mark 16:9-20 seem to be in perfect harmony with the rest of the book of Mark as well as with other New Testament books and the entire Gospel of Jesus Christ. W-H claimed that the KJV was not from reliable sources like the corrupted Codex B. Once they made this claim, many New Testament scholars and lots of Christians that loved the approval of men gullibly agreed with them that Mark 16:9-20 was added much later than 350 AD. If this were true, and if indeed Mark 16:9-20 were a later addition, then the most important question to ask would be, what purpose does this addition then serve? If we ask this question, we might see that these verses serve a perfect purpose and are in harmony with the rest of the Gospel of Jesus Christ. This should lead to the next question, why delete it? Why not look for other reliable sources that may have quoted these twelve verses instead of deleting them? The majority never asked and they simply jumped on the W-H bandwagon of deception.

Should you trust the modern day English Bibles such as the NIV, NASB, RSV, ESV produced from W-H's NTOG? How can the average Christian decide if W-H were just scholars doing honest academic work, or mean deceitful men, intentionally distorting the truth about Christ's deity and resurrection? By looking at the same types of tools W-H were using to try to deceive us, that is, historical records and books written before NTOG. There are several.

The first record can be found in *Against Heresies*, written by Irenaeus, in his Greek and Latin commentaries dated around 150 AD. He acknowledged these twelve verses almost two hundred years before the corrupt Codex Vaticanus was written. The second record confirming the existence of Mark 16:9-20 is found in *Diatessaron*, by Tatian, a disciple of Justin Martyr, who dissented from the faith after Justin was killed in AD 165. Several other writers from the second and third century also acknowledged the existence of these twelve verses. One of them was Cyprian, author of *The Seventh Council of Carthage* who died in 258 AD, and quoted verses 17 and 18 in his book. Tertullian, a third century prolific Christian author in Carthage and the father of Latin theology who died about 240 AD, acknowledged these verses in *On the Resurrection of The Flesh*. Yet they were missing in Codex Vaticanus. Coincidence? As eminent scholars, what excuse do Westcott or Hort have for ignoring the historical evidence in favor of these twelve verses? None! As Cambridge scholars of repute, W-H must have known about these men but chose to ignore their writings in order to carry out a hidden agenda. They intended to remove evidence for the deity of Christ and all they had to do was find manuscripts to support their position, not as Christians but as Satanists. The Gnostics removed these verses in order to leave Christians confused. If there was no resurrection, (Mark 16:9), Christians have nothing. While Codex Vaticanus and Codex Sinaiticus both omit these twelve verses, Codex Alexandrinus includes them. Mark 16:9-20, the last 12 verses of Mark, were intentionally deleted from the Codex Vaticanus and Codex Sinaiticus and belong to the Gnostics. While Mark 16:9-20 has been removed from many modern versions, it was part of the original letters, not an addition, as W-H claimed. Neither the NIV nor its cousins are reliable bibles for proper nourishment of your soul and spirit compared to the KJV. That's because they have too many keystone words deleted.

Even though logic and common sense often tell us there is something wrong with these controversial versions of the bible, we still use them as if they are the Divine standard for spiritual nourishment of the Christian soul. For more than 137 years, since 1881, we have been tricked into lowlier counterfeit versions of God's word without ever questioning the deficiencies that blatantly stare us in the face in these newer modern versions.

Faced with so many bible versions, you must ask yourself three questions about the origin of the modern versions. The first one is would you give a Christian a copy of the Quran, tell them to revise it to fit their own ideas of what Islam should be and then publish it as the Quran? The second question is similar: would you give a Muslim a copy of the Bible, tell them to revise it to fit their own ideas of what Christianity should be and then publish it as the Bible? In both cases, the answer should be no. You shouldn't be telling others how to practice their religion. The third question is would you give the Bible to a Satanist and tell them to revise it and publish it as the Bible? The answer again is a resounding NO in each instance. If that is the case, then why should Westcott and Hort, both of them occultists, rewrite the New Testament of the Holy Bible and have us sit down and read their revised Greek New trash while we try to justify reading such trash? It makes absolutely no sense except we have been deceived.

Finally, I'd like to share with you some of the advantages of memorizing the bible. First, when you memorize bible verses, you're digging spiritual wells from which your soul can draw water whenever you're thirsting for God's direction. The words you've memorized will speak to you and direct you when you need direction. Secondly, memorizing God's word requires and does build mental discipline. In turn, mental discipline is an important ingredient for success in life. Whether in business, ministry, athletics, or academics, those with the greatest mental discipline succeed the most. For his class recital as a young boy, Bill Gates, one of the richest men in the world today, recited from memory, the entire Beatitudes from Matthew 5 to Matthew 7. Those verses have served him well. Thirdly, memorizing God's word opens your mind to depths of divine wisdom, illumination and creativity. Fourthly, the bible verses in your mind create a positive stabilizing mental environment for your swinging moods. The more you memorize, the better you get at handling your emotions. Fifthly, your spirit, the part of you that rules everything else in your life, is energized by the power in God's word. That means you will have unlimited amounts of energy and spiritual power you can summon to your life situations when you have more bible verses committed to memory. Sixthly, the more of the word of God you have in you and obey diligently, the more your light fills the atmosphere around you and the spiritual atmosphere you create around you will be one of peace and joy. The seventh advantage is that demons will be subject to the increased authority that you have acquired through your intimate walk with God, your knowledge of the scriptures and obedience to the faith. The eighth advantage of memorizing bible verses is that you'll now have enough spiritual material with which to meditate and build great reserves of faith to accomplish just about anything you desire to. Last but not least, the only way for some people to heal from their varying levels of attention deficit, central nervous system hyperactivity or biochemical imbalances in the brain is to read the bible. The boring sections can be a real drag but if you take the time to read through the entire bible every year without skipping the genealogies, ADHD and other impulsive behaviors will give way to the words of God and gradually disappear from your life by the natural law of displacement.

If you use the King James Bible, you won't suffer any of the spiritual deficiencies experienced by those using anything other than the King James Bible. Regardless of its inevitable flaws, none of the modern versions, with their irreverent deletions, can match the King James in providing an accurate picture of all God would have us learn about his word.

Chapter 14

Personalizing Bible Vitamins

Praying and Prophesying
The bible tells us in Hebrews 4:12 that the word of God is quick and powerful, sharper than any two-edged sword. You can therefore use Bible Vitamins to pray and prophesy in a very profound way by direct application. For example, in II Kings 6:6 the axe that fell into the water and sank swam back up to the surface after Elisha threw a stick in the water. You can therefore pray when things seem impossible and say that according to II Kings 6:6

> *The iron will swim for my sake in Jesus' name. Amen.*

In the same manner you can speak and prophesy to someone who is in need of a miracle and say

> *"The iron will swim for your sake"* in Jesus' name. Amen.

If you are planning to start a project and need resources beyond your present capacity, you can pray according to Nehemiah 2:20 that

> *"The God of heaven, he will prosper us; therefore we his servants will arise and build"*. Nehemiah 2:20

If you know someone embarking on a project, you can pray for them, with them, or over them that

> *"The God of heaven, he will prosper YOU; therefore YOU his servant(s), arise and build"*. Nehemiah 2:20

The slight tweaking that personalizes these verses releases an invisible force into the atmosphere. I wish many a pastor would speak these kinds of verses, and what powerful words they are, over their members every Sunday! When a person leaves your church and is led by God to do so, this is the type of Bible verse a pastor should release into their heart, even when they're leaving your church to start a separate ministry. By speaking the words of God, you are initiating in the elements of both the seen and invisible world, forces that could bring about the powerful results you've longed for. The words of God that you speak will connect with the voice of God that is already upon the waters. Your words by themselves may not be enough, as there are often conditions of the soul and the spirit of the individual as well as the natural and spiritual environments that must often be met, before a prayer manifests. Nevertheless you ought to understand that the single most important advantage of praying using the word of God is promised power. Since you are speaking God's word into the situation and the atmosphere, a corresponding answer, based on your faith or that of the hearer, can trigger the impossible to become a reality. God's word has such surgical precision cutting through any mental or spiritual barriers like a laser beam, to get you results according to Isaiah 55:11, as long as you are equally prepared for the blessing and responsibility.

God's Word is Meant for You
Whether or not you believe in healing, speaking the words of the Bible can bring healing to the sick or tormented body. When the centurion met Jesus, he had so much faith he simply told Jesus

...but speak the word only, and my servant shall be healed. Matthew 8:8

So make it a habit to regularly speak Bible verses on health to your body and to others. Also, if you want to diminish the dangerous negative impact of anger on your body physiology, memorize these verses, and then meditate on them: Proverbs 12:16; 14:17,29; 16:32 and Isaiah 46:10. Find the most inspiring and moving bible verses you can relate with in this book or the Bible. Memorize, master and apply them by speaking them into your own life and watch the changes gradually take place to transform your life as you act on them. Before neuroplasticity was discovered to be the ultimate outcome of learning processes that lead to lasting changes in the brain, the term neurolinguistic programming was used to refer to changes in behavior created by speaking. So as you speak and believe what you say and hear, your brain will change. Faith will develop. You will become a different person completely.

The heart is where the greatest sins are committed. That's why God wants to change our hearts using the penetrating power of his word to change the heart of even the hardest sinner. *Bible Vitamins* provides you with a microwave version of the most powerful words on earth, bible verses. Memorize and ponder deeply upon them and they will change your life. The words will feed, fill, flush, fulfill, and fire you up while instilling the fear of God, wisdom and unwavering faith in you. That faith will occur at the anatomical, physiological, biochemical and behavioral levels. The bible is much more than I have revealed here in this book, and I hope you've truly been blessed.

Further Reading
1. *The Arithmetic of God.* Don Kistler.
2. *The Case for a Creator.* Lee Strobel.
3. *Numbers That Preach.* Troy Brewer
4. *The Revision Revised.* John Burgon
5. *How God Changes Your Brain.* A. Newberg & M. Waldman
6. *Switch on Your Brain.* Dr. Caroline Leaf
7. *Change Your Brain, Change Your Life.* Daniel G. Amen, MD
8. *The Authorized King James Bible*
9. *Kaplan and Saddock's Synopsis of Psychiatry*

About the Author

Dr. Caxton Opere is a board certified internist, researcher, ordained minister and the world's leading expert on the medical complications of divorce. He is a busy full time physician and pioneer of the 5-Minute Compatibility Tests™ and pastored Mercy Tabernacle in Baton Rouge Louisiana for 11 years. A passionate lover of God's word, he is neither a Hebrew student or scholar nor a theologian. He is happily married to Ade and they have three children, one of whom went to be with the Lord.

Other books by Caxton Opere, MD
1. *25 Things Every Pastor Must L.I.K.E. About Divorce
2. *Female Sexual Arousal and The Pink Pill
3. *5 Love Handles: Dr. Caxton's Marriage DNA
4. *Divorce Medicine: How Divorce and Toxic Relationships Affect Your Health
5. How Divorce Kills
6. *The 36 Well Kept Secrets of Successful Marriages & Divorce
7. 1 Roommate: Dr. Caxton's 7 Proven Steps for Choosing Your Ideal Mate
8. #1 Rule: Compatibility
9. *GSP: God's Success Program
10. *How To Enter a New Year & Reach Beyond The Stars
11. The DNA of Highly Successful Marriages

* Available at Amazon.com

Contact

https://www.facebook.com/caxtonopereministries/
www.caxtonopereministries.com

https://www.facebook.com/caxton.opere

https://www.linkedin.com/in/caxton-opere

www.ingramcontent.com/pod-product-compliance
Lightning Source LLC
Chambersburg PA
CBHW050801160426
43192CB00010B/1598